Lights, Camera, Execution!

Politics, Literature, and Film

Series Editor: Lee Trepanier, Saginaw Valley State University

The Politics, Literature, and Film series is an interdisciplinary examination of the intersection of politics with literature and/or film. The series is receptive to works that use a variety of methodological approaches, focus on any period from antiquity to the present, and situate their analysis in national, comparative, or global contexts. Politics, Literature, and Film seeks to be truly interdisciplinary by including authors from all the social sciences and humanities, such as political science, sociology, psychology, literature, philosophy, history, religious studies, and law. The series is open to both American and non-American literature and film. By putting forth bold and innovative ideas that appeal to a broad range of interests, the series aims to enrich our conversations about literature, film, and their relationship to politics.

Recent titles in the series:

Flannery O'Connor and the Perils of Governing by Tenderness, by Jerome C. Foss
The Politics of Twin Peaks, edited by Amanda DiPaolo and James Clark Gillies
AIDS-Trauma and Politics: American Literature and the Search for a Witness, by Aimee Pozorski
Baudelaire Contra Benjamin: A Critique of Politicized Aesthetics and Cultural Marxism, by Beibei Guan and Wayne Cristaudo
Updike and Politics: New Considerations, edited by Matthew Shipe and Scott Dill
Lights, Camera, Execution!: Cinematic Portrayals of Capital Punishment, by Helen J. Knowles, Bruce E. Altschuler, and Jaclyn Schildkraut

Lights, Camera, Execution!

Cinematic Portrayals of Capital Punishment

Helen J. Knowles, Bruce E. Altschuler, and Jaclyn Schildkraut

LEXINGTON BOOKS
Lanham • Boulder • New York • London

Published by Lexington Books
An imprint of The Rowman & Littlefield Publishing Group, Inc.
4501 Forbes Boulevard, Suite 200, Lanham, Maryland 20706
www.rowman.com

6 Tinworth Street, London SE11 5AL

British Library Cataloguing in Publication Information Available

Library of Congress Cataloging-in-Publication Data Available

ISBN 9781498579667 (cloth)
ISBN 9781498579674 (electronic)

In memory of Jenny

Table of Contents

Acknowledgments

One evening Helen's partner, John Gardner, suggested that they curl up on the sofa with their feline and canine menagerie to watch *Murder in Coweta County*, a little-known, made-for-television movie starring Andy Griffith and Johnny Cash. This book was borne of Helen's reaction to that film. To her, *Murder in Coweta County* was a death penalty film ripe for teaching in her undergraduate courses. Yet, upon researching the subject, she began to discover that literature speaking to the educational value of using such cinematic portrayals of capital punishment tended to focus on major motion pictures, and had not been brought together in a single, student-friendly volume.

When she pitched this project (designed to fill the aforementioned void) to Lexington Books for possible inclusion in their excellent *Politics, Literature, and Film* series edited by Lee Trepanier, it was an easy sell. This is because she was lucky enough to persuade two of her amazing State University of New York (SUNY) at Oswego colleagues to join her as co-authors. Had her emails and text messages to Bruce and Jackie been met with negative replies, this project would have been shelved; for in Helen's mind, there were no other individuals with whom she wished to collaborate.

As this book proceeded from conception to completion, the three of us benefited from the assistance, input, and wisdom of numerous individuals. Lee Trepanier (Saginaw Valley State University) is a series editor par excellence, and at Lexington it has been our pleasure to work with Madhumitha Koduvalli, Joseph Parry, and Bryndee Ryan. This team provided wonderful assistance, support, and patience as we strove to get this manuscript to and over the finish line. That goal would not have been achieved without the assistance of two very talented and hard-working students. Andre Nichols (SUNY Oswego '20) provided important research assistance, and Emily Tepfenhart (SUNY Oswego '19) checked all of the quotations for us. Together with Nicholas Stubba (SUNY Oswego '19), Emily also provided Helen with invaluable indexing assistance.

A very special expression of thanks goes to the incredibly talented Shanika Scarborough (SUNY Oswego–MA in Graphic Design '20) whom we commissioned to provide the cover art for this book (we are grateful to Professor Kelly Roe for recommending Shanika). Shanika's outstanding work not only enhances this volume, but also gives us a collective sense of institutional pride—this truly is a book borne of the talents of the SUNY Oswego community.

Last, but by no means least, are the friends and family members to whom we wish to say a huge "thank you." Helen extends her thanks to her mother, Rae, for her undying love and support; to Toffee (who wore his editor-in-chief cap every time Helen worked on this book) and his feline step-siblings Smokey, Clementine, and Faith; Bingo the dog; and Doc the horse. They all made a concerted effort to keep Helen emotionally and physically grounded (oftentimes in piles of hair). Above all else, however, Helen extends her loving thanks to John. Say you'll meow with me, John!

Helen (and John) dedicates this book to Jenny, who was taken from this world far too soon. May she fly high as our guardian angel.

Bruce would like to thank Helen and Jackie for asking him to join their project, which has proven a great way to continue to work with outstanding colleagues even after retiring. Thanks also to everyone who patiently listened to him talking at length about movies, most of which they had never seen and perhaps had never even heard of, particularly Rhonda, Steve, and Uncle Mel.

Jackie wishes to thank both Helen and Bruce for their collegiality as well as feedback on her chapters. This project was a true collaboration, and being able to work together to make it the best possible version of itself shows that as a team, we were successful in achieving that end. Like Helen, Jackie also wishes to thank her "puppy posse"—Bella, Bailey, and Chloe—for providing company during the movies and offering puppy kisses of encouragement when writing got tough. To her best friend, Rachel Lee, thank you for always being an endless source of support and guidance, and to her family, without whom none of this would be possible.

Introduction

Filming Death

Writing in 1931, Judge Benjamin N. Cardozo made the following observation about capital punishment. "Perhaps," he wrote, "the whole business of the retention of the death penalty will seem to the next generation, as it seems to many even now, an anachronism too discordant to be suffered, mocking with grim reproach all our clamorous professions of the sanctity of life."[1] Those words remain as relevant in the United States today as they were when they were written in the 1930s. Capital punishment is a subject of constant controversy; neither the retention nor the abolition of the death penalty has become an anachronistic topic. While an October 2017 Gallup poll reported that "Americans' support for the death penalty has dipped to a level not seen in 45 years," the new low was not that low. A majority (55 percent) of the country was still "in favor of the death penalty for convicted murderers."[2] Support was declining, but the nation was still profoundly divided on what, as Virginia Leigh Hatch and Anthony Walsh suggest, "may be the greatest moral issue facing American society."[3] The Eighth Amendment to the U.S. Constitution frames the constitutional aspect of the death penalty debate. However, the vagaries of its language—"nor cruel and unusual punishments inflicted"—do not beget any easy answers to questions about whether, and under what circumstances, it is legally permissible for the state to execute an individual.[4] Yet, even if one concedes the *constitutionality* of the death penalty, this certainly does not mean that one must also concede that this form of punishment is consistent with either one's own moral code or that of society.

The death penalty's ability to divide even the closest of friends, produce passionate differences of opinion, bring raw emotions bubbling to the surface, and generate bitterly fought and protracted legal dramas makes it an attractive subject for a movie. It is literally a matter of life and death, and its "unique finality"[5]—and the accompanying "social and philosophical drama[s]"—has been "expertly exploited" by Hollywood.[6] Quite simply, death sells. It is, however, death on Hollywood's own terms. Production companies are not charitable entities driven by a desire to make the world a better place; rather, they are capitalist enterprises in search of paying customers. Since they do not wish to bite the hands that feed them (i.e., the ticket-buying moviegoers), rather than taking a direct position on the profound moral questions that a subject like capital punishment raises, filmmakers tend to focus instead on depicting the subject using individual stories—the human-interest touch. In their iconic 1967 rock anthem, Jefferson Airplane rhetorically asked: "Don't you want [need] somebody to love?"[7] Hollywood makes the same assumption about its audiences—the people who pay to see their films "want" and/or "need somebody to love." They need a hero(ine) for whom they can cheer; they want a protagonist (or even an antagonist) that earns their trust and deserves their tears and sympathy.

Moral and legal questions do not necessarily have to take a back seat, but it is preferable that fictional characters in highly scripted settings raise them because this allows the filmmaker to establish the boundaries of the discussion. The average moviegoer does not go to the cinema because he or she wants a two-hour lecture on constitutional law or moral philosophy. Equally important, the average moviegoer does not want to leave the cinema with the feeling that he or she has been *subjected* to a two-hour lecture on constitutional law or moral philosophy. Paul Bergman and Michael Asimow astutely observe that, "[t]rial movies can . . . present controversial legal and moral issues in a sugarcoated package that we swallow with pleasure."[8] A movie about the death penalty is oftentimes a bitter pill for the viewer to consume (and oftentimes, as we will see, that is by the specific design of the film's producer and director). However, even that bitter pill is likely to come wrapped in packaging designed to offset some of the horrors associated with a state-sanctioned killing. For example, although *Last Dance* (the subject of chapter 8) was loosely based on the real life events associated with the execution of Karla Faye Tucker, in the film "the horror is toned down by having the murderer use a gun to kill her victims less slowly and painfully [Tucker used an axe]."[9] Filmmakers are, after all, acutely aware that the average moviegoer pays (increasingly high prices) to be *entertained*.

Although creating a sufficiently entertaining and audience-drawing cinematic portrayal of capital punishment inevitably involves taking shortcuts, the finished products are frequently inspired by or based on real-life events (as was the case with *Last Dance*). Indeed, its omnipresent nature makes the "law" a particularly attractive theme for filmmakers because it presents an opportunity to address historical events in a way that resonates (both morally and socially) with modern audiences. In this respect, capital punishment is no different from any other legal theme that might find its way on to the silver screen.[10]

Films based on actual events often take liberties with the facts for a variety of reasons. *Dead Man Walking* (see chapter 3) is based on Sister Helen Prejean's memoir about her counseling of death row inmates in Louisiana. The movie combines two of the actual men that she counseled into a single inmate who is made even less sympathetic than the actual murderers because he is portrayed as an unrepentant racist. If even such a repellant figure can be humanized, the case against the death penalty is made stronger. Given that the purpose of most movies is to entertain, it is not surprising that they take such dramatic licenses.

Even purely fictional films may incorporate elements of actual cases or real people. For example, in a scene in *The Chamber* (chapter 7), Sam Cayhall describes the botched execution of Teddy Meek at the Mississippi State Penitentiary (where Cayhall sits on death row). This is a clear reference to the events associated with the September 2, 1983 execution of Jimmy Lee Gray. Similarly, when writing the novel, *A Lesson Before Dying,* on which one of our movies is based (see chapter 5), Ernest J. Gaines began with a real death row inmate, Willie Francis. His "story was different from" the one being told by Gaines, who nevertheless still decided he "would use some of the information from the case material" to make an important point. [11]

Our book examines these and other films in detail to understand what messages they are attempting to convey. In addition to legal questions, these films present issues of race, class, and morality for their viewers to think about. How well, and to what effect, they present these issues is the focus of this volume. The inconclusiveness of studies on the deterrent effect (or lack thereof) of the death penalty allows those on both sides to point to statistics supporting their position. The two sides similarly disagree on the morality of capital punishment: Does taking the life of a murderer who has killed one or more innocent people justify the death penalty or does it make society complicit in a second killing? [12]

Movies have the advantage of presenting their arguments in a more dramatic, sometimes even melodramatic, fashion. Dry statistics generally will not cut it with the average audience. All of the films in this book use techniques such as musical scores, lighting, and camera angles to convey their messages in ways that go beyond plot and dialogue. Even nonfiction films use these methods. In *The Thin Blue Line* (see chapter 2), director Errol Morris added an original Philip Glass score to make the events leading up to Randall Adams's conviction seem inevitable. As Morris explains, "[a]ll my interviews are staged for the camera with the same lighting and poses." [13] In *Monster's Ball* (chapter 9), director Marc Forster created a film that featured measured pacing and a gritty look, giving the audience a sense of the depressing nature of the lives of the two main characters, a prison guard and the widow of an executed prisoner.

The films in this book were all made after 1976 because that is effectively the beginning of the modern era of capital punishment.[14] In 1972, the U.S. Supreme Court declared all existing death penalty laws unconstitutional because they provided no real guidance to the sentencing juries, thereby leading to arbitrary results. However, in 1976, the Court found that changes made by states were sufficient to allow the reinstatement of capital punishment. To explain this, we turn to a discussion of the current state of death penalty law and its development and evolution.

DEATH PENALTY JURISPRUDENCE

Although the vague language of the Eighth Amendment leaves the precise meaning of "cruel and unusual punishment" open to considerable interpretation, it generates an important constitutional question that must be answered before all others: Is the death penalty a "cruel and unusual punishment"? If not, then it is up to Congress and the legislatures of each state to decide whether they wish to have this form of punishment on the books as an option for their prosecutors to pursue in the relevant cases.

As numerous scholars have shown, the evolution of colonial, state, and federal capital punishment laws in America is inextricably intertwined with social and political trends in the nation's history.[15] There were no abolitionist governmental outliers in colonial America; every colony sanctioned public hangings as punishment for various crimes. Although Pennsylvania's decision, in 1793, to create different degrees of murder limited the incidences for which the ultimate penalty could be imposed in that state, and in the early decades of the nineteenth century some states took their executions "inside" (out of the public gaze), no state decided to abolish capital punishment in its entirety until Wisconsin in 1853 (it has never reinstated it).[16] The only other states to completely abolish the death penalty in the nineteenth century were Iowa (1872), Maine (1876), and Colorado (1897). However, all three restored this punishment within a few short years (1878, 1883, and 1901, respectively).[17]

As shown in table I-1, between 1900 and 1917, consistent with the basic societal principles of the Progressive Era, nine states either partially or completely abolished the death penalty. Once again, however, as table I-1 also shows, that trend was short-lived, primarily because of the social fear and upheaval caused by World War One. "[A] threatened and alarmed America wished to retrench, to oust any foreigners who might weaken its national stability and morale, and to subdue any violations of law and order."[18] This included restoring the ultimate penalty, which seven of the nine chose to do, most of them making that decision before the end of the century's second decade.

As Hugo Adam Bedau, who was one of the preeminent scholars of the subject, observed, the abolitionist "jurisdictions are and always have been the exception in this country."[19] However, it is important to note that there is a wide disparity between the different states' usage of the death penalty. Some states carry out capital punishment with such frequency that the numbers of the executions have for a long time far exceeded those of the majority of the states who retain this form of penalty. For example, since 1976, Texas (561), Virginia (113), Oklahoma (112), and Florida (98) have executed 884 individuals between them, a total that represents 58.9 percent of all executions carried out in the United States. Indeed, the 561 executions carried out by Texas alone represent 37.4 percent of the nation's total since 1976. In that same timeframe, fifteen states executed fewer than ten people.[20]

State	Partial Abolition	Complete Abolition	Restoration
Arizona	1916 (retained for cases of treason)		1918
Kansas		1907	1935
Minnesota		1911	
Missouri		1917	1919
North Dakota		1915	
Oregon		1914	1920
South Dakota		1915	1939
Tennessee	1915 (retained for cases of rape)		1919
Washington		1913	1919

Table I-1.   State abolition of the death penalty (1900–1917), and subsequent restoration of that punishment. Compiled using data from Bedau, "Background and Developments," 9.

Beyond the data pertaining to the abolition and retention of the death penalty by the states, four primary trends emerge when one examines the history, socio-legal, and sociopolitical evolution of the death penalty in the United States between the American Revolution and the decision in *Furman*.[21] First, the wide range of capital offenses that existed during the colonial and post-independence period was narrowed to just a few—primarily premeditated murder—in most states. This trend was less pronounced in the South where the penalty was often used in a racially discriminatory fashion both before and after the abolition of slavery. Second, juries were given discretion rather than being required to sentence all defendants convicted of certain offenses to death. Third, executions were moved from public places to private locations, usually state prisons. Fourth, attempts were made to adopt more "humane" methods of execution such as electrocution in the 1890s and, more recently, lethal injections.

These last trends are touched upon (to varying degrees) in several of the films analyzed in the chapters that follow. For example, although the actual prisoners upon whom *Dead Man Walking* were based were electrocuted, the film features a rather graphic depiction of lethal injection. Director Tim Robbins justified this dramatic license on the grounds that by the time the film was made, all states had adopted the newer method. However, this aspect of capital punishment is in flux. In 2017, Phil Bryant, the governor of Mississippi, signed House Bill 638 into law, changing the state's permissible methods of execution to include nitrogen hypoxia if lethal injection became unavailable or was ruled unconstitutional by the U.S. Supreme Court.[22] Alabama followed suit in 2018.[23] Moreover, after adopting this method in 2015, in 2018 Oklahoma announced that it would make it that state's primary way of executing condemned prisoners.[24]

New York offers a good example of these methods of execution trends in action. In 1888, it adopted reforms that made it one of the first states to use the electric chair and the first in which the state, rather than localities, administered the execution; at the same time, it retained the mandatory death sentence for premeditated murder. The first execution under the new law, however, was not a success as a second dose of electricity was required when the first failed to kill William Kemmler.[25] It was not until 1963 that the state repealed the mandatory death penalty, giving the jury the power to decide the sentence.

The *Furman v. Georgia* Thunderbolt

Surprisingly, while prior to 1972 the U.S. Supreme Court had ruled on the constitutionality of specific methods of execution,[26] it had refrained from issuing a judgment addressing the principal constitutional question. Until then, the death penalty was considered primarily an issue for states and localities, with reforms made by the political process rather than courts. That changed with the 1972 decision in *Furman v. Georgia*, a decision that "hit the country like a thunderbolt."[27] The court held that forty state laws violated the Eighth Amendment, a decision that necessitated the voiding of hundreds of death sentences. Beyond this, however, much remained unclear as the justices splintered into nine opinions. All that the five in the majority could agree upon, in a brief unsigned opinion, was that the death penalty in the specific cases the Court heard constituted "cruel and unusual punishment." Every member of that majority wrote his own separate concurring opinion explaining his specific position (every concurrence spoke for one justice and one justice alone). Only Justices William J. Brennan, Jr. and Thurgood Marshall believed that capital punishment was *per se* unconstitutional (unconstitutional under all circumstances). Justice William O. Douglas thought that the flaw in the state laws was that their use of jury discretion resulted in a system that discriminated against the disadvantaged. Justices Potter Stewart and Byron R. White criticized the lack of standards provided for jurors and the infrequency of death sentences; this was an infrequency that they believed resulted in random applications of this punishment that failed to serve any clear state interests. As Justice Stewart dramatically put it, these death sentences were cruel and unusual "in the same way that being struck by lightning is." The Constitution, he concluded, "cannot tolerate the infliction of a sentence of death under legal systems that permit this unique penalty to be so wantonly and so freakishly imposed."[28]

Hoping to modify their laws in a way that would secure a change of constitutional heart (and therefore a change of vote) by at least one of the five justices in the majority in *Furman* (probably Stewart or White), states sought to limit jury discretion in one of two ways after the decision. Most commonly, they adopted two-stage, or bifurcated, trials. Defendants found guilty of a capital offense during the trial phase would then be sentenced in a second phase in which the jury would determine the punishment to be applied. The other approach was to eliminate all jury discretion by mandating a death sentence for certain offenses, such as premeditated murder.

The *Gregg v. Georgia* Response

The bifurcated trial was upheld by a 7-2 vote in the 1976 decision in *Gregg v. Georgia*.[29] The court cited the thirty-five states that had adopted new capital punishment statutes and the significant number of death sentences imposed since *Furman* as strong evidence that the death penalty did not violate the public's standards of decency. Over the strenuous dissenting objections of Justices Marshall and Brennan, the court concluded that the state interests in retribution and deterrence both justified capital punishment. Additionally, for the majority in *Gregg*, the bifurcated trial, by requiring the jury to find at least one aggravating circumstance specified by statute and allowing the defense to present mitigating factors during the penalty phase, provided the jury standards that *Furman* had found fatally lacking in earlier laws.

Also decided in 1976, *Woodson v. North Carolina* rejected the imposition of a mandatory death sentence. Death is different from incarceration due to its irreversibility; consequently, juries faced with a choice between a guilty verdict and a mandatory death sentence might choose not to convict a guilty defendant because of the severity of the penalty. Furthermore, the single penalty for such a serious offense failed to treat each defendant as an individual. Finally, most states had rejected this approach, both before and after *Furman*.[30]

Life and Death After Gregg

Carol and Jordan Steiker characterize the Supreme Court's approach to capital punishment since *Gregg* as "retention of the death penalty with top-down regulation of capital practices by the American judiciary," resulting in a lengthy appeals process without substantially changing the penalty's arbitrariness and disproportionate imposition against racial and ethnic minorities and the economically impoverished.[31] Among the limits the court has placed on states have been bans on the death penalty for rape and the execution of juveniles and the mentally disabled (generally defined as those with an IQ of 70 or lower).[32]

After *Gregg*, a strong majority of the public supported capital punishment. Not only did most states reinstate the death penalty, but, according to the Gallup Poll in 1977, supporters outnumbered opponents by a margin of 66 percent to 26 percent.[33] After support peaked at 80 percent in 1994, it began a steady decline, although still retaining majority support, to (as we noted above) approximately 55 percent in favor in 2017.

As we can see in figure I-1, the number of executions shows a similar pattern. No individual was executed between 1968 and 1976 because of Supreme Court decisions (or pending cases). After *Gregg* permitted the resumption of capital punishment, the country would never see individuals executed with the dubious frequency that had defined previous decades (the high-water mark was reached in 1935, when 1,999 people were put to death). However, it was not until 1999, when the post-*Gregg* numbers peaked at 98, that we would begin to see the numbers decline, reaching a low of 20 in 2016.[34] Additionally, between 1996 and 2015, the death penalty was abolished in 7 of the 38 states that had adopted it after *Gregg*.[35]

There are two main reasons for these abolitions. First, and surprising to many, is the fact that capital punishment is significantly more expensive than life imprisonment, largely because of the high cost of the bifurcated trial proceedings and the lengthy appeals process that frequently lasts for a decade

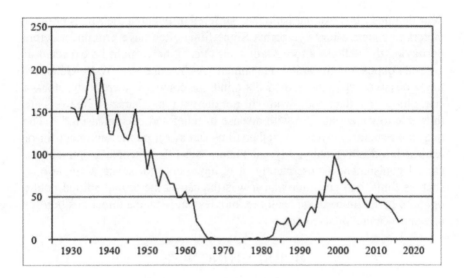

Figure I-1.   Executions in the United States, 1930–2017. Compiled using data from Bedau, "Background and Developments 11; "Executions By Year."

or more. Between 1973 and 2013, only 16 percent of those sentenced to death were executed, while 42 percent had their sentences overturned or commuted; 6 percent died of other causes and thirty-five percent remained on death row.[36] The second reason stems directly from the fact that a large number of defendants sentenced to death have since been exonerated. According to the Death Penalty Information Center, between 1973 and 2018, 162 such defendants were freed from death row. In Illinois in 2000, after thirteen people who had been sentenced to death were found to have been wrongly convicted, Governor George Ryan declared a moratorium on further death sentences and, a few years later, commuted to life imprisonment the sentences of all 167 inmates on death row. Eleven years later, Illinois abolished capital punishment.[37]

Over 2,700 persons remain on death row, and in 2017, juries sentenced 39 defendants to death.[38] As of 2019, 21 states had abolished the death penalty. That, however, means that a far greater number of states (29) have chosen to retain it, something which has always been the case in the United States.[39]

Essentially, this suggests that the public is ambivalent about the death penalty. While they support it in the abstract, when it comes to individual defendants, many find it more difficult to sentence them to death, especially if the alternative of life without parole is available as a severe punishment that will prevent future crimes by those convicted. In capital cases where there is little or no doubt about the defendant's guilt, their attorneys use a strategy of conceding that legal guilt while humanizing them by showing their families, abuse, or hardship they suffered throughout their lives or other factors to generate jury sympathy. Since films often have prominent actors portraying the defense attorneys or their clients, they might be expected to generate opposition to capital punishment. As Yvonne Kozlovsky-Golan astutely observes, "[i]n the audience's mind, the convict is merely an actor—a star, more often than not—who will not die with the character. Viewers are thus able to watch the film with a sense of relief and even pleasure."[40] The question remains, however, whether films can affect public sentiment for or against the death penalty. Myriad factors can affect people's opinions on capital punishment. Consequently, it is impossible to isolate a single one, such as films, and conclude that *it* was the causal factor that shifted public opinion. In addition, as we shall see, movies rarely take a direct position for or against capital punishment.

OUR STARTING NINE

Hollywood has not only "expertly exploited" capital punishment,[41] it has also *enthusiastically* embraced the subject matter as something deserving of cinematic treatment. There is no shortage of movies (and documentaries) that address (in some shape or form) some aspects of the death penalty. However, when we chose the nine films about which we would write for this book, we deliberately focused our attention upon those for which the death penalty was a central character. We have omitted movies such as *12 Angry Men* (1957) and *To Kill a Mockingbird* (1962) because they treat capital punishment in a qualitatively different way from those films featured in this book. They are not films *about* the death penalty *per se*; rather, they are better understood as courtroom and legal procedures dramas involving defendants who are on trial for their lives. The possibility that the accused will be sentenced to death is something that hangs over but is not itself a principal player in the legal proceedings, whose cinematic portrayals have been well discussed in other books.[42] Similarly, films such as *Paths of Glory* (1957), *Let Him Have It* (1991), and *Pierrepoint: The Last Hangman* (2005), while all meritorious, have been excluded because of our desire to focus the reader's attention upon the cinematic treatment of capital punishment in the United States.[43] Finally, we did not rely upon critical acclaim or box office receipts in order to arrive at our chosen nine. We have included some films despite the fact that they were broadly panned upon their release. Take, for example, *The Chamber*, the subject of chapter 7. To John Grisham, upon whose novel it was based, the film was "[a] train wreck from the very beginning."[44] The critics agreed. As Roger Ebert, the Pulitzer Prize-winning film critic, observed:

In the early days of X-rated movies, they were always careful to include something of "redeeming social significance" to justify their erotic content. Watching *The Chamber*, I was reminded of that time. The attitudes about African Americans and Jews here represent the pornography of hate, and although the movie ends by punishing evil, I got the sinking feeling that, just as with the old sex films, by the time the ending came around, some members of the audience had already gotten what they bought their tickets for. [45]

Ebert similarly criticized (as did most reviewers) *The Life of David Gale*, which we discuss in chapter 4. Believing the film did not merit receiving any starred rating, he wrote: "I am sure the filmmakers believe their film is against the death penalty. I believe it supports it and hopes to discredit the opponents of the penalty as unprincipled fraudsters." Referring to the movie's lead actor, and producer/director, Ebert went on to say:

[Kevin] Spacey and [Alan] Parker are honorable men. Why did they go to Texas and make this silly movie? The last shot made me want to throw something at the screen—maybe Spacey and Parker.

You can make movies that support capital punishment . . . or oppose it . . . or are conflicted . . . But while Texas continues to warehouse condemned men with a system involving lawyers who are drunk, asleep or absent; confessions that are beaten out of the helpless, and juries that overwhelmingly prefer to execute black defendants instead of white ones, you can't make this movie. Not in Texas. [46]

This does not mean that we have overlooked movies that received critical or audience acclaim. *The Thin Blue Line* won numerous awards including best documentary from the National Society of Film Critics. In a 2014 poll taken by the publication *Sight and Sound*, film critics voted it the best documentary of all time. [47] *Dead Man Walking* not only was a box office success, but was also nominated for four Academy Awards, with Susan Sarandon winning an Oscar for best actress. Finally, as discussed below, Halle Berry also won the best actress award for her role in *Monster's Ball*, the first African-American actress so honored. Although *The Green Mile* may not have won any of the four Academy Awards it was nominated for, it earned a whopping $136 million at the box office.

Chapter 1 analyzes *Murder in Coweta County* (1983), which casts Johnny Cash and Andy Griffith as the lead protagonist and antagonist, respectively, and depicts the true story of events that took place in rural Georgia in 1948. It is a compelling example of a made-for-television movie portraying a gruesome murder committed by a powerful landowner who thought he was above the law, without allowing that portrayal to descend into stereotypical exaggerations of lawlessness in the American South in the 1940s. Chapter 2 takes on *The Thin Blue Line* (1988), a non-fiction movie important enough to have been included in the Library of Congress's National Film Registry. [48] The subject of the film is Randall Adams, who was sentenced to death for a murder he did not commit. Although the death sentence was overturned on appeal due to a flaw in Texas capital punishment law, Adams served twelve years in prison before the findings of the film resulted in his release, making this a particularly important movie. It is also significant because of director Errol Morris's innovative use of re-enactments (a technique that has become quite common), as well as his unusual methods of interviewing and storytelling.

In chapter 3, we examine 1995's Hollywood blockbuster, *Dead Man Walking*. Based on Sister Helen Prejean's book, it seeks to humanize a defendant (played by Sean Penn) facing execution without losing sympathy for the families of the victims. This film serves as a nice point of comparison to *The Thin Blue Line,* because the narrative about the death penalty shifts between the chapters from discussion of an innocent man to discussion of an occupant of death row whose criminal guilt is never disputed. In chapter 4, analysis focuses on *The Life of David Gale* (2003), a film that examines the possibility of an innocent person being executed. Since the death penalty is irreversible, the film raises the crucial question (in a way distinct from the other films analyzed in the book) about whether the criminal justice system is fair enough to sentence someone to death.[49]

Race is a timeless and pervasive theme in many discussions of the death penalty. In chapter 5, we examine *A Lesson Before Dying*, the 1999 HBO adaptation of Ernest Gaines's novel of the same title. Like *Murder in Coweta County*, this is the story of a capital case that took place in the Jim Crow South. However, in this film the narrative is dominated by that socio-political, temporal context. Using an impactful combination of emotionally powerful dialogue and lighting techniques, the producers trace the story of a rural Louisiana schoolteacher, played by Don Cheadle, who takes it upon himself to educate an African American man who finds himself sentenced to death for a crime he did not commit. In light of the fact that Gaines's novel is broadly based on the facts surrounding the execution of Willie Francis, this chapter provides a useful way in which to expose readers to the extended discussion of legal doctrine as it relates to race and the Eighth Amendment. Also set in Louisiana and released in 1999, *The Green Mile*, a Hollywood blockbuster, is the subject of chapter 6. Although themes of race and prejudice are present in this film, they do not drive the narrative in the same way as *A Lesson Before Dying*. Our analysis of this motion picture version of Stephen King's award-winning novel focuses on the film's treatment of the execution of the intellectually challenged and the problems associated with the use of the electric chair.

Chapter 7's examination of *The Chamber*, a 1996 adaptation of John Grisham's novel, turns the analytical spotlight onto the lawyers whose clients are facing the ultimate form of punishment. Starring Gene Hackman as Sam

Cayhall, a Klansman who is scheduled to be executed by the state of Mississippi, the film raises profoundly important questions about legal ethics and family ties as it traces the efforts of Cayhall's grandson—an attorney played by Chris O'Donnell—to save his grandfather's life. Chapter 8 examines another 1996 movie, *Last Dance*. Distinguishable from every other movie treated in this volume, *Last Dance* features a female defendant. This film serves to emphasize that (a) there are women on death row, but that (b) the individuals who face state-sanctioned execution are disproportionately male.

Chapter 9—the final chapter that analyzes a film—takes on the major Hollywood production, *Monster's Ball* (2001). The film depicts a complex web of moral conflicts including the one that materializes between the characters played by Billy Bob Thornton and Halle Berry (she won an Oscar for her performance as the widow of a man whose execution she comes to learn was presided over by Thornton's prison warden character). The film serves as an important reminder that the impact of the "machinery of death"[50] extends far beyond the person being executed. As such, it is a fitting way to end the analysis in this book. This is because, as we demonstrate in our short Conclusion, while death penalty movies are usually driven by a focus on individual characters, the stories that those movies tell all bring to light myriad aspects of capital punishment, encouraging audiences (and, by extension, readers of this book) to ask as many questions as the films (and analyses of those films) answer.

NOTES

1. Benjamin N. Cardozo, *Law and Literature and Other Essays and Addresses* (New York: Harcourt, Brace, 1931), 93–94.

2. Jeffrey M. Jones, "U.S. Death Penalty Support Lowest Since 1972," Gallup, October 26, 2017, http://news.gallup.com/poll/221030/death-penalty-support-lowest-1972.aspx.

3. Virginia Leigh Hatch and Anthony Walsh, *Capital Punishment: Theory and Practice of the Ultimate Penalty* (New York: Oxford University Press, 2016), x.

4. Not to mention the fact that the due process language of the Fifth and Fourteenth Amendments ("No person shall . . . be deprived of life, liberty, or property, without due process of law") and ("No state shall . . . deprive any person of life, liberty, or property, without due process of law") is open to the interpretation that it explicitly permits capital punishment because it says that the government may deprive a person of their life providing it accords that person due process of law. For a useful discussion of this, see Joseph Blocher, "The Death Penalty and the Fifth Amendment," *Northwestern University Law Review Online* 111, no. 1 (2016).

5. Coleman v. Balkcom, 451 U.S. 949, 955 (1981) (Marshall, J., joined by Brennan, J., dissenting from the denial of certiorari).

6. Yvonne Kozlovsky-Golan, *The Death Penalty in American Cinema: Criminality and Retribution in Hollywood Film* (London: I. B. Tauris, 2014), 1.

7. "Somebody To Love," Spotify, track 2 on Jefferson Airplane, *Surrealistic Pillow*, 1967.

8. Paul Bergman and Michael Asimow, *Reel Justice: The Courtroom Goes to the Movies* (Kansas City, MO: Andrews and McMeel, 1996), xvii.

9. Kozlovsky-Golan, *The Death Penalty in American Cinema*, 221.

10. Ibid., 1–4.

11. Ernest J. Gaines, "Writing *a Lesson Before Dying*," *Southern Review* 41 (2005): 771.

12. For arguments for and against the death penalty, see Hugo Adam Bedau and Paul G. Cassell, *Debating the Death Penalty: Should America Have Capital Punishment? The Experts on Both Sides Make Their Case* (New York: Oxford University Press, 2004).

13. Peter Bates, "Truth Not Guaranteed: An Interview With Errol Morris," *Cinéaste* 17, no. 1 (1989): 17.

14. For a study of the relationship between social and political attitudes towards the death penalty, and cinematic portrayals of capital punishment, that looks at films from the entirety of the twentieth century and into the twenty-first century, see Kozlovsky-Golan, *The Death Penalty in American Cinema*.

15. See, for example, Hugo Adam Bedau, "Background and Developments," in *The Death Penalty in America: Current Controversies*, ed. Hugo Adam Bedau (New York: Oxford University Press, 1997); Marie Gottschalk, *The Prison and the Gallows: The Politics of Mass Incarceration in America* (New York: Cambridge University Press, 2006). On the history of capital punishment's evolution in individual states, see Andrew Welsh-Huggins, *No Winners Here Tonight: Race, Politics, and Geography in One of the Country's Busiest Death Penalty States* (Athens: Ohio University Press, 2009) (discussing Ohio); Alan Rogers, *Murder and the Death Penalty in Massachusetts* (Amherst: University of Massachusetts Press, 2008).

16. Bedau, "Background and Developments," 3–9. Michigan and Rhode Island partially abolished it in 1847 and 1852 respectively. Ibid., 9, 15.

17. Ibid.

18. Kozlovsky-Golan, *The Death Penalty in American Cinema,* 100.

19. Bedau, "Background and Developments," 3.

20. "Number of Executions By State and Region Since 1976," Death Penalty Information Center, accessed August 17, 2019, https://deathpenaltyinfo.org/number-executions-state-and-region-1976.

21. Carol S. Steiker and Jordan M. Steiker, *Courting Death: The Supreme Court and Capital Punishment* (Cambridge, MA: Belknap Press, 2016), 9.

22. Mississippi Legislature, 2017 Regular Session, House Bill 63: http://billstatus.ls.state.ms.us/2017/pdf/history/HB/HB0638.xml.

23. Kim Chandler, "Alabama 3rd State to Allow Execution by Nitrogen Gas," *Associated Press*, March 22, 2018.

24. Mark Berman, "Oklahoma Says It Will Begin Using Nitrogen for All Executions in an Unprecedented Move," *Washington Post*, March 14, 2018.

25. Deborah L. Heller, "Death Becomes the State: The Death Penalty in New York State—Past, Present and Future," *Pace Law Review* 28 (2008): 591.

26. See Wilkerson v. Utah, 99 U.S. 130 (1878) (upholding the constitutionality of execution by firing squad, but concluding that being "drawn or dragged to the place of execution" or being "emboweled alive, beheaded, and quartered" would violate the Constitution [see 99 U.S. at 135, 136]).

27. 408 U.S. 238 (1972); Helen Prejean, *The Death of Innocents: An Eyewitness Account of Wrongful Executions* (New York: Vintage Books, 2005), 201.

28. 408 U.S. at 309, 310 (Stewart, J., concurring).

29. 428 U.S. 153 (1976).

30. 428 U.S. 280 (1976).

31. Steiker and Steiker, *Courting Death*, 154.

32. Kennedy v. Louisiana, 554 U.S. 407 (2008); Roper v. Simmons, 543 U.S. 551 (2005); Atkins v. Virginia, 536 U.S. 304 (2002).

33. "In Depth: Topics A–Z; Death Penalty," Gallup, accessed April 18, 2019, http://news.gallup.com/poll/1606/death-penalty.aspx

34. "Executions By Year."

35. "Number of Executions By State and Region Since 1976."

36. Frank R. Baumgartner and Anna W. Dietrich, "Most Death Penalty Sentences Are Overturned. Here's Why That Matters," *Monkey Cage (Washington Post)*, March 17, 2015, https://www.washingtonpost.com/news/monkey-cage/wp/2015/03/17/most-death-penalty-sentences-are-overturned-heres-why-that-matters/?noredirect=on&utm_term=.c3168c8fb52e.

37. "Innocence: List of Those Freed From Death Row," Death Penalty Information Center, updated April 19, 2018, https://deathpenaltyinfo.org/innocence-list-those-freed-death-row; Jodi Wilgoren, "Citing Issue of Fairness, Governor Clears Out Death Row in Illinois," *New York Times*, January 12, 2003.

38. "Death Sentences in 2017," Death Penalty Information Center, accessed May 18, 2018, https://deathpenaltyinfo.org/2017-sentencing#Defendants2017.

39. It should be noted that the governors of 4 of those 29 states have, in recent years, imposed moratoria on capital punishment (Oregon [2011]; Colorado [2013]; Washington [2014]; and Pennsylvania [2015]). "States With and Without the Death Penalty," Death Penalty Information Center, accessed August 17, 2019, https://deathpenaltyinfo.org/state-and-federal-info-state-by-state.

40. Kozlovsky-Golan, *The Death Penalty in American Cinema*, 7.

41. Ibid., 1.

42. See, for example, Bergman and Asimow, *Reel Justice* (of the movies featured in our book, only *The Thin Blue Line* is discussed in this volume). See ibid., 49–54; Anthony Chase, *Movies on Trial: The Legal System on the Silver Screen* (New York: The New Press, 2002), (Chase does not discuss any aspect of capital punishment in this book); Kent Kauffman, *Movie Guide for Legal Studies* (New York: Pearson, 2010).

43. For an excellent comparative discussion of the use of capital punishment around the world, see Roger Hood and Carolyn Hoyle, *The Death Penalty: A Worldwide Perspective*, 5th ed. (New York: Oxford University Press, 2015).

44. "A Conversation With Bestselling Author John Grisham," Diane Rehm Show, November 17, 2016 (transcript at https://dianerehm.org/shows/2016-11-17/a-conversation-with-best-selling-author-john-grisham).

45. Roger Ebert, "Reviews: *The Chamber*," accessed April 18, 2019, https://www.rogerebert.com/reviews/the-chamber-1996.

46. Roger Ebert, "Reviews: *The Life of David Gale*," accessed April 18, 2019, https://www.rogerebert.com/reviews/the-life-of-david-gale-2003.

47. "Filmmakers' Poll," *Sight & Sound*, September, 2014, https://www.bfi.org.uk/news-opinion/sight-sound-magazine/september-2014-issue.

48. Of all the films discussed in this book, *The Thin Blue Line* is the only one to have this honor bestowed upon it.

49. In October 2017, the actor Anthony Rapp accused Kevin Spacey of making unwanted sexual advances toward him when Rapp was only fourteen years old. In the immediate wake of that breaking news, numerous other individuals accused Spacey of sexual harassment. This scandal had serious, negative implications for Spacey's career. See, for example, Sandra Gonzalez, "'House of Cards' Production to Resume without Kevin Spacey," *CNN.com*, December 4, 2017, https://www.cnn.com/2017/12/04/entertainment/house-of-cards-production/index.html. After the scandal broke, we carefully reconsidered our decision to include *The Life of David Gale* in this book because it stars Kevin Spacey. We collectively decided that the film is bigger (and important to discussions of cinematic portrayals of the death penalty) than just the sum of its cast. Consequently, we made the decision to retain a chapter about this film.

50. Callins v. Collins, 510 U.S. 1141, 1145 (1994) (Blackmun, J., dissenting from the denial of certiorari).

Chapter One

Murder in Coweta County: No Man is Above the Law

In 1983, the actor Andy Griffith was still best known to audiences as the loveable and endearing Sheriff Andy Taylor, the character that he played on the *Andy Griffith Show*. That aw-shucks sitcom, which generated a special brand of highly appealing nostalgic television, flew high in the network television ratings for much of the 1960s. Some of the titles of Griffith's subsequent works might suggest his career took a darker turn after Sheriff Andy turned in his badge, but titles can be deceiving. In *Winter Kill* (1974), *Street Killing* (1976), and *Murder in Texas* (1981), all made-for-television movies, Griffith played a sheriff, a prosecutor, and the father of a murder victim, respectively. When Griffith passed away in 2012, the title of the obituary that ran in the *New York Times* spoke volumes about the actor's image: "Andy Griffith, TV's Lawman and Moral Compass, Dies at 86."[1]

In 1983, musician Johnny Cash was best known to his fans as a prolific singer-songwriter whose work cut across genres and garnered widespread appeal. He had enjoyed country music chart success since the 1950s with hits such as "Cry! Cry! Cry!," "I Walk the Line," "Ring of Fire," and "A Boy Named Sue"—performed at a live concert at San Quentin State Prison in California. Cash was voted into the Country Music Hall of Fame in 1980, followed by induction into the Rock and Roll Hall of Fame twelve years later. At the same time, however, he had developed (and, perhaps, deliberately cultivated) a bad-boy reputation, running afoul of the law on numerous different occasions.

On Tuesday, February 15, 1983, American audiences tuned in to CBS to watch these two stars cast in the leading roles of that evening's made-for-television movie, *Murder in Coweta County*. They would have been forgiven for expecting Griffith and Cash to play the film's principal protagonist and antagonist, respectively. Instead, what they saw was a complete reversal of roles. Griffith excelled as the arrogant, "chillingly wicked,"[2] cold-blooded killer John Wallace, while Cash (for whom the project was a personal labor of love) shone as the crusading Sheriff Lamar Potts, determined to hold Wallace accountable for the ruthless murder he committed.

Murder in Coweta County tells the true story of the events that unfolded in rural Georgia in 1948. It is not a well-known film;[3] it was made for the small, rather than big, screen, and it does not typically find its way onto lists of movies about the death penalty. Nevertheless, it serves as a fitting way to open this volume about cinematic portrayals of capital punishment (Wallace goes to the electric chair for his crime). This is because, unlike some of the Hollywood blockbusters discussed in later chapters, this film neither (a) feels the need to engage in stereotypical, and exaggerated depictions of its subject matter (in this case, lawlessness in the pre-Civil Rights Movement South), nor (b) encourages or expects the audience to take a position on the morality or propriety of the death penalty. It raises issues that serve as a supporting cast of characters for the film's principal message—"that every human being—white or black, rich or poor—[is] . . . entitled to full justice under the law, and that neither money, power, nor influence should dilute that right."[4] In other words, it delivers the message that no person is above the law.

That message is conveyed to the audience at the very beginning of the film, when a southern voice reads the white text that scrolls upward against a black screen:

> In 1948, in rural Georgia, there was a vast estate known as "The Kingdom." Ruled by one man, his power was absolute and beyond the law. His family legacy was one of exploitation, corruption and ruthless violence. This is the story of the man who ran the Kingdom. And the man who brought him down.

In sum, it is the story of why "Wilson Turner was doomed." The story of why, "[w]ithout benefit of trial, judge, or jury, he was going to die."[5] A poor, white, tenant sharecropper, Turner was let go by Wallace simply for running Wallace's moonshine in a manner that this lord of all he surveyed did not appreciate. Turner had had Wallace's permission to do the liquor run, but that did not matter. Turner was dismissed, told to leave his home (on Wallace's land) immediately—taking his wife and their young baby with him—and (perhaps most significantly) ordered not to harvest the valuable crops he had planted. There was only one person entitled to them now—John Wallace.

Seeking a measure of revenge, Turner stole one of Wallace's prized Guernsey cows. Although he was arrested in a neighboring county, there was never any doubt that Turner would end up in the Meriwether County jail. The only surprise came when, citing lack of evidence, the Meriwether sheriff turned him loose, even being so kind as to ensure that Turner had the keys to his truck returned to him. At least, that is what Turner thought was happening. In actuality, it was a well-orchestrated set-up. Wallace and three of his men were waiting outside the jail. When Turner proceeded to drive off, a chase ensued, with the Wallace posse claiming that they were in pursuit of an escaped prisoner. At one point, Turner's truck, closely followed by the two chasing cars, is heading along a road, coming toward the camera. The camera pans right to follow the vehicles and, as it does, a sign comes into view. It reads "Coweta County." The men have crossed the county line. The driver of the car containing Wallace—who is hanging out the window firing his gun in the direction of Turner's truck—expresses concern, but Wallace orders him to keep driving. What the driver says next holds the key to the remainder of the story that the film tells: "but John, this is Lamar Potts's county."

This county is home to the Sunset Tourist Camp, where Turner is compelled to stop because he has run out of gas. It is here that Wallace kills Turner by smashing the man's skull in with his gun.

A "REAL APPRECIATION FOR SOUTHERN JUSTICE"

Murder in Coweta County was adapted for television from Margaret Anne Barnes's 1976 award-winning book of the same name, a book described by one newspaper critic as "one of the best crime trial recreations ever written."[6] Barnes was born in Newnan, the county seat of Coweta (pronounced Cay-eeta) County and home to the courthouse where the Wallace trial took place (when she was twenty-one); consequently, she brought an important, informed local perspective to the work. Her son recalls that it was Barnes's "'real appreciation for Southern justice' which led her to write about real-life events in Georgia and Alabama history."[7] Such was her commitment to uncovering and shedding light on these episodes in southern history (published in 1999, her third book told the story of the 1950s political corruption in Phenix City, Alabama that led to the assassination of the State's Attorney General-elect Albert Patterson);[8] she did not allow death threats to dissuade her from continuing to write about these subjects.[9]

"King" John Wallace

John Wallace was the self-anointed head of "The Kingdom" in Meriwether County, Georgia, and death threats were just one of what he considered to be the perfectly justifiable—and legal—tools of his trade. It was the Strickland family that "openly and arrogantly" designated the "half-moon corner" of the county, which it owned, as "'The Kingdom.'" A "fierce tribe," the Stricklands "had controlled the county for 150 years with fear, economic bondage, and an occasional dole."[10] After a federal revenue agent killed John Strickland in 1932, John's son, Tom, was passed over in favor of Wallace, who was John Strickland's nephew:

> In picking an heir apparent, the Stricklands put aside personal preferences and prejudices. Their key to survival was family solidarity. Whatever the crisis, they stood shoulder-to-shoulder, presenting an impregnable fortress to the world. To continue their rule of the county, the strongest clansman was selected, their sister's son, John Wallace.

Why? The answer becomes simple when one examines the way in which Wallace did business:

> John Wallace's reign was different from his uncle's. John Strickland's rule was based on absolute terror—even his friends were afraid of him . . . Wallace had a different way of doing things. He tolerated nothing but blind obedience, but he coupled this with a spontaneous generosity so remarkable that his mother called him "Double John." "Because," Miss Myrt once explained, "he's the best boy and the worst boy I ever saw."[11]

As a result, to a great many Georgians (although, generally only those that lived in Meriwether County), John Wallace was no less heroic and no less appreciative of "Southern justice." It was, however, heroism and justice on his own terms.

These attributes of Wallace are laid bare for all the audience to see from the very beginning of the cinematic adaptation of Barnes's book. After the opening text that scrolls on the screen, setting the scene for the audience, we get our first exposure to Wallace as he receives a large wad of bills from the two men to whom he is selling moonshine. As they finish stowing their illegal cargo beneath a tarp covering the bed of their pickup, we see another car—its side adorned by an official-looking badge—pull up. When the driver, wearing a sheriff's badge, steps out, we—the audience—are momentarily fooled into thinking that the look that has come across Wallace's face is a look of fear. This is the first of many times that this happens; such is the acting ability brought to the part by Griffith, that the audience is deceived every single time (just as Wallace would wish). The momentary flash of "fear" is immediately replaced by a broad smile as the two men warmly greet each other by their first names. Sheriff Hardy Collier (played by Danny Nelson) is an integral part of the "courthouse ring" in Meriwether County— the "little clique . . . of powerful men who had little or no respect for the rights of blacks" or any other men who dared to cross them.[12] Collier has not come to enforce the law, but instead to advise the moonshine purchasers to take a back roads route out of town in order to avoid the federal authorities.

That this is business as usual in "The Kingdom" is reinforced by what happens next. Before Collier can assent to Wallace's request for a ride into town, there's a piece of black business to take care of. Collier hauls a young African American man, caught siphoning gasoline from storage tanks on local farms, out of the back of his car. It is a man known to Wallace. Indeed, we are led to assume that he is one of Wallace's employees, and the man believes that, consequently, Wallace will show him some kind of mercy. He does—but it is a cruel kind of mercy designed to generate the aforementioned "blind obedience." At gunpoint, the young man is ordered by Wallace to place his arms and feet in the doorjamb of the car. We do not hear the crunching of skin and bones, and the painful wailing, as Wallace slams the door into the limbs of the man, but we do not need to. We have all heard the message, loud and clear.

With an appropriate degree of irony, we do not bear witness to the brutalization of the young man because the camera abruptly cuts away to a scene of a church choir singing "Onward Christian Soldiers." Although Wallace does not appear at the church until the services have ended, his arrival is greeted warmly, especially because he brings with him his own special brand of Christian charity. He produces a large wad of bills—which, as the audience knows,. is the same money he earned from selling illegal liquor—and presents them to the pastor, indicating that he has made good on his promise to help the church obtain new pews for the congregation. Representing the way in which the movie is a particularly faithful adaptation of Barnes's book, this is a depiction of one of the specific examples Barnes gives to illustrate Wallace's Janus-faced existence, and the "blind obedience" and absolute power it brought him. [13]

Sheriff Lamar Potts

The hero of *Murder in Coweta County* shared Barnes's "appreciation for Southern justice," and his generosity was legend just like Wallace's. That is where the comparisons between Wallace and Lamar Potts end. By the time the events depicted in the book—and the film—took place, Lamar Potts had already served twelve years as the sheriff of Coweta County (he would serve another two decades before retiring). After the Civil War and through until the 1960s, in Georgia, the county sheriff's "traditional role . . . was to defend the establishment against attacks on white supremacy." As Donald L. Grant explains, at this time, most "law officers and political insiders considered themselves above the law and took it upon themselves to mete out judgment and punishment without due process, often without consideration of constitutional restrictions against cruel and inhuman punishment." Potts "was an uncommon individual" who bucked this trend. [14] As Cash observes, in the quote from him that appears on the back cover of Barnes's book, "[i]t was my privilege to portray Sheriff Lamar Potts," an individual he describes as "a great American hero."

That heroism is on display from the very moment that we meet him in the movie. The witnesses to Turner's killing are in disbelief, but one of them knows exactly what to do. "I'm gonna call Sheriff Potts," he firmly declares. As the pair of Wallace cars speed away from the Sunset Tourist Camp, the scene shifts to the environs of a classic 1950s soda foundation. Initially, we just see a jacket bedecked with the sheriff's badge, but then the camera tilts up to reveal Potts's (Cash's) face. Talking with one of his deputies, he is concerned about the boy perusing the comics in the corner of the store. Potts knows the boy and knows that his family is dirt poor and cannot afford to replace the trousers that he has clearly grown out of. Go and buy the young man a pair that actually fit him, he instructs the deputy; then take the kid home but be sure that the family does not know that the money came from the sheriff's pocket. Potts does not want to embarrass the family more than he has to or to take credit for this act of charity. This one short scene speaks volumes about Sheriff Potts's character and standing in Coweta County.

SOUTHERN JUSTICE

After his questioning of witnesses at the Sunset Tourist Camp and gathering of initial pieces of information about the vehicles and likely individuals involved that leads him to suspect that Turner and Wallace were the victim and principal perpetrator, respectively, Potts drives over to the office of his opposite number in Greenville, the seat of Meriwether County. In the confrontation that ensues between Collier and Potts, it quickly becomes clear that while both consider themselves lawmen—as do the voters of their counties that elected them—only one is willing to act in accordance with, rather than "above" or "beyond," the law.

Collier is sitting at his desk, jacket- and hat-less. Potts is standing at the edge of the desk, and therefore towering over, and looking down upon, the other man. This camera angle deliberately conveys the impression that Potts is in charge, the fact that he is on "enemy territory" notwithstanding. Potts's appearance is far more formal—he is jacketed and wearing his hat—but he is also far more relaxed than Collier is as he delivers a firm, resolute message: "Now let me make something clear to you, Collier. I have jurisdiction on this case, and I didn't come here out of law. I came here out of manners. Now I want John Wallace and Herring Sivell brought to my office, and I want you to bring them." As Potts is speaking, the camera occasionally cuts to an increasingly agitated Collier, whose blood pressure is visibly rising. "You want them so bad, why don't you get them," he replies. Strongly, and calmly, his blood pressure not wavering, Potts has the last word: "That's your job."

Barnes describes Greenville in the following way: "Beneath its Southern slumber lay violence and injustice of the cruelest kind. There were those who were above the law, those who were beyond the law, and those who were at the mercy of the law."[15] Before engaging in a detailed discussion of the way in which the rule of law is portrayed in *Murder in Coweta County*, it is important very briefly to place the execution of Wallace (an execution that proves ultimately, in this case, that southern justice, not injustice, prevailed) in some historical context.

John Wallace was executed on November 3, 1950. He was one of six individuals (all men) that the state of Georgia has put to death since 1924 for capital crimes committed in Coweta County (the last such execution took place in 1955). Five of these men were African American. One—Wallace— was white.[16] The Jim Crow South is, in many important ways, very different from the American South today—the New American South.[17] Moreover, as figure 1.1 indicates, Georgia does not execute people at the rate it once did (reflecting nationwide trends). However, the fact remains that since 1976 (when the Supreme Court lifted its capital punishment moratorium with its decision in *Gregg v. Georgia*), only five states have executed more individuals than Georgia.[18] Additionally, as shown in figure 1.2, Georgia is located in the region of the country that has executed the overwhelming majority of individuals put to state-sanctioned death since 1976. The inescapable fact is that "[t]he history of the American death penalty has been . . . a history of profound regional division that is still clearly visible in death penalty practices today," and "[o]ne of the strongest predictors of a state's propensity to conduct executions today is its history of lynch mob activity more than a century ago."[19]

NO MAN IS ABOVE THE LAW

There are a number of different elements to the "no man is above the law" narrative in *Murder in Coweta County*; three are discussed here (when watching the movie, readers are encouraged to identify more elements). The first two speak to the principal reasons why the trial and subsequent execution of John Wallace are famous in American criminal justice history.

Wealth

In the 1950s, Judson Griffin and James Crenshaw were convicted of armed robbery; afterwards, their lawyers began to prepare their appeals. At the time, Illinois law stated that anyone seeking this particular kind of appellate review was required to submit a full, certified copy of the lower court proceedings and transcript to the appeals court. When the case eventually ended up at the U.S. Supreme Court in 1956, Illinois did not dispute Griffin and Crenshaw's claim that they were financially unable to pay the fees necessary to get a copy of the transcript. At issue, however, was whether the Fourteenth

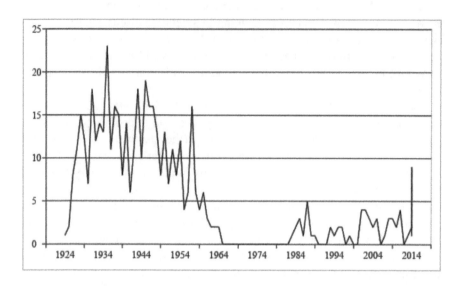

Figure 1.1.   Number of executions, per year, in Georgia, 1924–2017. Compiled using data from "Executions by Region"; "Executions in the U.S. 1608–2002: The ESPY File—Executions by State," Death Penalty Information Center, accessed August 3, 2018, https://deathpenaltyinfo.org/documents/ESPYstate.pdf; "A History of the Death Penalty in Georgia."

Amendment to the U.S. Constitution permitted states to deny appellate review to those who could not afford to secure the necessary documents. In his plurality opinion, Justice Hugo L. Black unequivocally concluded that it did not. "Providing equal justice for poor and rich, weak and powerful alike is an age-old problem," he wrote.[20] Continuing, he explained the importance of the appeals process and "equal justice under law" (the very phrase that adorns the west pediment of the Supreme Court's building):

> All of the States now provide some method of appeal from criminal convictions, recognizing the importance of appellate review to a correct adjudication of guilt or innocence. Statistics show that a substantial proportion of criminal convictions are reversed by state appellate courts. Thus to deny adequate review to the poor means that many of them may lose their life, liberty or property because of unjust convictions which appellate courts would set aside. Many States have recognized this and provided aid for convicted defendants who have a right to appeal and need a transcript but are unable to pay for it. A few have not. Such a denial is a misfit in a country dedicated to affording equal justice to all and special privileges to none in the administration of its criminal law. *There can be no equal justice where the kind of trial a man gets depends on the amount of money he has.*[21]

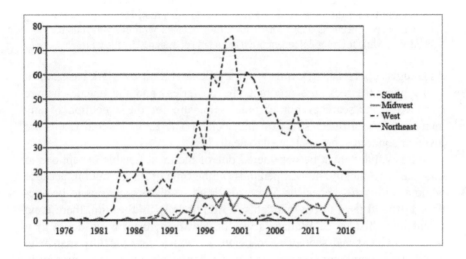

Figure 1.2.   Executions by geographical region, 1976–2017. Compiled using data from "Executions by Region."

Unfortunately, the administration of *un*equal justice due to disparities in wealth is rampant in the criminal justice system. As Professor Leroy D. Clark observes, "[n]o area of the law illustrates more the actual and perceived failure to ensure equal justice and serve the public interest by providing access to lawyers than the field of criminal representation."[22] In 1963, the Supreme Court issued its landmark ruling in *Gideon v. Wainwright*, which held that defendants in state criminal cases have a Sixth Amendment right to legal representation and that the states are constitutionally obligated to provide a lawyer to any such individual who cannot afford one.[23] However, what *Gideon* did not hold was that a criminal defendant is entitled to a *competent* lawyer. This problem is especially acute in capital cases, with the result that, simply put, America does not execute wealthy defendants.[24] In his concurring opinion in *Furman v. Georgia*, Justice William O. Douglas wrote, at length, of the disparities that plagued the administration of the death penalty in the United States. "In a Nation committed to equal protection of the laws," he wrote, "there is no permissible 'caste' aspect of law enforcement." Yet, as he detailed, this was exactly what existed—and for myriad reasons, not the least of which was the financial standing of a defendant.[25]

At one point in his concurrence, Douglas quoted from Warden Lewis E. Lawes's book about life in Sing Sing prison in New York:

> Not only does capital punishment fail in its justification, but no punishment could be invented with so many inherent defects. It is an unequal punishment in the way it is applied to the rich and to the poor. The defendant of wealth and

position never goes to the electric chair or to the gallows. Juries do not inten-
tionally favour the rich, the law is theoretically impartial, but the defendant
with ample means is able to have his case presented with every favourable
aspect, while the poor defendant often has a lawyer assigned by the court. [26]

As Douglas observed, "[f]ormer Attorney General Ramsey Clark has said, 'It
is the poor, the sick, the ignorant, the powerless and the hated who are
executed.' One searches our chronicles in vain for the execution of any
member of the affluent strata of this society. The Leopolds and Loebs are
given prison terms, not sentenced to death."[27]

John Wallace must be considered one of the most notable exceptions to
this rule. Technically, he was penniless at the time of his execution, because
while awaiting his appeal he arranged for all of his possessions to be auc-
tioned off and used to pay his debts.[28] Additionally, in the film, there is no
ostentatious display of Wallace's wealth. However, there is no doubt that,
when convicted and sentenced to death, he was a very wealthy man who
could afford good legal representation. As Barnes observes, those present in
the courthouse when the verdict was delivered and the sentence pronounced
"had witnessed an historic happening. Never in the history of Georgia had a
man of Wallace's prominence and wealth been convicted of so serious a
crime, and never had a man of such power been sentenced to the electric
chair."[29] This is something that the audience learns from the opening scene
of the film (showing Wallace's ill-gotten gain, and his Janus-faced, seemingly beneficent use of that gain essentially to generate loyalty and obedience).
At the same time, it is a scene that tells the audience that in John Wallace's
case, wealth equals power.

Race

Murder in Coweta County demonstrates that there are two reasons why this
was a landmark moment in the history of race and the American criminal
justice system: the wealth of Wallace was one; the other was the race of the
two men who testimonies brought Wallace down. This was one of the very
rare occasions in which a white man was convicted in a capital case in the
Jim Crow South primarily on the testimony of African American witnesses.
The Civil Rights Act of 1866 guaranteed that no individual would be denied
their right to give evidence in court based on their race. However, this did not
dramatically diminish (much less bring an end to) overt and subtle racial
discrimination against and hostility toward African American witnesses in
the courtroom (from judges, lawyers, and juries alike), especially in the
South.[30] Take, for example, the story of Willie Reed. An African American
sharecropper, Reed was famous for risking his life in order to testify at the
1955 Mississippi trial of the white men who gruesomely murdered fourteen-
year-old African American Emmett Till (the defendants were ultimately ac-

quitted by an all-white jury). As the prolific journalist and historian David Halberstam observed, the Till murder and trial was "the first great media event of the civil rights movement."[31] The murder generated immense shock and horror, as did the acquittal. Afterward, Reed fled to Chicago, living out the rest of life there, for many years living under an assumed name. "'He was a brave kid to do what he did,' said Moses J. Newton, a reporter who covered the Till case. 'Blacks weren't expected to do a lot of testifying against white people in court in Mississippi'" in the 1950s.[32] That was no less true in 1940s Georgia.

Wallace commands two of his African American farmhands, Robert Lee Gates (Brent Jennings) and Albert Brooks (Norman Matlock), to help him destroy Turner's body (discussed below). Upon finding out, from his lawyer, that the two men will testify against him, Wallace exudes defiance. "In all of Georgia, not one white man has ever gone to the chair on a nigger's word," he says. "And they're gonna testify against me? How long you think they're gonna be around to do that?" After we hear these words, the camera cuts abruptly to a scene in the foreground of which, positioned in one corner, is a deputy with a shotgun prominently hanging over his shoulder. It is clear he is standing guard as we see other police officers, including Sheriff Potts (identifiable by his hat and the presence of his distinct vehicle), helping a group of African American families move their belongings and themselves into a set of vehicles. We instinctively know, before we are told by the conversation that Potts has with his men, that these are the family members of Gates and Brooks, and that they are being shepherded to safety (i.e., beyond the bounds of Meriwether County). The two men will safely testify against Wallace, proving that in this instance, not even his race can shield Wallace from the clutches of the law.

Political influence

The final element of the "no man is above the law" narrative of *Murder in Coweta County* discussed here helps, in part, to explain why Wallace (and his circle of accomplices) was so arrogant and self-assured. On the third page of her book, Barnes writes the following: "For a man who wasn't scared of Hell itself, Wallace was sure careful about the revenuers. From the beginning, he had told Turner that caution was absolutely necessary. He'd been caught twice and sent to the Federal penitentiary. He was out on a presidential pardon, but if he was caught again, they'd put him away for good."[33] Wallace's use of this "I'm beyond the law because I'm protected by the law" excuse is briefly referenced by Barnes on two other occasions.[34] Generally, however, she does not discuss this aspect of Wallace's history in detail in the book and it goes unmentioned in the film. However, knowledge of its existence arguably helps anyone who watches the film to appreciate why Wallace believed that he was beyond the law; hence the value of providing some more explanation here.

In 1928, Assistant United States Attorney William A. Bootle (whom President Eisenhower later appointed as a judge to the United States District Court for the Middle District of Georgia) indicted twenty defendants on conspiracy to defraud the federal government of tax through moonshine-running activities. Of those arrested, Wallace and his three uncles—John, Mozart, and Maynard Strickland—were considered the principal players in the operation. Mozart and Wallace were indeed convicted, receiving jail sentences and fines, though Mozart received a pardon from President Franklin D. Roosevelt for the relatively small amount of the fine that had yet to be paid.[35] Why did the President do this? The simple answer is that it was just one of many such pardons issued by FDR after the repeal of Prohibition. John Wallace, however, did not view the pardon that way. To him, this act amounted to a Get Out of Jail Free card, good for use by *any* of the Strickland-Wallace clan, and applicable to *any and all future crimes* that any of the clan might commit. Likely, this was in no small part because the family supplied FDR with whiskey when he was staying in Warm Springs (the Meriwether County town situated less than ten miles from Wallace's "Kingdom").[36] That political influence (and potential presidential protection), however, was not going to help shield Wallace from the law beyond the borders of Meriwether County, something that he never came to terms with.[37]

Potts knew that it would not be easy to find the body of Wilson Turner, so he asked his deputies to solicit volunteers from the community to form a search posse. The next morning, a large crowd gathered outside the Coweta County courthouse. When Potts was met at the top of the steps by his brother J. H. (Earl Hindman), the ensuing dialogue emphasized just how much this was Lamar Potts's, rather than John Wallace's, territory. "Lamar. Okay, I've got it broke down into teams; every one of 'em's here because you asked 'em." As the Sheriff began to address them, the camera relocated down into the crowd, so that—along with the volunteers—it was looking up at, and taking directions from the Sheriff: "Hello fellas. There's a man who thinks he's above the law. Killed a fella, in our county. Thinks he's gonna get away with it. We're gonna see that he doesn't." Everyone in Coweta County is in agreement.

Sidebar: Stranger Than Fiction

While the Roosevelt-Wallace connection is fascinating, it is not the only truth-is-sometimes-stranger-than-fiction aspect of the political influence narrative of *Murder in Coweta County*. In addition to securing the role of the mystic, Mayhayley Lancaster, for his wife, June Carter Cash, Johnny Cash persuaded James Neal, one of the lawyers who had worked for him over the years, to play the part of A. L. Henson. This factoid does not sound particularly interesting until one learns about Neal's legal career. It was more than a little bit ironic that Neal should be asked to portray John Wallace's defense attorney, an attorney just as much part of the "courthouse ring" as everyone else in Wallace's "employment." This is because Neal was one of the principal federal prosecutors that successfully secured the prosecution of four members of President Nixon's inner political circle—John Mitchell, H. R. Haldeman, John D. Ehrlichman, and Robert C. Mardian—during the 1970s Watergate scandal. A decade after he worked to bring down participants in one of the biggest political disgraces in the nation's history, a scandal dominated by powerful figures who thought they could thumb their noses at the rule of law because they were above the law (as Nixon famously said in a 1977 interview, he firmly believed that "when the president does it, that means that it is not illegal"), Neal played a lawyer defending his client who thumbed his nose at the rule of law because he thought he was above the law.

Cash had "once asked him [Neal] for tickets to the Watergate cover-up trial." In 1983, he had a front-row seat to a very different type of performance by the lawyer, who "never shied from a camera," and got "'a kick every time it [*Murder in Coweta County*] is run.'"[38]

DIGNITY AFTER DEATH

In addition to race and politics, there is one other element of the story in *Murder in Coweta County* that plays out in several other films analyzed in this volume—the concept of human dignity. The role that this concept plays in cinematic portrayals of capital punishment is discussed extensively in *A Lesson Before Dying* (chapter 5) and *The Chamber* (chapter 7). In those two chapters, we see the way in which the state degrades the human dignity of the condemned prisoners. In *Murder in Coweta County*, the concept of dignity makes a different but nevertheless equally important appearance. It is not the dignity of John Wallace with which the film is concerned; indeed, it is not even the dignity of a living, breathing human being that our attention is focused upon. Rather, we, the audience, are taught an important lesson about the dignity, *after death*, of the body of Wilson Turner.

The "Burned Bones" Trial

In her book about the life and times of John Wallace, Dot Moore accurately describes his 1948 trial—for the murder of Turner—as the "Burned Bones" trial.[39] This is because the turning point in the proceedings was when people learned of the way in which Wallace had disposed of Turner's body. It was that act of desecration that, in so many people's minds, made this the most heinous crime possible. Professor William R. Ferris (who founded the Center for the Study of Southern Culture at the University of Mississippi) observes that, "[e]very Southerner has a healthy respect for death." Some of the traditions pertaining to that respect have, in recent decades, given way to the increasingly fast and frenetic pace of our lives.[40] In 1940s Georgia, however, that respect was a very important and prominent element of societal and cultural mores.[41]

It is difficult to make a crack in Wallace's arrogant, self-assured armor, and he firmly believes that he will be able to use an important aspect of the laws of Georgia for his own nefarious purposes. Literally translated from the Latin, *corpus delicti* means "body of the crime"; when the authorities suspect that a murder has taken place, their investigation will pursue the goal of putting together a "body" of evidence proving that someone has died at the hands of another. In 1948, in Georgia, prosecutors were required to provide physical proof that a death had occurred—in other words, the "body" they had to produce was the actual corpse. Initially, Wallace disposed of Turner's body by dumping it in an old abandoned well on his property. Far more afraid of Potts than Wallace, however, Sheriff Collier does not believe this will suffice. He reminds Wallace that Potts once pursued a suspect all the way into Kansas in order to secure a conviction. "Now I'm telling you John," says Collier, "if Potts can find a nigger in Kansas, he can sure find white trash in a swamp." Wallace's knowledge of the *corpus delicti* rule in Georgia leads to his defiant response: "he can't find a body if there ain't no body."

The "Package"

"When Sheriff Potts arrived on the square with John Wallace, the crowd parted to let Wallace pass. This was not the homage they might have offered him on Monday, nor the deference they might have shown him on Tuesday. Wednesday's opened path was a sign of withdrawal . . . a standing back from something incomprehensible and evil."[42] As Barnes explains, this is what happened on the third day of Wallace's trial after people learned of the way in which Turner was disposed of. In the film, this "evil" is conveyed to the audience through the scene that follows Wallace's visit to Lancaster. As he leads them on the search to find, and then retrieve, Turner's body from the abandoned well, Wallace never tells Brooks and Gates what they are looking for; to Wallace, it is nothing more than a quest to find "the package." This dehumanizes and strips Turner's body of its innate human dignity.

What happens next simply compounds Wallace's callous lack of respect for the dead. Brooks and Gates are instructed to wrap up the body and carry it slung from two sticks—in a manner that leaves the audience with a visual suggestion that the body is akin to an animal carcass being taken to a barbecue-roasting site—to a large moonshine pit. We see a large number of logs piled on top on the pit, logs that Wallace (and, to a lesser extent, Brooks and Gates) soaks with bottles of the liquor. We all know what is going to happen and, terrified of the spectacle that they are about to witness, Brooks and Gates find a large tree stump to hide behind. Wallace is far from terrified; his expression betrays his excitement. He lights a torch and eagerly throws it onto the log pile. As the blaze shoots up into the air, the camera repositions to watch Wallace creep closer to the fire, the foreground of brightly colored flames illuminating the sweaty but exuberant face of the man who believes he is now firmly beyond the reaches of the law. "All right Sheriff Potts; come get me now," he defiantly shouts. Gates's reaction is a study in contrasts: "Lord have mercy on me."

CONCLUSION: MAINTAINING THE RULE OF LAW

Speaking at the New York State Fair in Syracuse in 1908, President Theodore Roosevelt said: "We ask no man's permission when we require him to obey the law; neither the permission of the poor man nor yet of the rich man."[43] *Murder in Coweta County* is generally not a well-known movie, but it remains an important part of the history of Meriwether and Coweta counties and makes a powerful contribution to our understanding of cinematic portrayals of capital punishment by reinforcing the importance of the sentiment expressed by Roosevelt. When a new book on the life and times (and crimes) of John Wallace was published in 2011, the author held "audiences 'spellbound'" during her talk at the Coweta County Courthouse.[44] In 2016, the Newnan-Coweta Historical Society began stocking pamphlets entitled "John Wallace's Path to Death Row." Designed for use by tourists who want to "tour" the various sites associated with this infamous episode in Georgia's history, it was produced to coincide with "Flies at the Well," a new play put on by the Newnan Theatre Company.[45] Further, in July 2018, the seventieth anniversary of the conviction of Wallace and the thirty-fifth anniversary of the original airing of *Murder in Coweta County* were commemorated by special events organized by the Coweta County Convention & Visitor's Bureau (including a panel discussion, in the historic Newnan courthouse, featuring Dick Atkins, who produced the CBS movie).[46]

Visitors can even, if they are so inclined, drive down John Wallace Road in Meriwether County. Although that might strike some people as ghoulish and inappropriate, residents of the area—including, it should be noted, a grandson of Sheriff Potts—generally seem "untroubled" by the fact that there is a road named after the convicted killer. Perhaps they have good reason to be nonplussed by the road's existence. As one of Wallace's descendants suggests, "[m]aybe it's a good thing. Maybe it teaches people a lesson. And maybe the more they hear about it, the more they learn about it, the more they realize that everyone is accountable under the law."[47]

NOTES

1. Douglas Martin, "Andy Griffith, TV's Lawman and Moral Compass, Dies at 86," *New York Times*, July 3, 2012. To the generation of Americans that came of television age in the 1980s, Griffith's good-guy image was reinforced by his portrayal of the crusading defense attorney Ben Matlock, in the long-running television series *Matlock*.

2. Ibid.

3. One of us is indebted to John Gardner for bringing this movie to their attention long before the idea for this book was conceived.

4. Margaret Anne Barnes, *Murder in Coweta County* (Gretna, LA: Pelican Publishing, 1976), 29–30.

5. Ibid., 3.

6. The award she received was the "Edgar Allan Poe Special Award for an outstanding fact-crime study from the Mystery Writers of America." "Georgia Authors: Margaret Anne Barnes," Georgia Center for the Book, accessed June 19, 2018, http://www. georgiacenterforthebook.org/Georgia-Literary-Map/Georgia-Author-Detail.php?record_id= 157. The original book was published by Reader's Digest Press in 1976; after the movie came out, it was republished by Pelican Publishing. In her book about John Wallace's life—including the events discussed in Barnes's book—Dot Moore suggests that Barnes's book was originally called *Malice, Aforethought*. Dot Moore, *No Remorse: The Rise and Fall of John Wallace* (Montgomery, AL: NewSouth Books, 2011), 124. However, the Library of Congress record for the book clearly indicates that it was initially published, in 1976, as *Murder in Coweta County*.

7. Daniel Yee, "Obituaries: Southern History Writer Margaret Anne Barnes, 80," *Washington Post*, October 16, 2007.

8. Margaret Anne Barnes, *The Tragedy and the Triumph of Phenix City, Alabama* (Macon, GA: Mercer University Press, 1999).

9. "Georgia Authors: Margaret Anne Barnes."

10. Moore, *No Remorse*, 31; Barnes, *Murder in Coweta County*, 14.

11. Barnes, *Murder in Coweta County*, 15.

12. Jonathan Grant, ed., *Donald L. Grant, The Way it Was in the South: The Black Experience in Georgia* (Athens: University of Georgia Press, 2001), 509.

13. Wallace "was a master at presenting the unexpected gift and the dramatic dole…giving new pews to the church, replacing a widow's dead milk cow, rebuilding a farmer's burned-out barn. Whenever there was trouble, Wallace was always there, distributing whatever was needed from his great storehouse of possessions." Barnes, *Murder in Coweta County*, 15.

14. Grant, *Donald L. Grant*, 509.

15. Barnes, *Murder in Coweta County*, 51.

16. Over the same time period, it executed four men who committed their crimes in Meriwether County (the last in 1960). Another man was executed the same day as Wallace—Jimmie Richardson (a white man) went to the electric chair for murdering his wife during the course of a heated, drunken argument. Richardson was convicted in Crisp County. "A History of the Death Penalty in Georgia: Executions by Year 1924-2014 (2015)," State of Georgia, Department of Corrections (Office of Planning and Analysis: The Death Penalty), accessed August 3, 2018, http://www.dcor.state.ga.us/sites/all/files/pdf/Research/Standing/Death_penalty_in_ Georgia.pdf; Richardson v. The State of Georgia, 207 Ga. 373, 61 SE2d 489 (1950).

17. For discussions of this subject, see Numan V. Bartley, *The New South 1945–1980: The Story of the South's Modernization* (Baton Rouge: Louisiana State University Press, 1995); Charles S. Bullock, III, and Mark J. Rozell, eds., *The New Politics of the Old South: An Introduction to Southern Politics*, 6th ed. (Lanham, MD: Rowman & Littlefield, 2017); Sally G. McMillen et al., eds., *Major Problems in the History of the American South*, 3rd ed., vol. II: *The New South* (New York: Cengage Learning, 2011).

18. Texas, Virginia, Oklahoma, Florida, and Missouri. "Executions by Region," Death Penalty Information Center, accessed August 3, 2018, https://deathpenaltyinfo.org/number-executions-state-and-region-1976.

19. Carol S. Steiker and Jordan M. Steiker, *Courting Death: The Supreme Court and Capital Punishment* (Cambridge, MA: Belknap Press, 2016), 17.

20. Griffin v. Illinois, 351 U.S. 12, 16 (1956).

21. Ibid., at 18–19 (italics added).

22. Leroy D. Clark, "All Defendants, Rich and Poor, Should Get Appointed Counsel in Criminal Cases: The Route to True Equal Justice," *Marquette Law Review* 81 (1997): 48.

23. 372 U.S. 335 (1963).

24. Clark, "All Defendants, Rich and Poor," 49, 49n10.

25. 408 U.S. 238, 255 (1972) (Douglas, J., concurring).

26. Ibid., at 251, quoting from Lewis Edward Lawes, *Life and Death in Sing Sing* (New York: Doubleday, 1929), 155–60.

27. 408 U.S. 238, 255, 251–52 (1976) (Douglas, J., concurring).

28. Barnes, *Murder in Coweta County*, 261.

29. Ibid., 258.

30. Sheri Lynn Johnson, "The Color of Truth: Race and the Assessment of Credibility," *Michigan Journal of Race & Law* 1 (1996); Andrew Elliott Carpenter, "*Chambers v. Mississippi*: The Hearsay Rule and Racial Evaluations of Credibility," *Washington and Lee Race and Ethnic Ancestry Law Journal* 8, no. 1 (2002): 22–24; Martin Yant, *Presumed Guilty: When Innocent People Are Wrongly Convicted* (Buffalo, NY: Prometheus Books, 1991), 183–90. For an excellent study of race discrimination relating to legal case witnesses during the colonial period, see A. Leon Higginbotham, Jr., *In the Matter of Color——Race & the American Legal Process: The Colonial Period* (New York: Oxford University Press, 1978).

31. David Halberstam, *The Fifties* (New York: Villard, 1993), 437.

32. Emily Langer, "Willie Reed, Who Risked His Life to Testify in the Emmett Till Murder Trial, Dies at 76," *Washington Post*, July 24, 2013.

33. Barnes, *Murder in Coweta County*, 5.

34. Ibid., 19, and (more subtlely) 264–65.

35. "An Oral Interview with Judge W. A. Bootle, Part I," *Journal of Southern Legal History* 7 (1999): 170–72.

36. Ibid., 171. When the president came to Meriwether, he buoyed the mood of the county's residents, temporarily enabling them to forget about the Strickland-Wallace reign of terror. "When the presidential motorcade came down the Federal Highway from Atlanta, they [the residents] lined the streets and cheered. Roosevelt's warm response delighted them and they claimed him as their own." Barnes, *Murder in Coweta County*, 51.

37. It should also be noted that the U.S. Constitution only gives the president "Power to grant Reprieves and Pardons for Offenses *against the United States*, except in Cases of Impeachment." U.S. Const. art. II, §2. In other words, the presidential pardoning power only applies to federal crimes.

38. Stephen Miller, "U.S. News—Remembrances: Prosecutor of Hoffa, Watergate Figures," *Wall Street Journal*, October 23, 2010, https://www.wsj.com/articles/SB10001424052702303738504575568201047610126; Matt Schudel, "James F. Neal, 81; Lawyer Won Courtroom Battles Against Jimmy Hoffa and Watergate Conspirators," *Washington Post*, October 22, 2010. Two other obituaries of Neal that did not mention *Murder in Coweta County* are Bruce Weber, "James F. Neal, Litigated Historic Cases, Dies at 81," *New York Times*, October 23, 2010; Martin Childs, "James Neal: Lawyer Who Put Jimmy Hoffa in Jail and Prosecuted the Perpetrators of the Watergate Cover-Up," *Independent*, November 4, 2010. It is very appropriate that Henson was portrayed by a lawyer who "never shied from a camera," because as his memoir makes clear, Henson was also very fond of the media . . . Henson contends that during his incarceration in the Meriwether County jail, Turner was treated to a nice lunch with himself, Sheriff Collier, and Wallace. . . . As Dot Moore observed, "[n]ot likely." Moore, *No Remorse*, 51.

39. Moore, *No Remorse*, 65.

40. Ferris is quoted in Rick Bragg, "Almost Moribund Itself, a Courtesy Pause for Death," *New York Times*, May 1, 1997.

41. See, for example, the discussion in Moore, *No Remorse*, 69.

42. Barnes, *Murder in Coweta County*, 226.

43. Speech given at the New York State Fair, Syracuse, NY, September 7, 1903, quoted in Gordon Hutner, ed., *Selected Speeches and Writings of Theodore Roosevelt* (New York: Vintage, 2014), 47.

44. Noelle Matteson, "Dot Moore Presents New Book on John Wallace to Rapt Audiences," September 14, 2011, accessed June 19, 2018, http://www.newsouthbooks.com/pages/2011/09/14/dot-moore-presents-new-book-on-john-wallace-to-rapt-audiences/. The book in question is Moore, *No Remorse*.

45. Winston Skinner, "Brochure Offers Guide to Sites From 1948 Crime," *Newnan Times-Herald* (Newnan, GA), March 26, 2016.

46. Taylor Robins, "'Murder in Coweta County' Discussed By Descendants 70 Years Later," *Newnan Times-Herald* (Newnan, GA), July 22, 2018.

47. Mike Strickland, quoted in Doug Richards and Julie Wolfe, "Georgia Town Honors Bootlegger, Killer With Road," *USA Today*, February 7, 2015. Coincidentally, Andy Griffith also has a stretch of road named after him—the Andy Griffith Parkway in North Carolina—which he says was the best honor ever bestowed upon him. Martin, "Andy Griffith, TV's Lawman and Moral Compass."

Chapter Two

The Thin Blue Line: The Search For Truth

The danger of executing an innocent person has been the most effective argument for the abolition of the death penalty. As Robert Norris wrote, "The world is now more aware of wrongful convictions than ever and it may have an impact on public opinion, particularly regarding the death penalty. . . . [A]lthough many Americans still favor the death penalty, the prospect of errors is a key factor in eroding confidence in the practice."[1]

A wrongfully convicted defendant who has been sentenced to prison can be released and perhaps even financially compensated, but the finality of capital punishment makes it impossible to correct after an execution has been carried out. The 2011 repeal of Illinois's death penalty law presents a particularly dramatic example of the results of this argument. Eleven years earlier, after thirteen death row inmates had been exonerated, Republican Governor George Ryan declared a moratorium on executions, explaining that "'until I can be sure with moral certainty that no innocent man or woman is facing a lethal injection, no one will meet that fate.'"[2] To help him decide on a long-term solution, he appointed a commission to study the issue. In 2003, he decided that the process was so flawed that he commuted the sentences of all 167 prisoners on death row to life imprisonment. When a later governor, Democrat Pat Quinn, signed legislation ending capital punishment, his stated reason was that "our experience has shown that there is no way to design a perfect death penalty system, free from the numerous flaws that can lead to wrongful convictions or discriminatory treatment."[3] Between the law's enactment in 1977 and its repeal in 2011, twenty of the 305 defendants convicted and sentenced to death were exonerated.[4]

The Exonerated, a 2002 play that was adapted into a cable television movie in 2005, used documentary evidence and first-person narration to tell the stories of defendants wrongly convicted and sentenced to death who were later discovered to be innocent. At the end of the film, the actors morph into the five men and one woman who were eventually cleared.[5] The play ran off-Broadway for 600 performances and won numerous awards. It was staged for Governor Ryan and other politicians in December 2002, after Ryan's moratorium on executions but prior to his 2003 commutation of the sentences of all Illinois death row inmates.[6] Its continued relevance is attested to by frequent revivals all over the United States, including a tenth anniversary production in New York City by the Culture Project.[7] The growth of new media has led to an entire genre of programs devoted to examining convicted murder defendants who may be innocent. Two of the most prominent examples are the Netflix series *Making of a Murderer* and the podcast *Serial*, whose first season, according to CBS News, had 68 million downloads.[8]

Supporters of the death penalty counter that its benefits outweigh the possibility of erroneous conviction. Louis P. Pojman argues that although "an occasional error may be made, regrettable though this is," it "is not a sufficient reason for us to refuse to use the death penalty, if on balance it serves a just and useful function."[9] Instead, we should work to improve the judicial system, especially the appellate process.

THE ACCIDENTAL ORIGINS OF ERROL MORRIS'S FILM

Errol Morris' 1988 documentary *The Thin Blue Line* tells the story of Randall Dale Adams, who had been sentenced to death twelve years earlier for a murder he did not commit. The title comes from the prosecutor's statement in his closing argument that the police are a "thin blue line" separating society from anarchy. However, as Paul Bergman and Michael Asimow write, "only a large dose of good luck and a dedicated filmmaker saved Adams from an overzealous prosecutor."[10]

Morris's original intention was to make a movie about Dr. James Grigson, also known as "Dr. Death," a forensic psychologist whose expert testimony for the state was an important factor in the sentencing of about a third of Texas' death row inmates.[11] The Texas Code of Criminal Procedure requires that, for a death sentence to be imposed, the jury must find that "there is a probability that the defendant would commit criminal acts of violence that would constitute a continuing threat to society."[12] In his testimony, sometimes made without having interviewed the defendant, Grigson often asserted one hundred percent certainty, occasionally even "a one thousand percent chance," that the defendant presented a future danger. Not only did Grigson testify against Adams, he still maintained, even after Adams had been officially exonerated and released from prison, that Adams would kill in the future.[13] Despite his expulsion from the American Psychiatric Association (APA) and the Texas Society of Psychiatric Physicians in 1995, Grigson continued to testify until his retirement in 2003. He died the next year. [14]

In *Barefoot v. Estelle*, [15] by a 6–3 majority, the Supreme Court upheld the practice of admitting psychiatric testimony predicting future dangerousness. In response to the prosecution's hypothetical questions, asked because he had not interviewed Thomas Barefoot, Grigson concluded that there was "a one hundred percent and absolute chance" that the defendant would commit violent criminal acts in the future, even if incarcerated. In its *amicus curiae* brief, the APA noted that such predictions were wrong approximately two-thirds of the time. Nevertheless, a majority of the court believed that because the defense could contest such claims, the jury would be capable of making an appropriate decision.

It was Grigson who suggested to Morris, "You've got to go to death row and interview these people. They're not like you and me." [16] The director, who served as a private investigator before becoming a filmmaker, spoke to thirty-five death row inmates. He concluded that all but Randall Adams were guilty. Feeling the need to go beyond his suspicion, Morris launched a two-year investigation that confirmed his original instinct and provided the basis for *The Thin Blue Line*. He insisted that, because he does not know enough to generalize about the legal system, the film is "not about how the American justice system produces unfair convictions and puts the wrong people in jail." Instead, its subject is the inconvenience of truth because "our desire to seek the truth is a lot weaker than our desire to tell ourselves what we want to hear, to perpetuate our own beliefs." Once the police believed that Adams killed an officer, "they broke the rules, suppressed evidence, put perjured evidence on the stand." [17] Morris believed that by changing the objective of the justice system from finding the truth to justifying the penalty, capital punishment actually increases the likelihood of error. Despite the prosecution's obligation to act in the interests of justice, once charges are brought, the case acquires so much momentum that it is difficult to change directions, even if there is evidence supporting the defendant's innocence. These profoundly troubling aspects of the capital punishment system are portrayed in *The Thin Blue Line* using an impressive and innovative selection of cinematic techniques.

A DIFFERENT TYPE OF DOCUMENTARY

Although many of the techniques introduced by *The Thin Blue Line* were new when the film was made, even today many viewers who remain used to the more traditional direct address and cinema vérité (truthful cinema) styles will need to be aware of them. Direct address is the original documentary form, still used for most television news programs, in which a guiding voice explains the material to the viewer. Cinema vérité, first developed in the late 1950s, seeks to show real people and events as they occur, with minimal interference by the director who is primarily an observer. Some of its advocates, such as Frederick Wiseman, even go so far as to avoid interviews, voice-over, and a musical score.[18] In contrast, according to Morris, "[a]ll of my films break with the basic tenets of cinema vérité: No handheld cameras or shooting with available light, no running after the actions, no trying to remain as unobtrusive as possible."[19] No matter how inconspicuous a cinema vérité filmmaker may try to be, the participants will always be aware of the camera's presence and therefore become performers. In an interview featured on the Criterion Collection DVD, documentary filmmaker Joshua Oppenheimer argues that everyone in *The Thin Blue Line* is playing a part in order to be recognized and validated.

Morris also employs many of the techniques of *film noir* (French for "black film"), a style popular in low budget crime movies made during the post-World War II era. Their low-key lighting often illuminates only part of a scene, creating multiple shadows and sharp contrasts that can result in featured characters blending into the darkness. A variety of camera angles disorients the viewer. The result, according to Paul Schrader, is that "no character can speak authoritatively from a space that is being continually cut into ribbons of light." Adding to this effect, the audience is disoriented by the "use [of] a convoluted time-sequence."[20] Further disorientation comes from the lack of onscreen titles or narration identifying each of the witnesses speaking in this documentary. The atmosphere is heightened by Philip Glass's score.

Although *The Thin Blue Line* won many awards, including the National Society of Film Critics best documentary prize, and was subsequently placed on the National Film Registry of the Library of Congress, it was deemed ineligible for Oscar contention because of its use of techniques more common to fictional movies, and what was termed "scripted content."[21] As we discuss below, what are often called reenactments are reconstructions of the stories told at trial by those claiming to be eyewitnesses. These reflect their account of the truth, but not necessarily Errol Morris's belief about what actually occurred. As Bennett Gershman describes it, "the result is a portrayal, more vivid than any judicial decision or fictional account, of the vulnerability of the adversarial process of criminal justice, and the ease with which an innocent man could be put to death."[22]

In an interview featured on the DVD, Morris disputes the post-modern idea that truth is constructed, insisting instead that there is a fundamental reality even if we are not always able to discover it. *The Life of David Gale*, a fictional film discussed in chapter 4, opens with the opposite view, that all media, including the movie being watched, uses language to construct reality. That contrast should be kept in mind when watching the two films.

Randall Adams was convicted of the 1976 murder of a police officer primarily on the basis of the testimony of David Harris, who actually committed the murder, and several passersby, who testified as to what they claimed to have seen. Although Adams was convicted and sentenced to death, United States Supreme Court Justice Lewis Powell ordered a stay three days before his scheduled execution because of the exclusion of jurors who, despite expressing reservations about the death penalty, stated that they would follow Texas law in sentencing the defendant. [23] A year later, the full court overturned the death sentence but not the conviction. [24] Rather than risk a retrial on Adams's guilt, at the urging of District Attorney Henry Wade, [25] Governor Bill Clements commuted his sentence to life imprisonment. [26] Had it not been for this technical error, Adams likely would have been executed before this film demonstrated his innocence. An appeal claiming that the Supreme Court's decision required a new trial on his guilt rather than simply the penalty phase was filed by Adams but rejected by the Texas Court of Criminal Appeals. [27]

By interviewing these witnesses and staging versions of their testimony, the film converts its audience into a jury to decide Adams's (and ultimately Harris's) guilt or innocence. Instead of directly accusing any of the witnesses of lying, Morris permits their own words to reveal the ultimate truth. He believes that this technique allows the audience to ask: "Could it have happened that way? Does this make sense? Are there pieces missing? Have I elided something or has something been destroyed that I need to know about?" [28]

In a trial, each side competes to control the narrative. As Blume, Johnson, and Sundby explain, "[b]ecause jurors—like everyone else—make meaning of the world through the use of stories, the question of whether to sentence the defendant to death or to life imprisonment often depends upon whether the prosecution story or the defense story is more compelling." [29] Since this is equally true of the verdict of guilt or innocence, Morris's method of dramatizing these stories effectively creates a mystery for the audience to solve. As Richard Sherwin has written, "[p]eople prefer stories neat . . . And trial lawyers, especially prosecutors and defense attorneys, are only too glad to indulge a preferred image or storyline, if it will help win a case." [30] The public likes the logic and deduction of a detective story that ends in a definitive solution to the mystery. However, Sherwin argues, this desire for a neat resolution often ignores the complexities of events. "Especially in a case of capital murder," he explains, "we prefer causality, closure, and factual resolution over the discomfort of unending mystery." [31] This leads him to criticize *The Thin Blue Line* for preferring the clear conclusion of declaring Adams innocent and Harris guilty to the post-modern complexity of the non-linear and confusing aspects of this film that should make us uneasy. [32]

THE INVESTIGATION

The film's opening immediately invites the audience to be skeptical by trans-forming the color of the word "blue" in the all-white title to red. Adams explains how he and his brother stopped in Dallas on the way to California, then decided to stay when he was offered a job during his first day in the city. A few days later, when he ran out of gas, he was offered a ride by the sixteen-year-old David Harris, who then takes over the story. Witnesses look directly at that camera, giving the impression that they are directly addressing the audience.[33] The witnesses' accounts are supplemented by a series of docu-ments and pictures, such as a map of Dallas and a picture of a gun. Morris may be trying to show how unreliable such seemingly neutral materials can be as, for example, we have no way to tell whether the gun pictured is the one Harris states that he sold or simply a generic picture. Morris also provides an early signal of whom to trust by showing Adams wearing a white shirt and Harris in orange prison garb.

This scene is followed by a depiction of the murder of officer Robert Wood, beginning with the striking image of a stopped police car with red lights flashing. The reconstruction is intercut with diagrams of where the bullets struck. Newspaper accounts of the shooting are shown in such an extreme close-up that we can see the dots that make up their black and white photographs, thus exposing the artificial construction of what seem to be relatively objective stories. The movie repeatedly returns to the roadside where the murder occurred as it reconstructs the story told by each of the witnesses. Each new witness changes the reconstructed scene, inviting the audience to scrutinize it for new clues.

Another important image that will be seen frequently is the otherwise banal Burger King milkshake that was tossed to the ground when Wood's partner, officer Teresa Turko, left the police car. Morris shows the milkshake flying through the air in slow motion. Whether this happened before or after the gun was fired is important in judging the accuracy of her account. Did she leave the police car and therefore get a good view of the crime or did she remain inside as the critical events occurred? Police procedure would have required her, as the back-up officer, to stand behind the car that was stopped as Wood approached it, but, because she could not identify either the make of the stopped vehicle or its license number, investigators suspected that she was in the patrol car drinking the milkshake during the murder. She stated that there was one person in the car stopped by Officer Wood, a male with sandy blonde hair, a description that would seem more to resemble Harris than Adams. In essence, the reconstructed scenes enhance rather than resolve ambiguity. Unlike the other witnesses, Turko is not interviewed in the film.

As Adams narrates his interrogation by the police, the film zeroes in on ashtrays and a pistol. Despite threats by Detective Gus Rose, Adams refuses to sign a confession. The very different accounts by Rose and another officer are shown in a long shot. A clock and ashtrays with accumulating cigarette butts indicate a lengthy interrogation. We see Wood stopping a car to warn the driver that his lights were turned off, only to be shot and killed. We do not, however, see the shooter.

A return to the original investigation informs us that the big break in the case came when David Harris was arrested for stealing a car in his hometown of Vidor. Although Harris had boasted about shooting a police officer, his friends told the investigators that they did not believe him. After Harris denied any involvement in the murder, one of his friends led police to where the murder weapon had been hidden. Harris then told his interrogators that he had only been bragging but that he knew who committed the crime because he was present at the scene. According to one of the officers, Harris was "a friendly kid." Following this, Harris recounts his story that Adams shot Wood. Adams's lawyers believe that because at the time of the murder Harris was a minor who could not be sentenced to death, Adams was a more convenient defendant, even though Harris had stolen the car stopped by Wood, giving him a motive, and the gun used was his. One of those attorneys, Dennis White, was so disillusioned by this case that he later gave up practicing criminal law. The judge in Adams's trial refused to allow the defense to cross-examine Harris about his Vidor crime spree that also included several burglaries and an armed robbery to which he confessed. In the film, a Vidor neighbor explains that Harris told him that he had "been robbing these houses and held up a couple of stores . . . got me a pistol."

In Judge Metcalfe's interview, he describes a great respect for law enforcement stemming from his upbringing, particularly by his father who was an FBI agent in Chicago during the 1930s and was present at the Biograph Theater the night that notorious gangster John Dillinger was apprehended. Morris underlines this with a vintage clip from a movie about Dillinger as the judge, portrayed as a bit of a crime buff, explains that the famous "woman in red" who pointed Dillinger out to the FBI was actually dressed in orange. He recalls that the prosecutor's closing statement about the "thin blue line" of police that protects the public from anarchy caused his eyes to well up, although he does not believe his emotional reaction was visible to those in the courtroom.

Adams next explains that on the day of the murder, Harris had an arsenal that he asked him to place in his car trunk, except for a pistol that Harris put under the driver's seat. The pair then drank beer and went to a drive-in movie. Morris so thoroughly researched his film that the reconstruction of this account shows excerpts from the two obscure movies. Neither Adams nor anyone else in the film ever explains why he, at age twenty-eight, went out drinking and to see a soft-core pornography movie with a sixteen-year-old. After they returned to Adams's motel, Adams asked his brother if Harris could stay for the night, but the brother refused so Harris left. This is essentially the account given by Adams to the police in a statement that he signed.

According to Adams, Harris's story was two hours off because the murder took place two hours after he and Harris split up. The murder occurred at about half past midnight, but he and Harris separated at about half past nine. After Harris dropped him off at his hotel room, he remained in his room for the rest of the night. He watched the end of "The Carol Burnett Show" followed by the ten o'clock news, then went to bed. Neither the film nor the trial included testimony from Adams's brother, with whom he shared the room. Why did he not testify to either provide an alibi or state that his brother was not telling the truth? In contrast, the film shows huge kernels of popcorn to accompany evidence that the drive-in's concession stand closed early, which contradicts Harris's claim that he bought popcorn late on the night of the murder.

Adams also notes disparities between Turko's original statement and her testimony. She told investigators that the car that she and Wood had stopped was a Vega, but later corrected herself to state that it was a Mercury Comet. According to her statement, made fifteen minutes after the crime, the killer had a fur-lined collar, which at the trial Harris testified that he wore.

During the trial she omitted the collar, instead remembering bushy hair that Adams had at the time. Their stories are then reenacted.

THE EYEWITNESSES

Three people told the police that they witnessed the murder while passing by the murder scene. The most bizarre was Emily Miller, who claimed to have seen Adams shoot Wood. In her interview, she said that she had always wanted to be a detective, sees killings wherever she goes, and particularly enjoyed watching Boston Blackie films on television. The movie then shows an excerpt from one of them. When asked by Morris about picking the wrong man from a police lineup, she states on camera that a police officer corrected her. Ms. Miller claimed that, although her husband Robert was driving and it was late at night, she was able to get a good look through an open window on the driver's side of the car. According to Edith James, one of Adams's attorneys, because Miller had been fired two weeks before the shooting, her testimony about working that night was a lie.

The third witness's identification was somewhat uncertain, having first identified the killer as either Mexican or African-American, as did Emily Miller in her original account to the police. That witness, Michael Randell, could not remember whether the police car was in front of or behind the stopped vehicle and admitted he did not see any gunfire. He testified that he was alone in the car and on his way home from playing basketball, but a woman with whom he was having an affair that he did not want his wife to know about in fact accompanied him. The pair was returning from a bar in Fort Worth. While she was intoxicated, the film does not provide evidence about how much he had to drink.

Assistant District Attorney Douglas Mulder did not reveal the identity of the three eyewitnesses to the defense until just prior to their testimony, which was not part of the prosecution's original case. They were rebuttal witnesses, whose testimony was introduced to contradict that of Adams and came as a surprise to his lawyers. Mulder also did not inform them that a neighbor of the Millers had called him with the information that Robert Miller had told her that it had been too dark for him to see anything but that he would testify otherwise to obtain a reward that had been offered. She also said that his wife was a habitual liar, who had been fired from her job for theft. The neighbor's account is shown in the film. After the trial, Mulder falsely told Adams's attorneys that the witnesses had left the state, even though he had spoken to them by phone at their Dallas hotel. These omissions and misrepresentations, which violated state and federal law, prevented the defense from obtaining information that would likely have discredited the rebuttal testimony, but the trial judge neither declined to allow the witnesses to testify nor granted a continuance to give the defense time for further investigation. When the defense asked the judge to overturn the verdict based on this newly discovered evidence, he ruled that it was too late to raise these points.

Although Morris did interview Mulder, he chose not to include it in the movie because it was "boring" and the prosecutor was unresponsive to his questions. Rather than discussing the specifics of the case, the ADA spoke in very general terms, providing nothing of interest. [34]

During the trial's penalty phase, Grigson testified that, based on a fifteen-minute interview, Adams would commit future acts of violence, even though he had no record of crime or violence. In the film, attorney Dennis White points out that Harris stole a car and guns, had a criminal history, and bragged to friends about killing a police officer. The week after Adams was sentenced to death, robbery charges against Emily Miller's daughter were dismissed. These charges were serious enough to have carried a possible penalty of life imprisonment.

"I'M THE ONE WHO KNOWS"

In the film, Harris explains how he was prepared to testify by the prosecutor "who was deceiving the jury" and told him to lie about charges against him being dropped. After the trial, while Adams sat on death row, Harris was convicted of and incarcerated for a series of crimes.

After a reenactment of Emily Miller picking someone other than Adams out of a lineup, something she freely admits but did not mention at the trial, a police officer tells us (the audience) that when Harris was arrested for burglary and drunk driving, he claimed to have been shot by the boyfriend of a girl in a bar. In fact, he had committed murder, a crime for which he was sentenced to death. Like the other police officers, this one notes that Harris was always friendly and respectful to him.

In the film's climax, an audio-taped interview, we hear Morris's voice. Unlike all the other interviews, rather than showing Harris, only the image of a tape recorder, playing as its counter clicks, appears on the screen with Harris's words superimposed. We hear him speaking of Adams's bad luck and innocence. How does he know? "I'm sure he is" innocent, he states, because "I'm the one who knows." This image, which makes Harris's virtual confession all the more dramatic, was a fortuitous accident. Originally, Morris planned to show this interview in much the same way as every other but, because Harris was on death row, he was only permitted to be filmed through chicken wire, an image Morris rejected.[35] When, after two years of trying, Morris was finally allowed to shoot the interview in a Dallas jail, his camera jammed midway through. With no time to repair it or find an adequate replacement, Morris returned the next day with a tape recorder. This did result in one interesting omission. When Morris asked Harris whether he was alone in the car at the time the police stopped him on that fateful day, Harris, aware that there was no camera, silently smiled and nodded.[36] Since we hear the roughly recorded voice of a killer rather than the "friendly kid" questioned by the police or even by Morris earlier in the movie, it is easier for the viewer to visualize Harris as a murderer. The film ends dramatically with yet another view of the flashing red light of the police car.

CONCLUSION

The closing titles note that at the time of the final interview, Harris was on death row for a 1985 murder. Much like the killing of Robert Wood, Harris shot the victim at point blank range. He was executed by lethal injection in 2004.[37] For someone watching the movie today, this makes Harris's final confession even more chilling.

Despite the evidence presented in this film and the national attention it received, the prosecution opposed Adams's petition for a new trial. At a hearing before Judge Larry Baraka, Harris testified that his trial testimony was untrue and was given in exchange for having all charges dropped against him, including stealing the car and gun used in the murder of Wood. Together with ADA Mulder's misconduct in withholding the names of the eyewitnesses and lying about their having left the state at a time they were in

Dallas, it was enough new evidence for Judge Baraka to order another trial. Even this did not convince the state to drop the charges, but this time, the Texas Court of Criminal Appeals, which had upheld Adams's original conviction, rejected its appeal and granted Adams a new trial.[38] Finally, the prosecution decided that Adams perhaps was not guilty and dropped all charges. Adams was freed in 1989 after twelve years of wrongful imprisonment.

Texas has one of the most generous compensation laws for those wrongfully convicted; such individuals are eligible for payments of $80,000 for each year of imprisonment as well as an annuity, educational benefits, job training, and financial compensation.[39] Unfortunately for Adams, the Tim Cole Act was not passed until 2009. Cole was an African-American college student who had been convicted of rape in 1985 and sentenced to twenty-five years in prison. He refused to agree to parole because it would have required him to admit guilt for a crime for which he was innocent. After two asthma attacks that left him unconscious in his cell, a third in 1999 caused heart failure that killed him. In 2007, the actual rapist confessed, too late to help Tim Cole, but the Texas legislature, notorious for its tough on crime attitude, was so moved by the deceased's story (with some of its members seen in tears) that it enacted the new compensation law. This legislative history provides strong evidence of the power of stories of those wrongfully imprisoned in shaping public opinion and the law. The far more restrictive law in effect when Adams's conviction was dismissed did not, however, entitle him to any compensation for the twelve years that he had been incarcerated. Only those who had been pardoned by the governor were entitled to a $25,000 payment. Since his conviction was dismissed, Adams was not only ineligible for that sum, he did not even qualify for the $200 granted to those who were released either on parole or after the completion of their sentences.

While Adams was still in prison, Morris paid him a nominal sum for the rights to his story, promising an additional $60,000 and two percent of the profits if a commercial movie was made from this material. In retrospect, Morris believed that this contract was a mistake that led to a serious misunderstanding.[40] The film's box office gross of about $1.2 million,[41] while quite respectable for a documentary at the time, left him with a debt of $100,000. After Adams was exonerated and released, he sued for the $60,000, claiming that *The Thin Blue Line*, despite its lack of profit, was a commercial film. The suit was settled in 1989, with Adams retaining print and commercial film rights to his story but not receiving any payment.[42] In 1991, with co-authors William and Marilyn Mona Hoffer, Adams told his story in *Adams v. Texas*, a book published by St. Martin's Press.[43] During the remaining twenty or so years of his life, Adams gave some speeches urging abolition of capital punishment, lived in several states, but died in such obscurity that the media did not report his October 2010 death until June of the next year.[44]

Bennett Gershman explains how *The Thin Blue Line* demonstrates that virtually every aspect of the criminal justice system failed in this case.[45] Rather than undertake an investigation that fully examined all relevant evidence, the detectives settled on an innocent man despite evidence of guilt of another, then essentially stopped looking. Harris seemed like a "nice kid" while Adams appeared too vehement in his protestations of innocence. As one of the investigators put it in the film, Adams "almost overacted his innocence." In addition, "he had done other things that he told me about that didn't seem to bother him in the least." Probably because these "other things" had no relevance to the murder, the film never explains what they were. One possibility was that unlike the clean-shaven man with neatly trimmed hair we see in the documentary, at the time of his arrest, Adams had bushy hair and a droopy mustache that gave him a far less respectable appearance to his interrogators.

Although the defense attorneys were honorable people doing their best, they were easily manipulated by the prosecution and not nearly aggressive enough in their advocacy in contrast to a very zealous prosecutor who, rather than acting in the interests of justice, behaved dishonestly and in violation of his legal obligations in order to win a conviction. Since most criminal defendants lack the means to pay for legal counsel, they must rely on the state to provide them with an attorney. Approximately 90 percent of capital defendants are indigent. In these days of tight state budgets, funding for criminal defense ranks low on the list of the public's priorities, which means that the most capable attorneys are likely to turn to more financially rewarding areas of legal practice. For those who represent indigent defendants, heavy caseloads and limited resources for investigation, expert testimony, and other necessary aspects of preparing a case increase the possibility of wrongful conviction.[46]

Justice also requires an impartial judge, but Metcalfe was so sympathetic to the prosecution that he reacted emotionally to its arguments and failed to protect the rights of the defendant. Finally, the rules of evidence, meant to assure that the jury will be given an adequate factual basis for determining the defendant's guilt or innocence, were all too often ignored. An additional problem, not discussed by Gershman, is the failure of the appeals process to correct any of these injustices until Adams finally had the good fortune to be discovered by Morris. Only the Supreme Court's discovery of a technical problem in the Texas capital punishment process preserved Adams's life long enough to keep him alive until the film was made.

As serious as the flaws of this trial may have been, a single case does not necessarily prove that an entire system is unfair. While the film may have come to the correct conclusion about who committed the murder, its techniques, such as the use of a musical score, the reenactments, selective editing, flattering or unflattering lighting or camera angles, and the use of visual images, also can be abused in the hands of a less ethical filmmaker than Morris or by one whose investigation does not uncover all the relevant facts. Even if Morris came to the correct conclusion, he stacked the deck by excluding his interview with the prosecutor and with his use of images, such as Adams's white shirt and the use of vintage movie clips, to discredit Emily Miller and Judge Metcalfe. That is one reason why Sherwin argues that the film fails to capture the full complexities and ambiguities of the case.

The judicial system failed Adams by incarcerating an innocent man for a dozen years and coming close to executing him. It only came to a fair outcome because Morris happened on the case, investigated it, and made a successful film. Opponents of the death penalty would argue that this is a very slim reed on which to sentence people to death. Whether this is true is one of the issues that readers are encouraged to evaluate for themselves as they read analyses of the films presented in the other chapters.

NOTES

1. Robert J. Norris, *Exonerated: A History of the Innocence Movement* (New York: New York University Press, 2017), 18.

2. Quoted in Ken Armstrong and Steve Mills, "Ryan 'Until I Can be Sure'; Illinois Is First State to Suspend Death Penalty," *Chicago Tribune*, February 1, 2000.

3. Quoted in Rob Warden, "How and Why Illinois Abolished the Death Penalty," *Law and Inequality* 30, no. 2 (2012): 245.

4. Ibid., 248.

5. *The Exonerated*, directed by Bob Balaban, written by Jessica Blank and Erik Jensen, featuring Brian Dennehy, Danny Glover, Delroy Lindo, Aidan Quinn, and Susan Sarandon, aired January 27, 2005, on Court TV.

6. Chris Jones, "'Exonerated' An Enlightening Evening for Ryan," *Chicago Tribune*, December 18, 2002, https://www.chicagotribune.com/news/ct-xpm-2002-12-18-0212180080-story.html.

7. Ken Jaworowski, "When Justice Makes You Gasp," *New York Times*, September 19, 2012, https://www.nytimes.com/2012/09/20/theater/reviews/the-exonerated-revived-at-the-culture-project.html?mtrref=www.google.com&
gwh=E1C2666AE11DCA1B62930422C8440CD6&gwt=pay.

8. "New Hope for Inmate From 'Serial' Podcast," CBS News, accessed April 19, 2019, https://www.cbsnews.com/video/new-hope-for-inmate-from-serial-podcast/.

9. Louis P. Pojman, "Why the Death Penalty Is Morally Permissible," in *Debating the Death Penalty: Should America Have Capital Punishment? The Experts on Both Sides Make Their Case*, ed. Hugo Bedau and Paul Cassell (New York: Oxford University Press, 2004), 68.

10. Paul Bergman and Michael Asimow, *Reel Justice: The Courtroom Goes to the Movies* (Kansas City, MO: Andrews and McMeel, 1996), 53.

11. Eugenia T. La Fontaine, "A Dangerous Preoccupation With Future Danger: Why Expert Predictions of Future Dangerousness in Capital Cases Are Unconstitutional," *Boston College Law Review* 44, no. 1 (2002): 208–10. These figures were as of 1994.

12. Article 37.071, Section (2) (b) (1).

13. La Fontaine, "A Dangerous Preoccupation," 208–10.

14. Laura Bell, "Groups Expel Texas Psychiatrist Known for Murder Cases," *Dallas Morning News*, July 26, 1995.

15.   463 U.S. 880 (1983).

16.   Isaac Butler, "What Errol Morris Thinks of *Making a Murderer*," *Slate.com*, January 27, 2016, http://www.slate.com/articles/arts/culturebox/2016/01/errol_morris_q_a_on_the_thin_blue_line_and_making_a_murderer.html.

17.   Errol Morris and Peter Bates, "Truth Not Guaranteed: An Interview with Errol Morris," *Cinéaste* 17, no. 1 (1989): 16–17.

18.   Bill Nichols, *Engaging Cinema: An Introduction to Film Studies* (New York: W.W. Norton, 2010), 117.

19.   Morris and Bates, "Truth Not Guaranteed," 17.

20.   Paul Schrader, "Notes on Film Noir," *Film Comment* 8, no. 1 (Spring 1972): 11.

21.   Charles Musser, "*The Thin Blue Line*: A Radical Classic," March 25, 2015, https://www.criterion.com/current/posts/3500-the-thin-blue-line-a-radical-classic.

22.   Bennett L. Gershman, "*The Thin Blue Line*: Art or Trial in the Fact-Finding Process?" *Pace Law Review* 9 (1989): 276.

23.   Peter Applebone, "A Murder in Texas: 12 Years Later, Questions Linger About Justice System," *New York Times*, October 31, 1988.

24.   Adams v. Texas, 448 U.S. 38 (1980).

25.   Best known for defending Texas's anti-abortion law in Roe v. Wade, 410 U.S. 113 (1973).

26.   Applebone, "A Murder in Texas."

27.   Adams v. State, 624 S.W.2d 568 (1981).

28.   "Q&A: Errol Morris on Catching the Interview Bug," *Columbia Journalism Review*, July 14, 2017, https://www.cjr.org/special_report/qa-errol-morris-on-catching-the-interview-bug.php/.

29.   John H. Blume, Sheri Lynn Johnson, and Scott E. Sundby, "Competent Capital Punishment Representation: The Necessity of Knowing and Heeding What Jurors Tell Us About Mitigation," *Hofstra Law Review* 36, no. 3 (Spring 2008): 1043.

30.   Richard K. Sherwin, "Law Frames: Historical Truth and Narrative Necessity in a Criminal Case " *Stanford Law Review* 47, no. 1 (November 1994): 40.

31.   Ibid., 81.

32.   Ibid., 39–83.

33.   Later in his career, Morris invented the interrotron, a device that projects his video image on the camera so that whomever he is interviewing can look at him and the camera simultaneously, even when he is in another room. Grant Rindner, "Director Errol Morris: 'The Best Way to Make Something Look Spontaneous is to Make it Spontaneous,'" *Vox*, August 22, 2017, https://www.vox.com/2017/7/12/15947912/errol-morris-interview-podcast.

34.   Morris and Bates, "Truth Not Guaranteed," 16.

35.   Butler, "What Errol Morris Thinks."

36.   Ibid.

37.   Associated Press, "*Thin Blue Line* Figure Executed in Texas," *New York Times*, July 1, 2004.

38.   Ex Parte Adams, 768 S.W.2d 281 (1989).

39.   Anna M. Tinsley, "An Innocent Man Died in Prison: How His Legacy Helps the Wrongly Convicted in Texas," *Fort Worth Star-Telegram* (Fort Worth, TX), May 17, 2018.

40.   Teresa Turko, "Interview with Errol Morris," *The Thin Blue Line* DVD, Criterion Collection, 2015.

41.   *The Thin Blue Line* was the third highest grossing documentary of 1988. The two that took in more at the box office were two music related films: *U2: Rattle and Hum* ($8.6 million) and *Imagine: John Lennon* ($3.75 million)

42.   Associated Press, "Freed Inmate Settles Suit With Producer Over Rights to Story," *New York Times*, August 6, 1989. This is the source of Morris's claim of a $100,000 debt.

43.   Randall Adams, William Hoffer, and Marilyn Mona Hoffer, *Adams v. Texas* (New York: St. Martin's Press, 1991).

44.   Douglas Martin, "Randall Adams, 61, Dies: Freed with Help of Film," *New York Times*, June 25, 2011.

45.   Gershman, "*The Thin Blue Line*."

46. Virginia Leigh Hatch and Anthony Walsh, *Capital Punishment: Theory and Practice of the Ultimate Penalty* (New York: Oxford University Press, 2016), 260–63.

Chapter Three

Dead Man Walking: Redemption For the Guilty

"When Chava Colon from the Prison Coalition asks me one January day in 1982 to become a pen pal to a death-row inmate, I say, 'Sure.'"[1] From this modest beginning, Sister Helen Prejean would go on a remarkable journey to the land of men sentenced to death. At the time, she had been working for a year at St. Thomas, a housing project in New Orleans, whose residents were mostly poor African-Americans. Since nearly every family in St. Thomas had a relative in prison, corresponding with an inmate facing execution seemed, at least to this Catholic nun, to be a natural extension of her work utilizing religious faith to achieve social justice. However, when Sr. Helen learned of the crime for which Elmo Patrick Sonnier had been sentenced to die, she was horrified. In 1977, Sonnier and his brother kidnapped a teenage couple, raped the young woman, forced the pair to lie down, and then shot them in the head. Despite her revulsion at this deed and her fear that she would have nothing to say to the man found guilty of it, Sr. Helen did not change her mind about contacting Sonnier.

Sr. Helen assumed that Sonnier was black; he in fact turned out to be white. Statistics about Louisiana's imposition of the death penalty suggest why she may have made that mistake. Even though Louisiana's population is only about one-third African-American, of the 240 individuals sentenced to death between 1976 and 2014, 147 (61.3 percent) were black compared to the 93 (38.7 percent) who were white.[2] As other chapters in this volume demonstrate, racial disparities in the administration of the death penalty are often addressed in cinematic portrayals of capital punishment. *A Lesson Before Dying* (chapter 5) brings the issue into particularly stark relief. The frequency with which the subject makes an appearance in films about the death penalty is representative of its real-life pervasiveness.

51

The problems associated with racial bias are particularly acute in Louisiana. A study of the death penalty in the state concluded that "there is consistent racial bias in every metric of black and white death penalty rates," pointing out that, as of 2015, no white had been executed for killing a black person since 1752.[3] *Murder in Coweta County* (see chapter 1) presented the exceptionally rare wealthy individual who is executed in America; *Dead Man Walking* highlights the way in which it is unusual for a white man to be executed in Louisiana.

After receiving several letters from Sonnier, Sr. Helen began to think of him as human despite his monstrous deeds. Before committing to visiting him, she had to confront some moral questions, particularly whether choosing to help him would be a betrayal of the victims of his crimes. This question and the issue of whether she has an obligation to the surviving families are quandaries that neither her book nor the film on which it is based will ever fully resolve. However, she has no doubt about the importance of opposing the death penalty, which is also the position of the Catholic Church. Even if she was murdered, she would not want her death avenged by the execution of her killer, "*especially by government*—which can't be trusted to control its own bureaucrats or collect taxes equitably or fill a pothole, much less decide which of its citizens to kill."[4]

Since Sr. Helen began counseling death row inmates, the Catholic Church's opposition to capital punishment has become unequivocal. In 1992, Pope John Paul II allowed an exception when the death penalty was "the only practicable way to defend the lives of human beings effectively against the aggressor."[5] In his 2015 address to the U.S. Congress, however, Pope Francis argued for the global abolition of capital punishment because "every life is sacred, every human person is endowed with an inalienable dignity, and society can only benefit from the rehabilitation of those convicted of crimes."[6] In 2018, Pope Francis made this position official, adding to the Catholic catechism a declaration that the death penalty is impermissible in all cases as a violation of the "dignity of the person." Sr. Helen reacted with delight to the unconditional nature of the change: "It's a happy day. I'm clicking my heels." She cautioned, however, that, "It's on paper. We've still got to move it into the pews and make it active."[7]

The Church's position has had a significant influence on the death penalty. During a 1999 visit to the United States, Pope John Paul II encountered Missouri Governor Mel Carnahan at a prayer service in St. Louis. Although the governor, a Southern Baptist, was a death penalty supporter who previously had approved twenty-six executions, the pontiff urged him to, in Carnahan's words, "show mercy" to Darrell Mease, whose execution was scheduled for the next month. Carnahan commuted the death sentence to life without parole, not because he had changed his support for capital punishment, but because "I was moved by his concern for this prisoner."[8] The limits of Church influence can also be seen in survey results showing that a majority of Catholics (53 percent) favor the death penalty for murder, which is nevertheless a significantly lower percentage than the 73 percent of white evangelical Protestants and 61 percent of white mainline Protestants in support.[9]

It took several months for Sr. Helen to be approved as Sonnier's spiritual adviser. The final step was an interview by the Catholic priest who served as the prison chaplain. Sr. Helen describes him as "strictly an old school pre-Vatican Catholic" who told her that inmates are the scum of the earth who will try to take advantage of her. He believed that her main obligation was to help the prisoner save his soul by receiving the sacraments before he was executed.[10] When she was finally approved to visit Angola prison, Sr. Helen was struck by the regulation that all visitors are subject to searches so intrusive that they may even include strip searches extending to body cavities. However, perhaps because she is a nun, on her first visit Helen was only given a brief pat down.

WHAT ABOUT THE VICTIMS?

In the decade between this visit and her writing of *Dead Man Walking*, Sr. Helen had come to believe that, rather than devoting her efforts solely to Sonnier, she should also have approached the families of her victims. Now she tries to do both; although, despite a few acceptances by those families, "most angrily reject" her offer.[11]

Until the late twentieth century, the American criminal justice system sought primarily to adjudicate the guilt of the accused and determine the appropriate penalty for those convicted. After all, it is the state, not the victim or the victims, that brings a criminal prosecution. The idea of victims' rights has only recently been adopted by the criminal courts. Central to the movement is the belief that those harmed by criminal acts deserve a say in the proceedings and should be empowered or gain closure by being given that say in the courtroom. As historian Jill Lepore explains, "[t]he victims'-rights movement, which began decades ago, has lately reached new heights."[12] Lepore considers the 1997 trial that convicted and sentenced Oklahoma City bomber Timothy McVeigh to death to be the turning point for that movement because of the strong reaction to the judge's decision not to permit testimony from many of the members of the families of victims. Judge Richard Matsch even cautioned the jury against giving too much weight to victim impact statements that he feared would have an excessively emotional effect. Consider the difference when, twenty-one years later, before the sentencing of the former Olympics gymnastics doctor Larry Nassar, who had been convicted of seven counts of sexual assault, Judge Rosemarie Aquilina allowed nearly 150 women to testify about alleged crimes Nassar had committed against them, crimes for which he had never been charged.[13]

Until 1991, the Supreme Court had not allowed victim impact statements to be admitted as evidence in the penalty phase of capital cases. However, in a 6–3 decision in *Payne v. Tennessee*,[14] the court changed its mind in the belief that the victim's life and the effect of the crime on his/her family had to be included to provide balance in sentencing. Justice Thurgood Marshall's dissent argued that including these statements took the jury's attention away from the key factors of the defendant's character and the circumstances of the crime to illicit factors such as the status of the victim and the eloquence of the surviving family members.[15] In a separate dissent, Justice John Paul Stevens stated that in capital cases, victim impact evidence "serves no purpose other than to encourage jurors to decide in favor of death rather than life on the basis of their emotions rather than their reason."[16] In other words, jurors would be so moved by the suffering of these families, that all other evidence would be overwhelmed. A 2011 controlled experiment by Ray Paternoster and Jerome Deise, using a videotaped version of an actual penalty phase and jurors drawn from a state's jury list, provided some confirmation of these reservations by finding that those who viewed victim impact evidence were significantly more likely to vote for a death sentence.[17] Nevertheless, as of 2018, thirty-two states had adopted victims' rights amendments, with five more scheduled to be voted on in the November elections. Supporters are hoping for the eventual adoption of a victims' rights amendment to the United States Constitution.[18] In 1988, Sr. Helen herself obtained Church funding to establish a victim support group in inner city New Orleans.[19] The main problem for its largely African-American membership was that the police failed to pursue the investigation of their relatives' murders very energetically. If the killer is not caught, capital punishment is irrelevant.

In capital cases, victim-impact statements can be used to provide information to the sentencing jury or judge, serve as a therapeutic tool for family and friends of the victim, or allow those friends and family to confront the defendant.[20] Most states with capital punishment permit victim impact evidence to be admitted in the penalty phase of the bifurcated trial. Indiana's statute establishes a post-sentencing procedure that allows family and friends of the victim to make statements directly to the court and the defendant.[21] In the Boston Marathon bombing case, after Dzhokar Tsarnaev was sentenced to death, survivors of the bombing were permitted to testify.[22] The reasoning behind this is to give those affected by the murder a voice that may be therapeutic without prejudicing the jury that will be determining whether to sentence the defendant to death or life imprisonment. However, as Susan Bandes has asked, if the purpose of such testimony is healing, "are the criminal courts the best venue for making that happen?"[23] It is not just Sr. Helen who has faced the dilemma of how to balance compassion for the victims of crime and their families with the rights and humanity of the person convicted of that crime; it is the American criminal justice system as a whole.

FROM BOOK TO FILM

Although Pat Sonnier (he disliked using the name Elmo) seemed remorseful to Sr. Helen, the words of the prison chaplain left her in some doubt. She continued to act as his spiritual adviser and even arranged for prominent capital punishment defense counsel Millard Farmer to represent him in his last legal appeals and his request for executive clemency. Despite these efforts, Sonnier was executed by electrocution on April 5, 1984, six years after the murder he had been convicted of carrying out. According to the death certificate, the procedure took four to five minutes.[24]

In a telephone conversation with Sr. Helen, the Louisiana head of corrections, C. Paul Phelps, told her that he wanted executions to be carried out with *"dignity."*[25] By this, he meant professionally and without emotion, a meaning quite different from the concept of individual human dignity discussed in several chapters of this book. However, it is similar to the concept of institutional dignity featured in chapter 7's analysis of *The Chamber*. Phelps's remark so upset Sr. Helen that she asked to meet with him because he had expressed reservations about the death penalty but felt obligated to carry out state law. However, when she asked whether he would attend an execution as she did, he replied "Never in a million years."[26] To Sr. Helen, the carrying out of a killing without emotion by seemingly good people who do not believe that the death penalty accomplishes much, if anything, is truly horrifying. That this interesting encounter was not included in the movie is something that viewers of the film are encouraged to consider.

Emotionally exhausted by her experience as Sonnier's spiritual adviser, Sr. Helen decided to shift her energies into training others for that task and advocating against capital punishment. However, when Farmer urged her to advise one of two death row inmates, she agreed to take up the cause of Robert Lee Willie, whose crimes were at least as horrific as those of Sonnier. Willie was convicted of raping and murdering eighteen-year-old Faith Hathaway, a killing that was part of an eight-day crime spree that included assaults, other rapes, and kidnappings. Willie had a long record of criminal violence.

Although Faith Hathaway's stepfather, Vernon Harvey, had told reporters that he could not wait for Willie to "fry," this time Sr. Helen chose to reach out to the victim's family.[27] Meeting with Vernon and his wife Elizabeth at their home, she listened to their heartbreaking account of what they had been through and their strong belief that Willie should be executed. However, despite her sympathy she remained determined to continue her opposition to the death penalty and to serve as Willie's spiritual adviser while they persisted in advocating for his execution. Willie was executed on December 28, 1984.

In the film, Sr. Helen, played by Susan Sarandon, who won an Oscar for her performance, counsels Matthew Poncelet, portrayed by Sean Penn, who was nominated for, but did not win, best actor. Poncelet is a fictional composite, with many characteristics taken from Sonnier and Willie. By combining Sonnier's crime with Willie's personality, including his racism and stated admiration for Adolf Hitler, screenwriter and director Tim Robbins chose the worst features of each. Rather than making the argument that innocent people are wrongly executed, he chose "the more difficult question as to whether any life can be taken, even the contemptible."[28]

While making the film, Robbins explained several key ideas behind it to Sr. Helen. The death row inmate would be clearly guilty. The suffering of his victims' families would be depicted with sympathy. Sr. Helen would not be portrayed as a saint without fault. Finally, the movie would not be an anti-death penalty polemic.[29] Robbins explained this last point: "I don't think any film can change people's minds about a subject like capital punishment. What a film has to do to be successful is to make people rethink their position, no matter what side of the debate they're on."[30]

DEAD MAN WALKING ON FILM

The movie starts by intercutting scenes of Sr. Helen driving to her first prison encounter with Poncelet with others showing her becoming a nun who works with poor African-Americans in New Orleans; a black and white film of the brutal murders that Poncelet and his co-defendant (who was sentenced to life imprisonment) were convicted of also are looped in. Robbins chose to make these flashbacks, which are spread throughout the film, incomplete so that the audience does not learn which of the defendants committed the actual murders until Poncelet's execution. The stark use of black and white scenes emphasizes the viciousness of the crime. The scenes set in the St. Thomas houses were filmed on location using actual residents, rather than professional actors, to add to the film's sense of authenticity.

During the drive to the prison, Sr. Helen passes a "Get Tough! Join Governor Fredericks. Stop Crime!" billboard which, together with background views of television news stories sprinkled throughout the movie, illustrates the manipulation of the crime issue by politicians to gain electoral support. This required some dramatic license as the only sign mentioned in the book is hand painted and tied to a tree, with a message of encouragement: "Do not despair. You will soon be there."[31]

Sr. Helen's visit to Angola Prison begins with an ironic touch as her cross sets off the metal detector. As Edmund Arens explains, this signals "a lot of dissonance, disruption or interruption of the way things work will follow."[32] The prison chaplain who, as noted above, is described in her book as "an old-school pre-Vatican Catholic," introduces her to the institution.[33] He urges her to wear the habit, a suggestion she declines, then warns her that the prisoners "are all con men and will all take advantage of you." It is impossible to miss the contrast between the jaded chaplain and the idealistic nun.

Sr. Helen is separated from Poncelet by a grill that partially obscures her view of him. As they get to know and trust one another, the film symbolically reduces this barrier, first to Lucite plastic then, during the minutes prior to the execution, by allowing Sr. Helen to put her hand on his shoulder, their only physical contact in the film. These barriers also make their conversations much like religious confession as Sr. Helen encourages the condemned man to take responsibility for his deeds.

The first words uttered by Poncelet, who has spent six years on death row, are unlikely to gain him sympathy from the movie's audience. In a speech littered with racial epithets, he blames his plight on his co-defendant, drugs and alcohol, and everything but his own agency. Nevertheless, Sr. Helen gently prods him to show her a picture of the daughter that he has lost touch with. She is impressed by the ability of the uneducated inmate to have learned enough law to have written an appellate brief that he asks her to file on his behalf. She will try to find a lawyer willing to represent him in a last-ditch effort to prevent his execution.

That lawyer is Hilton Barber (Robert Prosky), a fictional version of Millard Farmer. Explaining how he will approach the upcoming pardon board hearing, Barber explains that his main goal will be to humanize Poncelet. "It's easy to kill a monster, but it's hard to kill a human being." This is the film's main theme, illustrated by Sr. Helen's visit to Poncelet's financially struggling but loving family. Sr. Helen's dinner with her own prosperous family, who oppose her work counseling death row inmates, presents a vivid contrast.

Barber's plea to the pardon board provides an opportunity for the film to express arguments for and against the death penalty without totally stopping the action or boring the audience with a lecture. He explains why those sentenced to death are virtually all poor—a subject addressed in other films analyzed in this volume (such as chapter 5's *A Lesson Before Dying*). Unable to afford an attorney, Poncelet was assigned a tax lawyer who spent little time on jury selection and raised only one objection during the entire trial. He follows this with a graphic description of lethal injection. Poncelet's mother is unable to conclude her testimony as she breaks down in tears. The prosecutor counters with horrifying photographs of the murder victims and a description of the effects of the crime on their families. The board quickly denies Poncelet's appeal.

In the book, Sr. Helen discusses the role of the pardon board in far more detail than is possible in a two-hour movie. Before the Sonnier hearing, she and Farmer met with Howard Marsellus, the board's chair, who seemed sympathetic to their arguments. Nevertheless, the board ruled against Sonnier by a 4–1 vote, with the dissent cast by Lionel Daniels, who was disturbed by the inadequacy of the defense lawyer in the penalty phase rather than by Marsellus. In 1986, Marsellus was convicted of accepting a bribe of $5,000 in exchange for a non-capital inmate's pardon. After he served his prison term, Sr. Helen was able to locate him to discuss how the pardon board operated while he was its chair. Marsellus claimed that in exchange for his appointment as chair, he was expected to show loyalty to the governor. By upholding death sentences, the board removed the responsibility (and any political problems a gubernatorial decision, whether it granted or refused a pardon, would have generated) by allowing Governor Edwin Edwards to state that he was simply following the board's recommendations. Under Marsellus, the board upheld all six death sentences that it considered.[34] In 2000, Edwards, who served four terms (not all consecutive), was convicted of extorting millions of dollars from businesses that applied for casino licenses; he was sentenced to ten years in prison.[35]

As she waits for the pardon board's decision, Sr. Helen is confronted by Earl Delacroix (Raymond J. Barry), who asks why she is not as concerned about his murdered son Walter as she is about his killer. Deciding to make up for her failure to meet with the families of Poncelet's victims, the conscience-stricken nun tries to visit Delacroix at home. Although the screen door at first serves as a barrier between the two, he lets her in after she apologizes. In a moving scene, Earl explains how his son's murder has been a nightmare that has led to the dissolution of his marriage. The boxes strewn around his house symbolize his now disordered life. Nevertheless, the scene's final shot of the two speaking quietly, as the camera moves into the distance, presents the possibility of future reconciliation. Sister Helen's visit to the parents of Hope Percy, the other murder victim, goes far less well when they realize that she is trying to console them while still counseling Poncelet. Believing that she is trying to have it both ways, they angrily demand that she leave. Even though the film is clearly opposed to capital punishment, its sensitive depiction of victims' families provides balance that requires audience members to think about their own views, whatever their position. In contrast, politicians are portrayed as cynical opportunists. Without informing Sr. Helen and Barber, the governor turns what was supposed to be a private meeting about possible executive clemency into a public spectacle during which he postures before the television cameras.

As Poncelet's spiritual adviser, Sr. Helen, the first woman to be approved for this role, was required to meet with him several hours a day for the week prior to his execution and the entire day of his death. Her job is complicated by a television interview in which Poncelet praises Hitler. When she confronts him, rather than sitting as in their previous scenes, the two are standing on either side of the partition. This allows them to express their emotional energy by moving, almost like caged tigers. Despite the prison chaplain's admonition that her only task is to convince Poncelet to accept the sacraments, Helen tells him that to die with dignity, he will have to take responsibility for his crimes.

Poncelet is allowed to spend several hours of his final day with his mother and three younger brothers (his father died when he was fourteen years old). As the family engages in friendly banter and reminiscences, we start to see Poncelet as a person rather than only as the racist monster responsible for the deaths of two young innocent people. When the family is forced to say its final goodbyes, Poncelet's mother is not even permitted to hug him, which seems designed more to take away a measure of his dignity than for any legitimate security purpose. Much of the process that follows takes additional measures to strip him of that dignity, from the replacement of his boots with white cloth slippers to shaving his head and eyebrows to fitting him with a diaper.

Poncelet's last meal shows how movies can circulate stories through our culture. When the film was being made, Sr. Helen objected several times to Poncelet's holding up a shrimp to explain how much he enjoyed it because it was the first time that he had eaten shrimp. Although, as she put it in her foreword to the published script, "Someone from Louisiana who never had shrimp? Unbelievable," Robbins retained the scene on the grounds that he enjoyed these types of "little incongruities." However, prominent death penalty scholar David Dow has pointed out that Robbins borrowed this idea from the BBC documentary *Fourteen Days in May*, in which the African-American death row inmate in Mississippi eating his final meal tells the warden he has never eaten that shellfish.[36]

Troubled by her inability to convince Poncelet to accept blame for what he did, Sr. Helen retreats to the ladies' room, where she is able to pray for divine guidance and release some of her emotions until the entrance of a nurse interrupts her solitude. In his notes to the published screenplay, Robbins refers to that nurse as "the angel of death, intruding on Sister Helen's pleas for strength from God, another violation."[37] One reason for that sentiment is that since 1983, the American Nurses Association has asked its members not to participate either directly or indirectly in executions.[38] It is also worth noting that the American Medical Association Code of Ethics Section 9.7.3 suggests that, "a physician must not participate in a legally authorized execution." Since both are merely guidelines, however, there is no punishment mechanism for violators.

Upon Sr. Helen's return, Poncelet finally confesses to killing Walter and raping Hope. When he says, "that boy, Walter, I killed him," it is the first time he has spoken the name of either victim, indicating that he is beginning to see them as people, while we are starting to see him as a human being as well. As both break into tears, Sr. Helen tells him that despite having done something terrible, taking responsibility for it gives him dignity. This confession is so important that the scene was filmed six times with three different cameras. Poncelet thanks the nun for loving him. She responds by singing "Be Not Afraid." The announcement "Dead Man Walking!" is made by one of the guards as he is led to the execution chamber with Sr. Helen allowed to rest a hand on his shoulder.

In the book, Sr. Helen has a long conversation with a troubled prison guard, Major Kendall Coody, who, after five executions, has difficulty sleeping. "I can't square it with my conscience," he tells her, "putting them to death like that."[39] She never sees him after Willie's execution as he first transfers, then takes early retirement, and, soon after, dies of a heart attack. A similar conversation with a fictionalized version of Coody was filmed, but Robbins cut it because it was so disturbing that it distracted from the main narrative. "The power of the scene," he wrote in the published script, "stopped our story."[40] The effect of participation in executions on corrections officers is an important theme of *Monster's Ball*, which is discussed in chapter 9.

Even though the prisoners counseled by Sr. Helen were executed by electrocution, Robbins chose to use lethal injection instead because, as he explains in his DVD commentary, at the time of the film's release in February 1996, lethal injection had become the primary method used in every death penalty state in the hope that it would be more humane.[41] Louisiana's first lethal injection took place one month after *Dead Man Walking* was released. The authorities found it so difficult to find one of Antonio James's veins in which to insert the catheter that they asked for his assistance, which he provided. Between 1996 and 2010, Louisiana used lethal injection to execute six men.[42] Since then, however, the state has found it so difficult to obtain the necessary drugs that it has been unable to execute anyone else, despite the fact that there were 72 prisoners on death row by 2018. For that reason, in July 2018, a federal judge extended the moratorium for another twelve months as, unlike some other states, Louisiana allowed no other methods of capital punishment.[43] As indicated in the introduction to this volume, the method of executing an individual plays a central role in current debates about the death penalty in the United States. This book will return, in chapter 7's treatment of *The Chamber*, to problems associated with the drugs used for lethal injection.

The portrayal of Poncelet's execution has generated considerable discussion. Edmund Arens views it as a ritual with religious music: the hymn *Sacred Love* played during the prisoner's final walk and Pakistani Sufi chanting. More controversially, he sees Poncelet, strapped to the gurney in a vertical position with his arms outstretched at his side, as the victim of a crucifixion rather than the recipient of legitimate societal vengeance by the most humane method available.[44] Edward Guthmann also views the execution scene in this manner by describing a "gurney that resembles a crucifix."[45] In his DVD commentary, however, Robbins denies any such intentions, explaining that this is simply the way the actual gurney is designed. Roy Gundmann and Cynthia Lucia agree, pointing out that the easiest way for the guards to deal with prisoners who struggle when their handcuffs are removed is to strap them to the table with their arms spread, then to return them to a horizontal position.[46] Sr. Helen's vigorous rejection of Poncelet's attempt to compare himself to Jesus because both are rebels provides some support for Robbins's view. If anyone in the film is analogous to Christ, it is Sr. Helen, whose emphasis on forgiveness and nonviolence is contrasted with the Old Testament "eye for an eye" defense of the death penalty as legitimate societal vengeance by a number of characters in the movie.

Cross-cutting between the execution and a now complete Technicolor version of the murders committed by Poncelet is subject to more than one interpretation. By showing the two killing scenes side by side, is it suggesting equivalence between the criminal actions Poncelet is being executed for and his death at the hands of the state? Poncelet's last words ask for forgiveness but also argue that killing is wrong, no matter who does it. However, the superimposition of images of the two victims indicates that they should not be forgotten. Austin Sarat suggests that by showing the behind-the-scenes preparation for the execution together with the flashbacks of the crime, the execution is made less shocking.[47] George Dionisopoulos takes a third position, arguing that, "the power of the scene is grounded in its ambiguity—in not providing a sense of neat closure."[48]

Ending a movie on such a downbeat note seems inconceivable, yet this scene is so powerful that anything after it is certain to be anticlimactic. Not surprisingly, Robbins had difficulty finding a satisfactory finish. The original script included the reading of a letter from Poncelet, an African-American mother lamenting the lack of prosecution for the murder of her two sons, a scene of the Percys still angry over the murder of their daughter despite Poncelet's execution, Sr. Helen writing her book, and an African-American boy in handcuffs being put into a police car. Instead, Robbins decided that the movie needed to end more quickly and on a note of reconciliation rather than with a scene that hammered home the obvious points. This was accomplished first by a brief scene of brightly colored signs by the children taught by Sr. Helen, welcoming her back. Finally, through a church window, we see

Earl Delacroix and Sr. Helen kneeling together in prayer. Avoiding the standard movie dissolves, the camera lingers on the two figures, slowly moving
away as the film ends. As Robbins describes it, "Two people alone in the
early morning, an audience thinking of the nature of love, the terror of
violence, and the possibility of forgiveness and the redemption it might offer
us all."[49]

RESPONSE TO THE FILM

A movie about a nun counseling a man guilty of a brutal murder, which
reaches its climax in his execution, would hardly be expected to make a big
splash at the box office. Despite approaching some twenty possible backers,
Robbins was able to raise a relatively small $12.25 million, enough for a low
budget movie that was only able to attract such well-known stars as Susan
Sarandon (the director's wife, who had originally approached him with the
project) and Sean Penn because they and Robbins agreed to work for a
fraction of their usual compensation.[50]

Yet, to the surprise of most, *Dead Man Walking* grossed more than $39
million in domestic box office receipts. Even such a financial success, however, was dwarfed by the forty-one films that made more money, with *Toy
Story* taking in $192 million that year and *Batman Forever* $184 million.[51] It
is no wonder that Hollywood prefers to make films designed primarily to
entertain rather than those putting forward a serious message, most of which
are far less successful than *Dead Man Walking*.

Critical reaction was extremely enthusiastic with the *Rotten Tomatoes*,
summary of reviews giving the movie a 95 percent certified fresh rating.
Roger Ebert called it "absorbing, surprising, technically superb, and worth
talking about for a long time afterward," while Owen Gleiberman praised it
as possibly "the most complexly impassioned message movie Hollywood has
ever made" with a "climax . . . so intense it left me shaking."[52] David Dow
claimed that fictional films such as *Dead Man Walking* and several others
discussed in this volume make a stronger argument against capital punishment than documentaries like *The Thin Blue Line* (chapter 2) because they
"hold up guilty men and say that all this talk of innocence is a moral distraction." "Death row," he argued "is full of guilty men, but they are yet men;
human beings who committed vile and despicable acts, yet still human beings."[53] Some, albeit a small fraction, are also women, as we shall see in the
chapter 8 discussion of *Last Dance*.

Austin Sarat believes that "the death penalty has been transformed from a
dramatic spectacle to a cool bureaucratic operation," which limits public
exposure to a carefully selected group of witnesses, thereby keeping the
brutality of capital punishment away from public attention. This makes fic-

tional representations of the death penalty such as films one of the main sources of public knowledge.[54] Sarat criticizes *Dead Man Walking* and *Last Dance* for focusing more on individual responsibility for crime than on its social causes. Sympathy for Poncelet and Cindy Liggett is largely due to their eventual acceptance of guilt, suggesting that death may be an appropriate penalty for those who do not repent. The main subject of *Dead Man Walking*, he argues, is less the legitimacy of the death penalty than Sr. Helen's efforts to convince Poncelet to accept responsibility for his crimes. "Without the confession," Sarat writes, "*Dead Man Walking* would give viewers little reason for opposing the execution."[55] Sister Helen's emotional reactions to the Percys' account of their suffering, the repetition of the crime reenactments in *Dead Man Walking*, and the intercutting of crime scene photos and Rick Hayes' reaction to them in *Last Dance* reduce the likelihood that audiences will accept structural explanations for the causes of crime.

Given that so many factors go into people's views on an issue as visible and emotional as the death penalty, it is impossible to determine whether a single movie had a significant effect on public attitudes. While the Gallup Poll shows a decline in the percentage of the public "in favor of the death penalty . . . for murder" from 77 percent in 1995, before the film's January 1996 release date, to 71 percent in February 1999, no one would attribute that limited reduction in support to reaction to the film, especially since the decline continued for the next two decades, reaching 55 percent support in October 2017.[56] After the movie's release, Sr. Helen's book surged to the top of the *New York Times* bestseller list, where it remained for eight months. Robbins wrote a theatrical version of the screenplay designed for student productions that has been performed at more than 200 high schools and colleges.[57] An opera version written by Jake Hegge with a libretto by Terrence McNally had its premiere in 2000 by the San Francisco Opera and has since been performed around the world. Despite our inability to measure the specific effect of this movie, it is clear that it continues to have an influence on the death penalty debate.

NOTES

1. Helen Prejean, *Dead Man Walking: The Eyewitness Account of the Death Penalty That Sparked a National Debate* (New York: Vintage Books, 2013), 3. Unless otherwise noted, this chapter's account of how Sr. Helen came to work with death row inmates is based on this book.

2. Tim Lyman, "Race and the Death Penalty in Louisiana: An Actuarial Analysis," May 23, 2017, https://ssrn.com/abstract=2972627.

3. Frank R. Baumgartner and Tim Lyman, "Louisiana Death-Sentenced Cases and Their Reversals: 1976–2015," *Journal of Race, Gender & Poverty* 7 (2016): 74.

4. Prejean, *Dead Man Walking*, 21.

5. Elisabetta Povoledo and Laurie Goodstein, "Pope Francis Declares Death Penalty Unacceptable in All Cases," *New York Times*, August 2, 2018.

6. Ibid.

7. Ibid.

8. Gustav Niebuhr, "Governor Grants Pope's Plea for Life of a Missouri Inmate," *New York Times*, January 29, 1999.

9. David Masci, "5 Facts About the Death Penalty," Pew Research, August 2, 2018, http://www.pewresearch.org/fact-tank/2018/08/02/5-facts-about-the-death-penalty/. The Pew Center has a separate category for African-Americans, probably because a majority (52 percent) oppose capital punishment.

10. Prejean, *Dead Man Walking*, 25.

11. Ibid., 32.

12. Jill Lepore, "The Rise of the Victims'-Rights Movement," *New Yorker*, May 21, 2018, https://www.newyorker.com/magazine/2018/05/21/the-rise-of-the-victims-rights-movement.

13. Benedict Carey, "More Than 150 Women Described Sexual Abuse by Lawrence Nassar," *New York Times*, January 26, 2018.

14. 501 U.S. 808 (1991).

15. 501 U.S. at 844–856 (Marshall, J., joined by Blackmun, J., dissenting).

16. 501 U.S. at 866 (Stevens, J., joined by Blackmun, J., dissenting).

17. Ray Paternoster and Jerome Deise, "A Heavy Thumb on the Scale: The Effect of Victim Impact Evidence on Capital Decision Making," *Criminology* 49, no. 1 (2011).

18. Lepore, "The Rise of the Victims' Rights Movement."

19. Prejean, *Dead Man Walking*, 232.

20. Susan Bandes, "What are Victim-Impact Statements For?" *Atlantic*, July 2016, https://www.theatlantic.com/politics/archive/2016/07/what-are-victim-impact-statements-for/492443/.

21. Indiana Code IC 35-38-1-8.5 (page 11–12), accessed April 20, 2019, http://iga.in.gov/static-documents/1/6/4/5/164563c6/TITLE35_AR38_ch1.pdf.

22. Bandes, "What are Victim-Impact Statements For?"

23. Ibid.

24. Prejean, *Dead Man Walking*, 91–94.

25. Ibid., 101.

26. Ibid., 105.

27. Ibid., 118.

28. Carole Shapiro, "Do or Die: Does *Dead Man Walking* Run?" *University of San Francisco Law Review* 30, no. 4 (1996): 1151.

29. Helen Prejean, foreword to *Dead Man Walking: The Shooting Script*, by Tim Robbins (New York: Newmarket Press, 1997), xi.

30. George N. Dionisopoulos, "To Open a Door and Look Inside: *Dead Man Walking* as a Prima Facie Case," *Western Journal of Communication* 74, no. 3 (2010): 293.

31. Prejean, *Dead Man Walking*, 24.

32. Edmund Arens, "*Dead Man Walking*: On the Cinematic Treatment of Licensed Public Killing," *Contagion: Journal of Violence, Mimesis, and Culture* 5 (Spring 1998): 17.

33. Prejean, *Dead Man Walking*, 25.

34. Ibid., 169-74.

35. "Former Louisiana Governor Gets 10-Year Prison Term in Corruption Case," CNN.com, January 9, 2001, http://www.cnn.com/2001/LAW/01/09/edwards.sentenced/index.html

36. Prejean, "Foreword," xii; David R. Dow, "Fictional Documentaries and Truthful Fictions: The Death Penalty in Recent American Film," *Constitutional Commentary* 17, no. 3 (Winter 2000): 543.

37. Robbins, *The Shooting Script*, 168.

38. Carol Potera, "ANA Expands Opposition to Capital Punishment," *American Journal of Nursing* 117, no. 6 (2017).

39. Prejean, *Dead Man Walking*, 180.

40. Robbins, *The Shooting Script*, 167.

41. Kate Pickert, " Lethal Injection," *Time*, November 10, 2009, http://content.time.com/time/nation/article/0,8599,1815535,00.html.

42. "Death Penalty Statistics from the US," Datablog, accessed April 20, 2019, https://www.theguardian.com/news/datablog/2011/sep/21/death-penalty-statistics-us.

43. Julia O'Donoghue, "3 Reasons Why Executions are on Hold in Louisiana," NOLA.com, July 24, 2018, https://expo.nola.com/news/erry-2018/07/52b2715a414476/3-reasons-why-executions-are-o.html.

44. Arens, *"Dead Man Walking,"* 14–29.

45. Edward Guthmann, "Sarandon Dead-On in Prison Drama," *San Francisco Chronicle*, January 12, 1996, https://www.sfgate.com/movies/article/Sarandon-Dead-On-In-Prison-Drama-2999586.php.

46. Roy Grundmann, Cynthia Lucia, and Tim Robbins, "Between Ethics and Politics: An Interview with Tim Robbins," *Cinéaste* 22, no. 2 (1996).

47. Austin Sarat, "The Cultural Life of Capital Punishment: Responsibility and Representation in *Dead Man Walking* and *Last Dance*," *Yale Journal of Law and the Humanities* 11, no. 1 (January 1999).

48. Dionisopoulos, "To Open a Door and Look Inside," 303.

49. Robbins, *The Shooting Script*, 169.

50. Lucy Silvio, "Raking in the Money?" *America* 8 (March 1996): 10.

51. "Feature Film, Released between 1995-01-01 and 1995-12-31 (Sorted by US Box Office Descending)," IMDb.com, accessed April 20, 2019, https://www.imdb.com/search/title?year=1995&title_type=feature&sort=boxoffice_gross_us,desc

52. Roger Ebert, *Roger Ebert's Video Companion* (Kansas City, MO: Andrews McMeel, 1998), 202; Owen Gleiberman, "A View to a Kill," *Entertainment Weekly*, January 19, 1996, 36.

53. Dow, "Fictional Documentaries," 552.

54. Sarat, "The Cultural Life of Capital Punishment," 159.

55. Ibid., 171.

56. "Death Penalty," Gallup, accessed April 20, 2019, https://news.gallup.com/poll/1606/death-penalty.aspx.

57. Generally, see *"Dead Man Walking*: The Book, the Movie, and the Play Project," In Deeds and Words: Sr. Helen Prejean's Ministry Against the Death Penalty, accessed April 20, 2019, https://dpuspecialcollections.omeka.net/exhibits/show/prejean/dmw.

Chapter Four

The Life of David Gale: A Paradoxical Execution

Charles Randolph hoped to use the 2003 film *The Life of David Gale* to focus the nation's conversation about capital punishment upon the question of whether the possibility of the execution of an innocent defendant provided an adequate reason to abolish the death penalty.[1] To do so, he crafted a screenplay whose principal protagonist—David Gale—was a professor who employed the Socratic method of instruction. The movie's director, Alan Parker, agreed that rather than taking a position for or against the death penalty, the goal of the film should be to stimulate discussion.[2] Since this was Randolph's first screenplay,[3] he may not have realized how reluctant Hollywood is to budget mainstream films whose primary goal is to engage in a serious discussion of capital punishment, as we suggested in the introduction. Tim Robbins had difficulty raising a far more modest budget for the independent film *Dead Man Walking* (analyzed in chapter 3). Parker has explained that he was only able to get studio funding for *The Life of David Gale* because he pitched it as a thriller—further proof that Hollywood believes a film about the death penalty is unlikely to succeed financially.[4]

Ultimately and ironically the very things that made *The Life of David Gale* a thriller—such as its complicated plot and structure—served to distract the audience's attention from the debate about capital punishment that was the original vision of Randolph and Parker.

THE TRIAL AS A SEARCH FOR TRUTH

"After explaining the concept of proof beyond a reasonable doubt, many trial courts will conclude their instructions by telling jurors 'not to search for

67

doubt' but instead 'to search for the truth.'"[5] Despite the common belief that a criminal trial is a search for truth, as Michael Cicchini points out in this quote, the requirement that the prosecution prove guilt beyond a reasonable doubt is supposed to provide a counterweight. The instructions he cites may cause a jury to ignore that high standard of guilt, instead leading to a conviction based on a preponderance of the evidence. If the state presents more convincing evidence, even if only slightly more convincing, jurors will be more likely to return a guilty verdict because "in a search for truth, the jury would be obligated to convict."[6] Even if they are probably correct, the possibility of an erroneous conviction is substantially increased.

There are other reasons why a criminal trial is not simply a search for truth. Perfectly reliable evidence may be excluded if it is the result of an illegal search. For example, if the police break into someone's house and find drugs, those drugs provide evidence of the truth of drug possession charges, but the Exclusionary Rule, established by the U.S. Supreme Court in its interpretation of the Constitution's Fourth Amendment, prevents a jury from learning about that truth. There also are a variety of privileges, such as those of lawyer and client, doctor and patient, or husband and wife, that prevent reliable evidence from being admitted in a trial. Finally, even if the defendant is the only witness to the crime, he or she cannot be forced to testify. The purpose of a criminal trial is to come to a just outcome. Truth is an important, albeit secondary, factor. In the 1992 film *A Few Good Men*, Colonel Nathan R. Jessup (played by Jack Nicholson) famously exclaimed during cross-examination, "You can't handle the truth."[7] There are, however, important differences between legal fact and legal movie fiction. Sometimes fundamental legal procedures work to privilege "justice" at the expense of "truth." These exclusions are based upon the premise that the penalty for a criminal conviction is so severe, literally life and death in the case of capital punishment, that the burden of proof is borne by the prosecution, which must prove the defendant guilty beyond a reasonable doubt. For supporters of the death penalty, despite Cicchini's caution, this protection along with the additional safeguard of the bifurcated trial minimizes the possibility that an innocent person will be executed.

In *The Thin Blue Line* (chapter 2), Errol Morris argued that there is a truth that can be found: if not necessarily in a criminal trial, then when the facts can be established through careful investigation. He used such an inquiry to exonerate Randall Dale Adams. In contrast, *The Life of David Gale* argues that there is no absolute truth because the facts are often ambiguous.

In an early scene, college professor David Gale (played by Kevin Spacey) explains the theories of Jacques Lacan to his class at the fictional University of Austin. His focus is on the importance of fantasy in people's perception of reality. Fantasies are deliberately unrealistic, he tells his students, because it is the quest that is desired and achieving its goal ends that quest. He believes that the only measure of the significance of our lives is how we value the lives of others. Although this lecture does not go into detail about Lacan's argument, the film, whose script was written by Charles Randolph (a philosophy teacher before he wrote this screenplay), seems to embrace some of Lacan's ideas of truth. Rose Pacatte believes that this is a key to the film because it indicates that the media uses language as a construction of reality. "All media are 'constructions,'" she writes, "including this movie."[8]

Lacan rejected the idea that language simply provides words that correspond to objects. He emphasizes the relationship between the sign (the word) and the language itself. For example, the word "needle" means far more than the device used to give immunizations. Thus, words often express a meaning not consciously intended by the speaker. The unconscious forms a chain that gives each signifier meaning in its connection to the chain's other signifiers.[9] In essence, the words used by the characters in the film do not necessarily convey to others the meaning consciously intended by the speaker.

The Life of David Gale stresses this subjectivity of meaning by presenting its story through a flashback within a flashback. It opens with a long shot of an automobile traveling along a rural road. When the car breaks down, the driver jumps out and, holding a videotape in her hand, begins running furiously. This scene will be shown in its full context near the end of the film, but at this point, without explanation, the movie, in what we will soon learn is its first flashback, cuts to a newsroom. A television is broadcasting an account of David Gale's conviction for murder and the failure of his final appeal.

This structure is used by Randolph to show that there is no single, fully accurate truth. The first apparent truth is Gale's conviction for the murder of Constance Harraway. The proof at trial appears overwhelming, with relatively little controversy over the verdict and sentence. However, when Gale decides to grant an interview shortly before his scheduled execution date, his story presents a different "truth" that the reporter listening to him finds convincing. Yet Gale's account, told in flashbacks that make it seem more accurate, proves subjective as we soon learn his motives for leading reporter Bitsey Bloom (Kate Winslet) astray. As David Parkinson has written, flashbacks can "reveal information that has previously been suppressed," but also can "deliberately obfuscate and mislead."[10] Gale proves to be a less than trustworthy narrator of his own story, intending both to reveal and deceive.

The film provides yet another twist or two to supply more "truths" for the audience. Even apparently reliable objective evidence such as a videotape of the killing proves misleading. The movie seems to be suggesting that, if Lacan is correct, we can never be sure which account is true. Is the audience's understanding of Gale's guilt or innocence any more correct than that of the trial jury? That uncertainty suggests that the movie is arguing that it provides enough doubt to abolish the death penalty.

A REPORTER IS SUMMONED TO TEXAS

This newsroom is where we first meet reporter Bitsey Bloom, who serves as a surrogate for the audience. Gale's lawyer, Braxton Belyeu (Leon Rippy), has offered her magazine an exclusive interview with the condemned murderer during the three days prior to his execution. The interview offer comes with the condition that Bitsey is the sole interviewer and that the magazine pays the lawyer half a million dollars. That a respectable news magazine would unhesitatingly pay such a large amount, in cash no less, to a convicted murderer for a story, is one of many implausible actions in this film. The *New York Times* ethics policy, for example, very clearly states, "we do not pay for interviews."[11]

Bitsey seems to have been selected because she was recently jailed for refusing to reveal confidential sources, but the movie fails to follow up on this potentially interesting point. Gale, a prominent capital punishment opponent, has been on death row for the past six years after being convicted of the rape and murder of Constance Harraway. Although Bitsey prefers to work alone, the magazine requires that intern Zack Stemm (Gabriel Mann) travel to Texas to assist her.

The selection of Texas allows the movie to explore the death penalty through the cultural divide between rural and urban populations. Part of this is due to the contrast between pro-death penalty red states, like Texas, and northern and western blue states, represented by Bitsy and Zack, the latter of whom reminds the audience to avoid states with "more churches than Starbucks." However, as important as the red–blue state divide might be, what *The Life of David Gale* does remind us—through its version of Texas—is that even in a profoundly pro-capital punishment state, there is a split between rural Texas and the university city of Austin.[12]

Nevertheless, there is little doubt that Texas was chosen as the film's setting because it is, as James Acker has written, "this country's undisputed leader in making use of the death penalty."[13] In 1982, it was the first state to use lethal injection. Between that execution (the state's first since 1964) and July 2018, Texas put 553 prisoners to death, more than one-third of the United States' total.[14] Consistent with nationwide trends, even in Texas, there has been a significant reduction in executions since *The Life of David Gale* was made in 2003. The peak was reached with forty in 2000. By 2017, the number had declined to seven. One reason is that in 2005, the state allowed juries to sentence convicted defendants to life without parole as an alternative to death, replacing the previous option of a life sentence *with* the possibility of parole. By the end of 2017, the state's death row population had been reduced to 234 from 460 in 1999. Nevertheless, the seven executions still constituted thirty percent of the national total of twenty-three carried out that year.[15]

BITSEY INTERVIEWS DAVID GALE

Bitsey and Zack's drive through Texas provides a way to advance the plot. Bitsey, who believes Gale to be guilty, argues with Zack, who has doubts, thus supplying information about the case to the audience. Although their rental car's check engine light goes on and the engine smokes, they fail to trade the auto in. This omission will lead to a development near film's end that increases the suspense. A menacing cowboy in a pickup truck seems to be following them. During most of the cowboy's appearances in the film, he will be listening to Liu's aria from Puccini's opera "Turandot," which will prove to be a major clue to the plot's main mystery as Liu sacrifices her life to save that of another.

Director Alan Parker was able to give a sense of realism to the prison scenes in several ways. The authorities gave him permission to use Ellis Prison, the site of Texas' executions until 1999, to film exterior scenes. Although he was allowed inside the prison to observe, for obvious security reasons filming there was not possible. Instead, he had as close to an exact replica built as a set.[16] The film's final scenes were filmed outside the Huntsville prison where death row prisoners are currently incarcerated.

Once inside, Bitsey and Zack are briefed by the community relations officer before meeting with Gale's lawyer. Zack and Belyeu then leave Bitsey alone with Gale for their interviews. There will be a two-hour session on each of the next three days. Each day's interview is told in flashback form that ends with a transition from Gale's version of the past to Bitsey's point of view in the present. Spinning the camera and using quick, almost subliminal, pictures of relevant words such as "guilty," "abolish," or "deranged" makes these transitions more understandable to the audience. Since Bitsey, supposedly a serious journalist, does not ask any questions during Gale's narration, the interviews are completely his story, which proves to be less than totally reliable.

As the first flashback to Gale's story begins, the audience learns that Gale is a death penalty abolitionist who works with his academic colleague, Constance Harraway (Laura Linney), for a group called Death Watch. Harraway is worried that at the next day's televised debate with Governor Hardin (Michael Crabtree), Gale will be so preoccupied with self-promotion that he will fail to prepare adequately. Her fears seem justified when Gale decides to go to a party that night rather than study the issue. Just before the debate, the usually confident Gale appears to be a nervous wreck, ignoring Harraway's attempts to present the governor's likely arguments and leaving his notes containing relevant statistics at home. Although Harraway does not know it, Gale's distraction is due to his actions at the party, which are discussed below. Nevertheless, he starts out well until, at the very end, when the governor asks whether, having stressed the danger of an innocent defendant being executed, he can name a single such person. Ill-prepared for this obvious question, Gale is stunned into silence as the debate ends.

Some critics have suggested that the film's governor resembles George W. Bush, who held that office when the script was written and was president when it was filmed. However, Parker explains that although both the real and fictional governors share a position on capital punishment, the actor cast in the part bears no significant physical resemblance to Bush. Too strong an analogy would be a "cheap shot" that would take attention away from the substance of the film. [17]

GALE'S LIFE FALLS APART

At the end of Gale's earlier lecture on Lacan, a student that the film refers to only as Berlin (played by Rhona Mitra), enters the classroom. After the rest of the class has left, she tells Gale that she "will do anything" to pass this course. In a provocative gesture, he places his face so close to hers that he appears to want to kiss her, only to whisper advice that she should study. He quickly leaves the room. This recklessness will be the first step in the unraveling of Gale's life.

At the party, Berlin walks into the bathroom where Gale is washing. She seduces him, asking him to rip off her clothes, be rough with her sexually, and to bite her shoulder. The less-than-sober Gale follows her directions. After the debate, Gale is arrested for raping Berlin. Although she soon drops the charges and leaves Austin, his career is ruined and his wife files for divorce, taking their young son, who Gale dotes on, to Spain.

According to Parker, he made this sequence even more frenzied by intercutting it with dancers at the party. It is hard to imagine such a scene being filmed in today's society given the growing focus on sexual harassment in colleges and the influence of the #MeToo movement. In 2017, actor Kevin Spacey himself was accused of sexual misconduct by more than a dozen men and boys. As prosecutors investigated some of these charges, he became unemployable as an actor. He was removed from his starring role in the streaming series *House of Cards* and his already filmed scenes in the film *All the Money in the World* were deleted and reshot with Christopher Plummer replacing him. [18]

Before the second day's interview, Bitsey and Zack drive to what used to be Harraway's house but has since been transformed into the creepy "David Gale Death House and Museum," so named because it was the site of Harraway's killing for which Gale was convicted. When the interview resumes, Gale explains that he had written an article about the brutal murder method that was later used to kill Harraway. At the murder site, a camera and tripod were left behind without any film or tape. He theorizes that this is evidence that he was framed because of his anti-death penalty activism and the real murderer removed a tape exonerating him.

Having lost his job, Gale wanders the streets, drunkenly ranting about Socrates drinking poison in acceptance of the unjust death sentence imposed against him for his teaching. As with Liu's aria from "Turandot," Socrates's gesture of self-sacrifice despite his innocence is meant to foreshadow Gale's fate. Belyeu's advice that he get treatment for alcoholism convinces Gale to begin attending Alcoholics Anonymous meetings. He even accepts a demeaning job as a manager of a (fictional) Radio Shed store with the hope of putting his life back together.

Gale visited Harraway because he wanted to continue working with Death Watch that is arguing against the execution of a seventeen-year-old girl. Although their advocacy would prove unsuccessful, two years after the movie was released the real U.S. Supreme Court ruled that executing minors violated the Eighth Amendment.[19] Dusty, the mysterious cowboy who had been following Bitsey, is revealed to be a friend of Harraway's who is helping her by performing yard work. After learning that due to his rape arrest Death Watch no longer wants anything to do with him, Gale resumes drinking. He tries to call his wife and son from a payphone, only to smash it when she hangs up. Gale's life seems to have spiraled totally out of control but matters become even worse when Harraway, his last friend, collapses. At the hospital, he learns that she has withheld her diagnosis of leukemia from him. As the flashback ends, Bitsey is moved to tears, suggesting that she is no longer skeptical about Gale's innocence.

WHO IS THE REAL MURDERER?

Zack's research on the trial indicates that Belyeu, who had been previously sanctioned (presumably by the bar association), did a poor job of representing Gale at the trial, particularly in the penalty phase, yet Gale had turned down lawyers with more death penalty experience who had offered to represent him pro bono. Zack and Bitsey return to their motel carrying a suitcase with the half-a-million dollar payment, only to discover that while they were out, someone had broken into Bitsey's hotel room and, rather than stealing anything, left them a videotape. It is hard to believe that a major magazine would entrust such a large amount of cash to this pair, staying at an unsecured motel susceptible to a break-in, without at least some sort of armed escort. The tape seems to be evidence of Harraway's murder, showing her naked and handcuffed with a plastic bag over her head as she struggles to escape before dying. A warning to viewers—the tape is quite graphic and is shown in different versions several times during the movie.

On the final interview day, Bitsey and Zack give Belyeu the money and the tape (that Belyeu does not believe will provide enough evidence to obtain a postponement of the next day's execution). When the interview resumes, Gale explains that the cowboy who has been conspicuously following Bitsey is Dusty Wright (Matt Craven), who was fired by Death Watch after punching a death penalty supporter at a rally. In the final flashback, Harraway and Gale discuss Elizabeth Kubler Ross's five stages of grief before dying. After Harraway regrets not having had enough sex in her life, they have intercourse that, if true, would explain why Gale's semen was found in her corpse. The next morning, Gale is shown in the back yard of his former house, lying on his back with his arms outstretched in what director Parker admits was deliberately meant as a crucifixion pose (here, the reader is encouraged to consider the similarities between this scene and the ending of *Dead Man Walking*). After the flashback ends, Bitsey suggests that Dusty, who had visited Harraway that morning, must have been the killer. Rather than agreeing or disagreeing, Gale retorts, "You're not here to save me. You're here to save my son's memory of his father."

On the day that Gale is scheduled to die, Bitsey and Zack race to Harraway's house with the tape in order to try to reenact her death. Convinced from this that Harraway committed suicide to prove that an innocent person could be executed, Bitsey believes that Dusty must have the evidence. For the plan to succeed, Gale would have to die to prove that the system does not work. Zack lures Dusty away so that Bitsey can break into his shack, where she finds a more complete tape, not realizing that Dusty never left and is watching her from outside. Returning to its opening scene, the film shows Bitsey desperately racing to the scene of Gale's impending execution, symbolically running through a cemetery, only to arrive too late.

However, when she releases the tape that proves Gale's innocence, the governor continues to defend capital punishment. Dusty uses a false passport to escape to Spain, where he turns the magazine's payment over to Gale's former wife. The suitcase also includes a note of apology from Berlin from her current home in San Francisco. Dusty's final appearance is at a performance of Puccini's opera "Turandot," listening to Liu's aria that celebrates self-sacrifice.

The film has one last twist up its sleeve as Bitsey receives a package sent by Gale (or more likely a confederate he gave it to) with yet another tape that starts where the previous one ended. It shows Dusty saying "it's over" as Gale enters to check Harraway's body. We now know that Gale has made the ultimate sacrifice, like Socrates, Liu, and Christ, in order to prove that innocent people can be wrongly executed. If this ends the death penalty, it will justify Gale's framing of himself by saving future lives.

THE MEANING AND SIGNIFICANCE OF
THE LIFE OF DAVID GALE

Before evaluating whether the film succeeded in establishing the discussion of the merits of the death penalty as explained at the beginning of this chapter, it will help to look at a 1956 film and its 2009 remake because, as Richard Kelly has written, Gale and Harraway's plan "echoes Fritz Lang's *Beyond a Reasonable Doubt*."[20] The three films also tell us a lot about the Hollywood approach to making movies about capital punishment. Lang opened his film with a scene of a man being led from his prison cell to the electric chair. As the switch is pulled, the camera cuts away to show the witnesses, who include novelist Tom Garrett (Dana Andrews), who was asked to attend by his future father-in-law Austin Spencer (Sidney Blackmer), a newspaper publisher opposed to the death penalty. This scene was not part of the original screenplay but was added in preproduction by director Lang. However, when producer Bert Friedlob learned of Lang's version, he demanded that it be weakened, resulting in the compromise seen in the final cut.[21]

Tom and Austin hatch a plan to discredit capital punishment by framing Tom for the unsolved murder of a burlesque dancer. After the trial, but just before his electrocution, Austin will step forward with evidence to exonerate Tom, thus proving that the system could condemn an innocent person to death. They tell no one else, not even Tom's fiancé Susan Spencer (Joan Fontaine), about this plan. At the time of this film, executions occurred far more quickly after conviction and sentencing than they do today. In 1956, according to the Bureau of Justice Statistics, there were 146 death row prisoners and 65 executions. The comparable figures for 2013 were 2979 on death row and 39 executions.[22] Unfortunately, in *Beyond a Reasonable Doubt* the plan goes awry when, just before the jury starts its deliberations, Austin dies in a fiery car crash that also destroys the evidence of how Tom framed himself. A desperate Tom reveals the plot in court, but without that evidence this seemingly preposterous story fails to prevent the jury from finding him guilty and the judge sentencing him to death.

At the last minute, however, a letter from Austin documenting their plan is discovered in his papers, causing the prosecutor to recommend a pardon to the governor. In a final twist, Susan is permitted to visit Tom in prison, where he reveals knowledge of the victim's real name, inadvertently indicating that he actually committed the murder. He then confesses that the victim had been threatening to reveal that they had been secretly married, but that she had failed to obtain the promised Mexican divorce, meaning that Tom could not marry Susan. After Tom killed his wife to avoid further blackmail, he saw Austin's plan as a method of getting away with murder. Susan contacted the governor just as he was about to sign a pardon. Tom then is returned to his cell to face electrocution.

At first, the movie seems opposed to capital punishment, but the convoluted plot with its final revelation suggests otherwise. The original opening scene might have been intended to show the brutality of the electric chair, but the milder version eventually filmed makes no real point about the death penalty. After the final twist, Tom is revealed as a despicable person who used Austin and Susan in an attempt to get away with murder that, to many, will make his execution a just penalty. Additionally, his scheme does not make very much sense as the police investigating the dancer's murder were so lacking in evidence that they seemed to have reached a dead end. Tom was not even on their radar screen, let alone a suspect. Had the plan succeeded, Austin and Tom would likely have been prosecuted for obstruction of justice. As Bosley Crowther put it in his review, "[t]his one may get by at Loew's State [movie theater], but it wouldn't stand up in court."[23]

The 2009 remake of *Beyond A Reasonable Doubt* is barely about the death penalty at all. Instead, director Peter Hyams has stated that he intended to tell "the kind of story that young people can relate to."[24] He started by replacing two of the leads previously played by middle-aged actors Dana Andrews and Joan Fontaine with much younger performers and eliminating the part of the newspaper publisher played by the even older Sidney Blackmer entirely. Instead of a death penalty scene, this film opens with a blindfolded woman. However, there is nothing dastardly happening; it is a completely innocuous scene because the woman is taking a television reporter's (C. J. Nicholas, played by Jesse Metcalfe) coffee taste test. In his DVD commentary, Hyams explains that the opening scene and the entire film are about seduction, with a goal of misdirecting the audience.[25]

After this opening scene, Nicholas rushes to a courtroom where prosecutor Mark Hunter (Michael Douglas) is delivering his summation to the jury in a murder case. Suspecting that Hunter has been falsifying evidence, Nicholas asks Assistant District Attorney Ella Crystal (Amber Tamblyn) for tapes of interrogations. Unfortunately, because Nicholas has no evidence to support his suspicions, his editor not only kills the story but also eliminates Nicholas's investigative unit, citing budgetary reasons. Nicholas then receives two mysterious phone calls but puts the caller off.

Nicholas subsequently convinces his cameraman to help him frame himself for murder. Instead of seeking to demonstrate defects in the death penalty, Nicholas's goal is to prove that Hunter is willing to use false evidence to obtain a conviction. However, the DA proves even more dastardly than Nicholas suspected as his investigator murders the cameraman and destroys the true evidence before it can be presented by the defense. Even after Nicholas takes the stand to explain his scheme, the jury convicts him and imposes the death penalty. A desperate Nicholas asks ADA Crystal to investigate. She finds enough evidence to have Hunter arrested and the case declared a mistrial. However, when she continues to look into the crime, she discovers that the murder victim was blackmailing Nicholas. With his elaborate plot revealed as simply a scheme to get away with murder, the film ends with Nicholas's arrest. Since the previous result was a mistrial rather than a guilty or not guilty verdict, he can be tried a second time.

The remake of *Beyond a Reasonable Doubt* proved a critical and financial disaster. It earned a mere $32,917 at the box office and a meager 7 percent fresh rating on Rotten Tomatoes, based on twenty-eight reviews.[26] As critic Melisa Anderson wrote, "Lang's film . . . exposed the immorality of the death penalty; Hyams's retread offers only more plot and longer, louder car chases."[27]

These films demonstrate the reluctance of movie studios to take on capital punishment directly. Lang's *Beyond a Reasonable Doubt* tried to raise important issues but changes in the opening scene and its extra twist at the end made it more of a thriller than an exploration of the morality or wisdom of the death penalty. Hyams made no effort at all, hoping to appeal to younger viewers by changing the plot to one of exposing prosecutorial misconduct (not a very controversial subject), using younger actors, adding more action sequences, and transforming the occupations of the characters into more glamorous ones of television reporter and assistant district attorney.

Hyams's film, made more than a decade after Robbins's *Dead Man Walking* for about twice the cost, provides more evidence that given a choice between a relatively mindless thriller and a serious examination of capital punishment, Hollywood will opt for the former.

How well does *The Life of David Gale* achieve its goal of encouraging viewers to think about the morality and wisdom of the death penalty? Any impact it might have had was limited by the relatively small audience it reached with a gross of only $20 million,[28] about half of what *Dead Man Walking* had earned eight years earlier. Nor did the critics help. The nineteen percent favorable rating on Rotten Tomatoes fails to show how vitriolic some of the criticism was. David Denby wrote that "[t]he picture is practically an ad for the dysfunctions of the current system of making movies," while Roger Ebert described the film as "about as corrupt, intellectually bankrupt and morally dishonest as it could possibly be."[29] C. A. Wolski believed that the case against the death penalty is undermined by the film's portrayal of Gale and his fellow activists as "stunningly irrational loudmouths who will do anything to further their cause."[30] Perhaps because of this negative reception, Parker, who had directed such successful films as *Midnight Express*, *Fame*, *Evita*, and *Angela's Ashes*, and who won the British Film Academy's highest award, has not directed a film since *The Life of David Gale*.[31]

Given that the possibility of wrongful conviction and execution is one of the most effective arguments against capital punishment, the film's Texas governor rebuts it directly by asking Gale to cite a single innocent person executed by the state at the end of their debate. Even though Gale is supposed to be a brilliant professor and a leading anti-death penalty activist, he is flustered by this obvious question. That failure eventually leads him to devise a plan to sacrifice his own life to provide an example that will refute the governor's point. The terminally ill Harraway helps him by making her suicide look like murder.

Instead, Gale might have investigated some questionable Texas executions. One reason that there are so many more exonerations of inmates on death row than of those put to death is that once the sentence is carried out, the legal and investigating team looking for reasons to stop the execution disperses, moving on to other cases. Few resources are devoted to continuing an inquiry into the innocence of someone who is already dead in the hope of exoneration. The families of those executed rarely have the resources to carry out such an inquiry on their own. Even when they do, the best they can hope for is a posthumous pardon, which is generally awarded at the discretion of the state's governor or pardon board rather than as a matter of right when an appellate court orders a new trial for a living defendant.

Nevertheless, the Death Penalty Information Center publishes a list of the "executed but possibly innocent" on its website which would have provided a good starting point for Gale.[32] Real-life professors have uncovered evidence that has exonerated defendants who were unjustly executed, even in the film's state of Texas. Columbia Law School Professor James Liebman and a group of his students discovered strong evidence that Carlos DeLuna, convicted by a Texas court in 1983 and executed six years later, was not the person who fatally stabbed a convenience store clerk. Another man, Carlos Hernandez, who had a record of committing similar crimes and even confessed, was the more likely murderer. They even published a book arguing for DeLuna's innocence.[33]

Had Gale pursued that alternative, however, there would have been either no movie or a very different one. Since Gale's innocence was an artificial construction, the film's evidence for his argument that the danger of wrongfully executing an innocent defendant is too great to justify any beneficial effects of the death penalty is weak. Nevertheless, the film does present an opportunity for its audiences to discuss the death penalty even if they have to do their own research. In that respect, the movie raises two important issues. The unreliability of Gale's tale of events substantiates Lacan's argument that seems to suggest that no testimony of witnesses in a murder case can provide a fully accurate picture of what happened. When the facts are contested, how can a jury find guilt beyond a reasonable doubt? The very phrase "guilt beyond reasonable doubt" will have a different meaning for each of the twelve jurors, the judge, the prosecution, and the defense. As Daniel Wright and Melanie Hall put it, "*reasonable doubt* is a difficult concept for legal experts to define and even more difficult to explain to jurors, who are unlikely to be trained in legal terminology."[34]

Another question is the one that has been raised by other films in this volume. Assuming that no system of criminal justice will ever be perfect, do the benefits of capital punishment, whatever they may be, outweigh the harm done by executing some, even if only a very small number, of innocent people? Gale makes no effort to balance one against the other, believing that the loss of life from a wrongful execution is so great that no benefit can outweigh it.

Mathew Manweller, who is critical of *The Life of David Gale*, believes that it does raise important questions, even if rather ineffectively. "If one can wade through the heavy handed manner in which director Alan Parker makes his anti-death penalty, anti-conservative views known," he writes, "the film raises interesting questions for students of law. For example, how many mistakes can be tolerated in a system that issues the ultimate penalty?"[35] Manweller thinks that the film's message of self-sacrifice, although not necessarily suicide, for the benefit of others may be its most important legacy. He cites with approval Gale's admonition to his students early in the film before his own downfall begins: "'The only way we can measure the significance of our own life is by valuing the lives of others.'"[36] Pacatte, revisiting the film ten years after it was made, is more favorably disposed, believing that "it opened a door to talk about the social construction of language and meaning surrounding the death penalty."[37]

There is little evidence that any film, let alone one as poorly received by audiences and critics as *The Life of David Gale*, has much effect on public attitudes concerning the death penalty. However, perhaps the most convincing ones can play a small part in a larger conversation.

NOTES

1. Dana Kennedy, "In Film, Still a Missionary," *New York Times*, February 23, 2003.
2. Rose Pacatte, "The Life and Lies of David Gale," Reel Spirituality, April 15, 2013, https://www.brehmcenter.com/initiatives/reelspirituality/film/articles/the-value-of-a-life-like-david-gales.
3. He has since written several more, winning an Oscar for co-writing *The Big Short*.
4. "*The Life of David Gale* (2003): Trivia," IMDB.com, accessed April 20, 2019, https://www.imdb.com/title/tt0289992/trivia.
5. Michael D. Cicchini, "The Battle Over the Burden of Proof: A Report From the Trenches," *University of Pittsburgh Law Review* 79, no. 1 (Fall 2017): 63.
6. Ibid.
7. *A Few Good Men*, directed by Rob Reiner (Columbia Pictures, 1992).
8. Pacatte, "The Life and Lies of David Gale."
9. For a far more complete explanation of Lacan's ideas, see Lionel Bailly, *Lacan: A Beginner's Guide* (London: Oneworld Publications, 2009).
10. David Parkinson, *100 Ideas That Changed Film* (London: Laurence King, 2012), 122.

11. John Cook, "Pay Up," *Columbia Journalism Review*, May/June 2011, https://archives.cjr.org/essay/pay_up.php. In her review, Stephanie Zacharek sarcastically writes about the $500,000 payment "which, of course they paid in cash, as most newsmagazines in real life are all too happy to do." Stephanie Zacharek, "'The Life of David Gale,'" *Salon*, February 22, 2003, https://www.salon.com/2003/02/21/david_gale/.

12. It bears noting that Austin is also an urban city. Moreover, while the majority of Texas is red, Austin and other major urban areas (Dallas, San Antonio, Houston) historically are blue and the more liberal areas of the state.

13. James R. Acker, "Snake Oil With a Bite: The Lethal Veneer of Science and Texas's Death Penalty," *Albany Law Review* 81, no. 3 (2018): 751.

14. "State by State Database," Death Penalty Information Center, accessed April 20, 2019, https://deathpenaltyinfo.org/state_by_state.

15. Jolie McCullough, "Texas Leads the Nation in Executions, But its Death Row Population is Dropping," *Texas Tribune* (Austin, TX), December 14, 2017.

16. "*The Life of David Gale*: The Making of the Film," Alanparker.com, accessed April 20, 2019, http://alanparker.com/film/the-life-of-david-gayle/making/.

17. Unless otherwise cited, all statements attributed to director Parker are based on his DVD commentary.

18. See, for example, Sandra Gonzalez, "'House of Cards' Production to Resume without Kevin Spacey," *CNN.com*, December 4, 2017, https://www.cnn.com/2017/12/04/entertainment/house-of-cards-production/index.html.

19. Roper v. Simmons, 543 U.S. 551 (2005).

20. Kelly, "*The Life of David Gale*," 42. Similarly, see David Stratton, "*The Life of David Gale*," *Variety*, February 7, 2003, https://variety.com/2003/film/reviews/the-life-of-david-gale-1200543554/.

21. Chris Fujiwara, "Beyond a Reasonable Doubt and the Caesura," in *A Companion to Fritz Lang*, ed. Joe McElhaney (Malden, MA: John Wiley & Sons, 2015), 165. Lang's version of the death penalty scene does not seem to have been preserved.

22. BJS began publishing this last statistic in 1984.

23. Bosley Crowther, "Screen: Suspense Story; Beyond a Reasonable Doubt at the State," *New York Times*, September 14, 1956.

24. "The Whole Truth: The Making of *Beyond a Reasonable Doubt*," featurette on DVD of *Beyond a Reasonable Doubt* (2009).

25. Ibid.

26. "*Beyond a Reasonable Doubt* (2009)," Rotten Tomatoes, accessed April 20, 2019, https://www.rottentomatoes.com/m/1212946_beyond_a_reasonable_doubt.

27. Melissa Anderson, "Michael Douglas Collects a Paycheck for Beyond a Reasonable Doubt," *Village Voice*, September 8, 2009, https://www.villagevoice.com/2009/09/08/michael-douglas-collects-a-paycheck-for-beyond-a-reasonable-doubt/.

28. "*The Life of David Gale* (2003)," IMDB.com, accessed April 20, 2019, https://www.imdb.com/title/tt0289992/?ref_=nm_flmg_dr_1.

29. David Denby, "Compromises: 'The Life of David Gale' and Daredevil,'" *New Yorker*, March 3, 2003, https://www.newyorker.com/magazine/2003/03/03/compromises; Roger Ebert, "Reviews: The Life of David Gale," RogerEbert.com, February 21, 2003, https://www.rogerebert.com/reviews/the-life-of-david-gale-2003.

30. C.A. Wolski, "The Ultimate Liberal Thriller," Box Office Mojo, accessed April 20, 2019, https://www.boxofficemojo.com/reviews/?id=76&p=.htm.

31. "Alan Parker," IMDB.com, accessed April 20, 2019, https://www.imdb.com/name/nm0000570/?ref_=nv_sr_1?ref_=nv_sr_1.

32. "Executed But Possibly Innocent," Death Penalty Information Center, accessed April 20, 2019, https://deathpenaltyinfo.org/executed-possibly-innocent.

33. James S. Liebman, *The Wrong Carlos: Anatomy of a Wrongful Execution* (New York: Columbia University Press, 2014).

34. Daniel B. Wright and Melanie Hall, "How a 'Reasonable Doubt' Instruction Affects Decisions of Guilt," *Basic and Applied Social Psychology* 29, no. 1 (2007): 91.

35. Mathew Manweller, "Film Review Essays," *Contemporary Justice Review* 7, no. 3 (September 2004): 339.

36. Quoted in ibid., 340.

37. Pacatte, "The Life and Lies of David Gale."

Chapter Five

A Lesson Before Dying: **A Dignified Date With Death**

Jefferson is going to die. He did not commit the murder-robbery of which he stands accused, but that really does not matter to the all-white jury that convicts and sentences him to die. Jefferson is African American; the victim of the crime was white; the setting is 1940s Louisiana. Jefferson was always going to die.

His family accepted this reality (as did Jefferson), but (unlike Jefferson) they were convinced his attitude had to change before he was sent to the electric chair. The story of why they felt like that, and how they achieved their goal, is the story told by Ernest Gaines in his award-winning 1993 novel, *A Lesson Before Dying*. How that story is conveyed in the 1999 HBO-produced, made-for-television movie adaptation of the same name is the subject of this chapter. The focus of the chapter is upon the *lesson* that the movie teaches the audience. This is because it is the same lesson that is imparted to Jefferson by his teacher Grant Wiggins (who, along the way, comes to realize just how fundamentally important that lesson is—infinitely more important than "what the white folks tell me to teach—reading, writing, and 'rithmetic"). Jefferson is taught that even though he is a death row inmate, he is still, first and foremost, a "member . . . of the human race." As U.S. Supreme Court Justice William J. Brennan, Jr. astutely observes in the following quotation, this is a crucial lesson to learn and remember:

> The calculated killing of a human being by the state involves, by its very nature, an absolute denial of the executed person's humanity. The most vile murder does not, in my view, release the state from constitutional restraints on the destruction of human dignity . . . For me, then, the fatal constitutional

infirmity of capital punishment is that it treats members of the human race as nonhumans, as objects to be toyed with and discarded. [1]

Far too often—as Jefferson is—prisoners are treated as "nonhumans," especially within a capital punishment system that seems effortlessly capable of dehumanizing the condemned. *A Lesson Before Dying* teaches us that no one deserves to die without human dignity.

"HOG: *N. & V.* • *N* . . . A DOMESTICATED PIG, ESP. ONE . . . REARED FOR SLAUGHTER"[2]

In the film, Miss Emma (Irma P. Hall) knows that her godson Jefferson (Mekhi Phifer)[3] is going to die; she just does not "want them killing no hog; I want a man to go to that chair on his own two feet." Grant (Don Cheadle), the local schoolteacher and nephew of Emma's close friend Tante Lou (Cicely Tyson), is initially far less concerned with Jefferson's fate. Early on in the film, he responds to Miss Emma by saying, "I'm sorry; a white man's been killed, and a colored boy has to die. That's all there is to it." As unsympathetic and callous as those words might sound, they reflect the reality of the situation, a reality that the film does not try to sugarcoat. As Gaines observed in an interview that addressed his body of literary work:

> You must understand that in this country the black man has been pushed into the position where he is not supposed to be a man. This is one of the things that the white man has tried to deny the black ever since he brought him here in chains . . . *My heroes just try to be men*; but because the white man has tried everything from the time of slavery to deny the black man this chance, his attempts to be a man will lead toward danger . . . So whenever my men decide that they will be men regardless of how anyone feels, they know that they will eventually die. [4]

Professor Carlyle Thompson reinforces this point in his article about *A Lesson Before Dying*: "When a white man dies at the hands of a black man in America's Jim Crow South, the expeditious death of that black man, regardless of his culpability or innocence, is as certain as the change of the seasons."[5] The film's audience knows this, too. Unlike many of the cinematic works discussed in this volume, *A Lesson Before Dying* does not encourage us to root for an ending wherein Jefferson walks free or has his death sentence commuted to life in prison. What it does do, however, is to emphasize to us that Miss Emma was always right. No one should ever go to the electric chair (or any other method of state-sanctioned execution) believing they are a hog.

It is his court-appointed lawyer that plants the dehumanizing idea that his client is a hog, rather than a man, in Jefferson's (and everyone else's) mind (in 1932, the U.S. Supreme Court held that defendants in capital cases did have a constitutional right to counsel, but it was not until 1984 that the court actually gave any guidelines about what would make such counsel "effective" or "ineffective").[6] The "absolute denial of" Jefferson's "humanity" in *Lesson Before Dying* comes as the defense attorney (portrayed by Sonny Shroyer (famous for playing the bumbling Deputy Enos on the 1970s–1980s television series *Dukes of Hazzard*) launches into his closing argument. This is a shining example of just how much the odds are stacked against Jefferson. After we witness the crime, the film cuts to a courtroom scene, but before we see the room, we hear a deep, male, southern voice pleading his client's case to the jury. When the courtroom comes into view, we quickly realize that this is the defense attorney speaking:

> Gentlemen of the jury, I ask you to look at my client. Ask yourselves, is that a man you see sitting there? Do you see anyone who could plan a murder? Would you call this a man? A fool perhaps; a fool who is not aware of right and wrong. A fool who stood by and watched this happen, not having the sense to run. No gentlemen, not a man. What you see there is a thing that acts on command, a thing to hold the handle of a plough, to chop your wood and pull your corn, but not a thing capable of planning a robbery or a murder. He is innocent of all charges brought against him.

As the lawyer begins to ratchet up his summation, Miss Emma, to whom the camera intermittently cuts, grows increasingly anguished and distraught, and with good reason:

> But let us for a moment say he was not. Even so, what justice would there be to take his life? Justice, gentlemen. You might as soon put a hog in the 'lectric chair as this.

Deep, ominous, sorrowful music begins to play, and Miss Emma begins to cry.

> Just a poor, dumb hog.

Jefferson's defeated face fills the screen while a haunting musical motif, repeated at key points throughout the film and dominated by a violin solo, fills the air. The music continues to play as the courtroom shot fades to a view of Jefferson standing in the corner of his jail cell facing the stark walls. He is engulfed by the shadows cast by shafts of light that come in through the barred window. We are viewing Jefferson from overhead, looking at him from the other side of the bars that form the ceiling of his cell. Reinforcing the validity of Jason Stupp's observation that "*A Lesson Before Dying* is, first and foremost, a prison novel" (and prison movie)[7] and reinforcing the notion that Jefferson is animal, not human, only twice does the camera join Jefferson inside his cell. In every other scene, the camera is outside, using a shallow depth of field that brings the prisoner into focus while blurring the foreground bars of his cage. In this way, the audience is imprisoned alongside Jefferson, not permitted to feel free until he feels free.

A "VAGUE BUT POWERFUL IDEA"

"So what you think you can teach him, there, boy?" This is the question that Sheriff Guidry (played by Frank Hoyt Taylor) puts to Grant. "To die with some dignity, I suppose." This, Grant's response, comes at the stage in the film when Grant begins (ever so slowly) to succumb to Tante Lou and Miss Emma's repeated "requests" (they are issued as commands) that he meet with the imprisoned Jefferson. It is one of only two uses of the word "dignity" in the film. This stands in stark contrast to "hog," which is uttered eighteen times. [8]

Although the actual *word* is used so infrequently, the *concept* of dignity is on full display throughout the film as we are constantly told that the goal of Grant's teachings is to make Jefferson feel as though he is a *man*. This focus on dignity is one of two important themes that make this film a timeless cinematic portrayal of capital punishment (as discussed below, the other theme is race). The concept of "dignity" is an omnipresent component of debates about capital punishment. "Dignity" is a "vague but powerful idea"[9] that influences and defines the direction of the death penalty dialogue, in no small part because its vagueness and power enable it to be invoked in support of myriad different views. Abolitionists, death penalty defenders, and neutral observers. Practitioners, politicians, and academics. "Dignity" is useful to all of these groups. Further, it is rare for the U.S. Supreme Court to issue a decision in a death penalty case without at least one accompanying opinion that speaks of dignity or one of that word's etymological relations. When the justices give voice to their interpretations of the "cruel and unusual punishments" language of the Eighth Amendment, they invariably feel the need to speak using the language of dignity.

Dignity and Supreme Court Jurisprudence

As we observed in the Introduction to this volume, in *Furman v. Georgia* (1972), the court imposed a temporary nationwide death penalty moratorium; it was, however, a decision that deeply divided the justices just as much as it divided the nation. [10] Justice Brennan's separate concurring opinion was famous for its effusive embrace of human dignity and its statement of what would become his fixed position in capital cases (a position shared by Justice Thurgood Marshall). This position was that under *all* circumstances the death penalty was unconstitutional. Brennan's interpretation of the Eighth Amendment rested on his view that it contained the "moral principle...that the state, even as it punishes, must treat its citizens in a manner consistent with their intrinsic worth as human beings." He wrote dissenting opinions in capital cases in order to set forth one simple argument—that dignity lies at the heart of this "intrinsic worth" and the Constitution cannot tolerate the death penalty because it strips individuals of this worth. As Brennan observed, "this type of dissent constitutes a statement by the judge as an individual: 'Here I draw the line.'"[11]

In Brennan's concurrence in *Furman*, the death penalty's affront to human dignity played an important role, as evidenced by the opinion's twenty standalone references to the concept.[12] Brennan concluded that, "[a]t bottom . . . the Cruel and Unusual Punishments Clause prohibits the infliction of uncivilized and inhuman punishments. The State, even as it punishes, must treat its members with respect for their intrinsic worth as human beings. A punishment is 'cruel and unusual,' therefore, if it does not comport with human dignity."[13] The problem for judges, a problem that Brennan freely acknowledged, was that the process of translating this bold unequivocal statement into a workable formula of constitutional interpretation could not be guided by this "formulation" alone. This is because it "does not of itself yield principles for assessing the constitutional validity of particular punishments." For this reason, Brennan undertook a thorough analysis of the court's prior decisions, and the principles underpinning the Eighth Amendment, in order to arrive at a list of four principles that would facilitate this assessment. He provided the following summary of the relationship between dignity and these four principles:

> Death is an unusually severe and degrading punishment; there is a strong probability that it is inflicted arbitrarily; its rejection by contemporary society is virtually total; and there is no reason to believe that it serves any penal purpose more effectively than the less severe punishment of imprisonment. The function of these principles is to enable a court to determine whether a punishment comports with human dignity. Death, quite simply, does not.[14]

When the court lifted the moratorium in *Gregg v. Georgia* (1976), Brennan penned a decidedly brief dissent that contained only one standalone reference to the concept of dignity. The court's duty of interpreting the Constitution, he wrote, was guided by moral principles. When this interpretive process involved giving meaning to the "cruel and unusual punishments" clause of the Eighth Amendment, it was his belief that he and his colleagues were judicially bound to consider a principle "inherent in the Clause." Namely, " . . . the primary moral principle that the State, even as it punishes, must treat its citizens in a manner consistent with their intrinsic worth as human beings—a punishment must not be so severe as to be degrading to human dignity."[15]

The explanation for the relative brevity of Brennan's *Gregg*'s dissent was simple. It was a reaffirmation of what he had said in *Furman*. It was his "judicial determination" that there could never be constitutional comportment between human dignity and capital punishment.

As the analysis of *The Chamber* in chapter 7 explains, some members of the court have, in recent years, endorsed a different concept of dignity, one that focuses on the state rather than the condemned. This is an *institutional* understanding of dignity. In the cinematic portrayal of capital punishment that appears in *A Lesson Before Dying*, there is only one concept of dignity at stake: human dignity.

A DIFFERENT KIND OF "SUSPECT CLASSIFICATION"

The philosopher Alan Gewirth described dignity as "a kind of intrinsic worth that belongs equally to all human beings."[16] This should be a universally accepted truth. However, as *A Lesson Before Dying* clearly shows, racial bigotry can all too easily get in the way of achieving that normative goal. One of the abiding strengths of the film, however, is that it does not try to sensationalize the racial bigotry that drives the dehumanization of Jefferson (and, to a lesser extent, all of the other African American characters in the story). Race is an important theme, but it is not overblown; this is simply because it does not need to be.

In the novel, Gaines does not explicitly tell us the timeline for the story. As Michael Zeitler observes, "the events . . . take place between October and April, unfolding alongside the annual, timeless, and symbolic cycle of the religious calendar around which the inhabitants of Bayone, Louisiana, organize and give meaning to their communal lives."[17] Yet which specific October and which specific April are we dealing with? The answer is less obvious. The painful influence of Jim Crowism sends a strong message about the time period, but it is only a passing reference to the fact that Jackie Robinson has just finished his second year playing for the Dodgers that gives us a particular chronological point of reference in the book.[18] By contrast, in the film, we are told exactly when the events we are about to witness took place. As the car carrying Jefferson and two acquaintances (who would carry out the robbery-murder and die in the ensuing gunfight) pulls up in front of Mr. Gropé's store, "St. Raphael Parish Louisiana—1948" appears on the screen.

In many ways, the *concept* of describing *governmental* race-based classifications as "constitutionally suspicious" first appeared in a U.S. Supreme Court opinion in *West Virginia v. Strauder* (1880), which struck down a state law prohibiting blacks from serving on juries.[19] However, the word "suspect" was not used by the court, in regard to this aspect of law, until 1944. Writing for the court in *Korematsu v. United States*, the infamous decision upholding the federal government's internment of Japanese Americans during World War II, Justice Hugo L. Black said "all legal restrictions which curtail the civil rights of a single racial group are immediately *suspect*."[20] This means that in terms of its timeline, *A Lesson Before Dying* is set against this constitutional backdrop.[21] It would be decades before substantive, race-related reforms would come to the nation's criminal justice system.

One could make the argument that important, race-related elements of *constitutional* reform came to the nation in the immediate aftermath of the Civil War. The ratification of the Reconstruction Amendments brought a *de jure* constitutional end to slavery (Thirteenth Amendment [1865]); gave citizenship to former slaves and provided a constitutional guarantee of "equal protection of the laws" (Fourteenth Amendment [1868]); and prohibited race-based denial of voting (Fifteenth Amendment [1870]). However, these were mere words, and while they set the stage for some important decisions advancing civil rights—such as *Strauder*—American history remains (to this day) replete with examples of *de facto* racial discrimination that thumbs its nose at these changes to the nation's "supreme law." As Douglas Blackmon masterfully demonstrates in his Pulitzer Prize-winning book, from the late nineteenth century through the middle of the twentieth century these were best described as pervasive, white supremacy-maintaining examples of "Slavery by Another Name."[22]

The very troubling relationship between race and capital punishment that persists today—and which helps to maintain the continuing relevance of *A Lesson Before Dying*—is, in part, a legacy of the U.S. Supreme Court's 1987 decision in *McCleskey v. Kemp*.[23] This was the first case in which the nation's highest court explicitly considered whether the death penalty was imposed and carried out in a manner that met the requirements of strict scrutiny that became the standard judicial review test for race-based governmental actions. By a 5–4 vote, the court rejected the relevance, to the case at hand, of the Baldus Study (named after its lead author, law Professor David C. Baldus) that the attorneys for Warren McCleskey, the African American defendant in the case, submitted as evidence of pervasive racial bias in death penalty cases. The study demonstrated that of the 2,500 murder cases, from Georgia, in its dataset, those that involved crimes against white individuals were over four times more likely to generate death sentences for the defendants than when the victim of the crime was black. In debates about the morality and constitutionality of capital punishment, one might be inclined to think of the person condemned to die as a "victim" of the death penalty system, and that they might be a victim of societal attitudes toward their race. By contrast, this particular aspect of the Baldus dataset focused on the correlation between the race of the person murdered and the sentence imposed upon the person convicted of carrying out that murder. Despite the compelling nature of those data, a bare majority of the court concluded that these data were not sufficient evidence that race had tainted the process that had put McCleskey on Georgia's death row.[24]

Today, it is difficult to ignore what contemporary statistics tell us about race and the death penalty. Although, as shown in figure 5.1, the percentages of blacks and whites currently on death row are about even, those percentages are misleading because one must keep in mind that "minority"—referred to by the U.S. Census Bureau as "people who reported their ethnicity and race as something other than non-Hispanic White"—are not projected to make up fifty percent of the country's population until 2042. In 1980, they constituted only 20.4 percent of the population, 24.4 percent in 1990, 30.9 percent in 2000, and 36.3 percent in 2010.[25] Additionally, historically (at least, since 1976), figure 5.1 also tells us that a far higher percentage of defendants sentenced to death have been black than white, and the racial disparity of the victims is even more stark. We obviously cannot say with certainty that the race of a defendant or their victim is the factor that ultimately leads a jury to choose death over life during the sentencing phase of a capital case. Similarly, this was exactly the point that the court made in *McCleskey*—that, "[i]t is the ultimate duty of courts to determine on a case-by-case basis whether these laws are applied consistently with the Constitution. Despite McCleskey's wide-ranging arguments that basically challenge the validity of capital punishment in our multiracial society, the only ques-

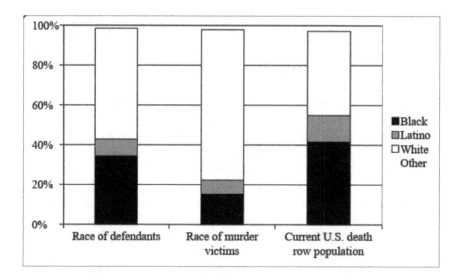

Figure 5.1.   Race-related death penalty statistics, 1976–2017. Compiled using data from "National Statistics on the Death Penalty and Race," Death Penalty Information Center, accessed June 8, 2018, https://deathpenaltyinfo.org/race-death-row-inmates-executed-1976#defend.

tion before us is whether, in his case . . . the law of Georgia was properly applied."[26] Regardless, the statistics certainly give us pause for thought about whether a decision is being made based upon a suspicious classification.

Looking beyond the Supreme Court's Eighth Amendment jurisprudence and its evaluative language of "suspect classes," one finds that in *A Lesson Before Dying* there is a different type of suspicious classification going on in and around Bayonne, the Louisianan setting for the story. To almost every white character, any African American they encounter is inherently suspicious. When readers watch this film, they are encouraged to consider to what extent Henri Pichot (played by Stuart Culpepper) views African Americans differently from all of the other white men and women. To the sheriff, Grant is suspicious because he found his way off the plantation, all the way to university; and Reverend Ambrose (Brent Jennings) is suspicious because, as discussed below, he fails to see that there is a crucial difference between Jefferson and Jesus Christ. To Edna, the sheriff's wife, Miss Emma and Tante Lou are suspicious because they refuse to believe it is acceptable to be made to meet Jefferson in the cramped confines of his jail cell. By now, however, we all know why Jefferson is suspicious.

Of course, it is obvious why these white men and women want us to believe that Grant, the reverend, Miss Emma, Tante Lou, and Jefferson are suspicious. Therein lies further confirmation of the second reason why *A Lesson Before Dying* is a valuable way for twenty-first century audiences to understand how capital punishment works in the United States.

As we noted in the introduction to this volume, when writing his novel Gaines began with a real death row inmate, Willie Francis. There is no doubt that Francis's "story was different from" the one being told in *A Lesson Before Dying*. Like Jefferson, Francis was a young black man (sixteen years of age when sentenced to die) who was convicted of murdering a white business owner in 1940s Louisiana. From there, however, the two stories diverge. Francis's case remains one of the most famous, and troubling episodes in American criminal justice history, because in May 1946 he survived the state's first effort to execute him using the electric chair. Only after his appeal—on "cruel and unusual punishments" grounds—went all the way up to and was decided against him by the U.S. Supreme Court was Francis finally executed a year later.[27] Although the facts of this story differed from those of the one Gaines wanted to write, he nevertheless decided he "would use some of the information from the case material" to make an important point[28]—an important point about the relationship between capital punishment, race, and humanity.

"I ONCE WAS LOST, BUT NOW AM FOUND"

In her *Variety* magazine review of the filmic adaptation of *A Lesson Before Dying*, Laura Fries writes that, "[u]nlike 'Dead Man Walking,' this death row drama is not about a guilty man coming to terms with his life, but rather an innocent man coming to terms with his death."[29] That transformation takes place over the course of Grant's eight visits (sometimes alone, sometimes accompanied by myriad other characters) with Jefferson.

The first three visits all follow the same pattern: Jefferson does not want to learn anything, because he has been wholeheartedly convinced—not just by his defense attorney but by all the white figures who have determined the course of his entire life—that he is indeed "just a poor, dumb hog." "You brought some corn?" he asks Grant. To Jefferson, this question is so simple. "Corn what a hog eat," he states, before pushing the basket of food prepared by Miss Emma and brought to the cell by Grant on the floor and lying on his back on his cot. The bars of the ceiling hold more interest than food, for Jefferson, and they are significant regarding what remains of his life. The following visit goes no better as Jefferson continues to emphasize the depressing, dehumanizing implications of his assigned existence as a "hog." Grant fails to persuade him to eat some of Tante Lou's homemade praline candy. Why should Jefferson refuse to consume this foodstuff? The answer seems obvious to him as he gets on his hands and knees and grunts like a hog. "Hog don't eat no candy, Mr. Teacher."

Grant does not make any real headway with Jefferson until the fourth visit. On this occasion, frustrated at both the lack of progress and the fact that he is being made to undertake this assignment against his will, Grant desperately tries to break the ice by finding something to talk about that would make Jefferson happy to be alive (before dying). Gaines explains that, "[t]he idea of the radio was not planned, but it turned out to be a most important turn in the story."[30] The film very nicely conveys this importance because the subject that transforms Jefferson is music. Neither the reverend, Tante Lou, nor Miss Emma are happy that Jefferson is finding solace in the radio that Grant subsequently buys for him. Yet as Grant defiantly explains, the radio brings light into Jefferson's life. Yes, God is supposed to do that, but if the radio does a better job, then so be it because Jefferson has but one more month left on this earth.

The other thing that triumphantly leads Jefferson out of the shadows of his "hog" label is the composition book that Grant leaves with him with the encouragement that he can write his thoughts in there when Grant is not around to discuss them. It is in this book that Jefferson writes "Man Walk on Too Foots; hog walk on four hoofs." To invoke a line from the song "Amazing Grace," while Jefferson "once was lost," he "now . . . [is] found."

In Gaines's novel, this "diary" plays a far more significant role than in the film. It literally *is* chapter 29; the words of the diary alone occupy the nine pages of this section of the book[31] and "signal" Jefferson's "resistance to the narrative the community fashions to coincide with his death."[32] As Stupp explains, its strategic placement "immediately after Grant has discussed the execution with Jefferson and immediately before the arrival of the truck carrying the electric chair and generator" only serves to strengthen its contribution to the journey that Jefferson takes in the book.[33]

In the film, several passages from the diary are read—either by Grant while in the cell with Jefferson, or by Jefferson (as a voice-over for the final scene—discussed below), and sections of other passages appear in the film's dialogue but not in the form of passages from the diary. The following is a perfect example:

> mr wigin you say you like what i got here but you say you stil cant giv me a a
> jus a b cause you say i aint gone deep in me yet an you kno i can if i try hard an
> when i ax you what you mean deep in me you say jus say whats on my mind so
> one day you can be save an you can save the chiren and i say i don't kno what
> you mean an you say i do kno what you mean an you look so tied sometime mr
> wigin i just feel like tellin you i like you but i dont kno how to say this cause i
> aint never say it to nobody before an nobody aint never say it to me[34]

The very fact that only the last "sentence" of this passage appears in the film—and as a verbal dialogue between Grant and Jefferson which gives us no clue that the words come from the latter's "diary"—might strike some viewers (who have also read the book) as an unfaithful adaptation of the novel. However, as film and literature scholars are quick to point out, asking whether a film is a "faithful" adaptation of a novel is not a very helpful form of evaluative inquiry.[35] As Robert Stam succinctly observes: "The question of fidelity ignores the wider question: Fidelity to what?"[36] If, regarding *A Lesson Before Dying*, the answer to that question is "the main point of the story," then one can definitely make the argument that the cinematic adaptation of this aspect of Jefferson's diary is an entirely faithful adaptation.

Yvonne Kozlovsky-Golan astutely observes that, "American attitudes toward the death penalty among both policy makers and the general public must be understood in relation to the two main ideological templates governing America's public agenda: the religious and the constitutional."[37] As is the case in *Dead Man Walking* (chapter 3), religion plays an important role in *A Lesson Before Dying*. This is, in part, because some of the film's characters are deeply religious (although, equally significantly, because Grant has lost his faith). There is one scene, however, wherein the importance of the role played by religion stems from the way in which it is intertwined with another, but distinctly secular, force. This scene, where Grant and the reverend are informed of the reasoning for the choice of Jefferson's execution date, serves to underscore the abiding truth of this line from *Dune*, Frank Herbert's acclaimed science fiction novel: "[w]hen religion and politics travel in the same cart, the riders believe nothing can stand in their way."[38]

Jefferson is to be executed on April 8. Shortly after the sheriff delivers this news to the prisoner, he summons Grant and the reverend to his plantation home in order to inform them of this development. It is a powerful scene that underscores the position of authority held by the two white men, because the sheriff and his friend Pichot are on horseback while the other two men are walking. This ensures that, from the camera's perspective, the two white men will always be looking down upon the two African Americans.

Matter-of-factly, the sheriff declares: "It'll be the second Friday after Easter, and I don't want you making any trouble for him." Why will the execution take place after Easter? The sheriff's answer speaks volumes about the fact that the political machinery cares nothing about the condemned. One other individual has already been scheduled to die before Lent and, "Well, the governor don't want to upset the Catholics." So forty days and forty nights will pass; the crucifixion and death of Jesus will be commemorated and then his resurrection will be celebrated before Jefferson is sent to the chair. As the sheriff explains to Grant and the reverend, "I think that we're real fortunate to have a governor who is mindful of his duty to the people." The dehumanizing way in which the sheriff still views Jefferson is underscored when he is asked about the timing of the execution. It will be between midday and three o'clock. Refusing to look the sheriff in the eyes and choosing instead to express his disdain in a subtler manner, the reverend replies despondently: "same time the Lord on the cross." The sheriff conveys no hint of any emotions when he has the final words of the scene: "Now that's not a connection I would have made with a convicted killer, reverend."

AN IMAGINED EXECUTION

Unlike many of the films studied in this volume, *A Lesson Before Dying* does not show the execution. In *Murder in Coweta County* (chapter 1), we see John Wallace strapped into the electric chair; in *Dead Man Walking* (chapter 3), Matthew Poncelet's execution by lethal injection is graphically portrayed; in *Monster's Ball* (chapter 9), we are witnesses to the way in which Sonny Grotowski breaks down as he leads Lawrence to the chair; and in *The Green Mile* (discussed in the next chapter), three different executions take place on screen, including that of Eduard Delacroix, who dies in botched circumstances so gruesomely detailed that nothing is left to our imagination. No such scene takes place in *A Lesson Before Dying*. We know that Jefferson dies, but any details of his electrocution are left to our imagination.

In 1940s Louisiana, there was no single state prison for housing those condemned to die; prisoners were routinely imprisoned and then executed in the parish where they committed their crimes—executed using the "traveling electric chair."[39] Gaines became aware of this during his conversations with Willie Francis's lawyer, and this fact from Louisiana's capital punishment past contributed to his decision to set the story in the 1940s.[40] Consequently, the omission of any of these details about executing a prisoner using "Gruesome Gertie"—as the Louisiana electric chair was known by death row inmates—might be considered problematic. This is especially true when one considers that as compared to the novel, which is a "single-track, uniquely verbal medium," the film is a distinctly "multitrack medium."[41] Including scenes—such as an execution—that can make good use of cinematic techniques like foreboding music and dramatic lighting, would seem to be very appropriate. However, *A Lesson Before Dying* is just that—a lesson (for the characters and audience alike) to be learned *before* anyone dies; thus, just as Gaines felt little need to include gruesome execution details in the book, such specifics were also shrewdly omitted from the film.

Rather than featuring his death, the final two scenes of the film emphasize Jefferson's humanity and, appropriately, the lessons that we have all learned before his death. The penultimate scene finds Jefferson, his head freshly shaved, folding up the blanket on his cot, and neatly arranging his belongings. He will never return to collect them, but he—now a man rather than a hog—takes pride in the things that the authorities will see when they come to clear out his cell. Further reinforcing the humanity of the condemned, for only the second time in the film the camera joins Jefferson inside that cell. Yet this time, the light that streams in through the barred windows possesses a heretofore-absent warmth.

The final scene shifts our focus to Grant but continues the emphasis on warmth and humanity. As we see Jefferson's face fading from view, we see a scene bathed in sunlight. It is a scene that is at once both inspiring and upsetting. For the camera slowly zooms in on Grant, who sits on the steps of the wooden one-room schoolhouse, contemplating the events that are at that time taking place at the nearby courthouse. As the camera zooms in, it passes happy children who are playing games in the sunlight-bathed, dusty yard. Even though the words that we hear—Jefferson's words—are the last we will ever hear, they are *his* words and it is *his* voice reading them, reading them as he writes them at the end of his "diary" before dying:

> Goodbye Mr. Wiggins. Tell the children I'm strong. Tell 'em I'm a man.
> Thank you Mr. Wiggins.
> Your friend, Jefferson

CONCLUSION: "THE EYES OF THE LAW ARE HUMAN EYES"

As the 1996 movie *A Time to Kill* (an adaptation of the John Grisham novel of the same name) builds to its conclusion, attorney Jake Brigance (played by Matthew McConaughey) delivers a powerful closing argument on behalf of his client. He successfully persuades the jury to find Carl Lee Hailey (Samuel L. Jackson) not guilty of capital murder, in large part because he *does not* ask them to view the crime in a color-blind manner (Hailey gunned down the two white men who abducted, raped, beat, urinated on, and unsuccessfully tried to lynch his ten-year-old daughter). Brigance has come to realize that in Clanton, Mississippi, you will get nowhere by asking an all-white jury to look beyond the fact that the defendant is African American. This is a passage from his summation:

> I set out to prove a black man could receive a fair trial in the South. That we are all equal in the eyes of the law. That's not the truth, 'cos the eyes of the law are human eyes, yours and mine. And until we can see each other as equals, justice is never going to be even-handed. It will remain nothing more than a reflection of our own prejudices. So until that day, we have a duty under God, to seek the truth; not with our eyes, not with our minds with fear, and hate that turn commonality into prejudice. But with our hearts.

Ernest Gaines emphasizes that, "the story" in *A Lesson Before Dying* "is not whether Jefferson is innocent or guilty, but rather how he feels about himself at the end."[42] The filmic adaptation tells that very same story, but it does something extra (in a way that a movie can arguably do more powerfully than a book). It asks us to consider how we feel about ourselves, and our fellow human beings. That is *A Lesson Before Dying*.

In 1993, the year it was published, Gaines's novel won the prestigious National Book Critics Circle Award in the fiction category. Four years later, it would gain widespread recognition and go to the top of the *New York Times* paperback bestseller list, thanks, in large part, to its selection as the October 1997 reading for Oprah's Book Club, the popular book discussion section of Oprah Winfrey's television talk show.[43] This meant that even before the HBO adaptation, "[t]elevision had a powerful role to play in this story."[44] Two years later, when the movie appeared, more honors were bestowed. At the 1999 Primetime Emmys, it took home the award for the Outstanding Made for Television Movie and Ann Peacock won for her adaptation of Gaines's novel. Critics were united in bestowing their acclaim upon the film. In his review which ran in the *Washington Post* with an extremely appropriate title—"'Lesson Before Dying': A Higher Education"—Ken Ringle made the following observation:

It might be too much to hope for, that television would treat such a work with respect, much less reverence. But, praise God, that has come to pass. HBO premieres it tonight at 8 and you're unlikely ever to see a more intelligent, compelling and beautifully crafted film anywhere. Miss it at your peril.[45]

In order to understand the different ways in which capital punishment has been (and can be) portrayed cinematically, *A Lesson Before Dying* is a must-see.[46] It has many lessons to teach us.

NOTES

1. William J. Brennan, Jr., "The Constitution of the United States: Contemporary Ratification," in *Interpreting Law and Literature: A Hermeneutic Reader*, eds. Sanford Levinson and Steven Mailloux (Evanston, IL: Northwestern University Press, 1988), 23.

2. *The Oxford American Dictionary and Language Guide* (New York: Oxford University Press, 1999), 463.

3. Afterwards, Phifer would become well known to general audiences for playing the longstanding role of Dr. Greg Pratt on the hit television show *ER* (from 2002 to 2008).

4. Quoted in John O'Brien, "Ernest J. Gaines," in *Conversations With Ernest Gaines*, ed. John Lowe (Jackson: University Press of Mississippi, 1995), 30 (italics added).

5. Carlyle V. Thompson, "From a Hog to a Black Man: Black Male Subjectivity and Ritualistic Lynching in Ernest J. Gaines's *A Lesson Before Dying*," *CLA Journal* XLV, no. 3 (2002): 280. Indeed, as Thompson further observes, "[u]nder Jim Crowism, black people are killed before they die; the daily humiliation they experience represents ritualistic lynching." Ibid., 282. Viewers of the film will encounter numerous examples of this.

6. Powell v. Alabama, 287 U.S. 45 (1932); Strickland v. Washington, 466 U.S. 668 (1984).

7. Jason Stupp, "Living Death: Ernest Gaines's *A Lesson Before Dying* and the Execution of Willie Francis," in *Demands of the Dead: Executions, Storytelling, and Activism in the United States*, ed. Katy Ryan (Iowa City: University of Iowa Press, 2012), 45.

8. The word "hog" appears fifty-two times in Gaines's novel. Thompson, "From a Hog to a Black Man," 281n2.

9. Ronald Dworkin, *Taking Rights Seriously* (Cambridge, MA: Harvard University Press, 1977), 198.

10. 408 U.S. 238 (1972).

11. William J. Brennan, Jr., "In Defense of Dissents," *Hastings Law Journal* 37 (1986): 436–37.

12. "Standalone" references differ from "dependent" ones—which might include, for example, quotations from other opinions or from secondary sources, the descriptions of the holdings of other cases that explicitly rely on "dignity" or a related word, or simply references (usually negative ones in a separate opinion) to a judicial colleague's invocation of the concept. When a judge writes an opinion in which he uses the concept of "dignity" to make a distinct point about his own arguments, this is considered a standalone use. Helen J. Knowles, "A Dialogue on Death Penalty Dignity," *Criminology & Criminal Justice* 11 (2011): 116.

13. 408 U.S. at 270 (Brennan, J., concurring).

14. Ibid., at 305.

15. 428 U.S. 227, 229 (1976) (Brennan, J., dissenting).

16. Alan Gewirth, "Human Dignity as the Basis of Rights," in *The Constitution of Rights: Human Dignity and American Values*, eds. Michael J. Meyer and William A. Parent (Ithaca, NY: Cornell University Press, 1992), 12.

17. Michael Zeitler, "'Mr. Joe Louis, Help Me': Sports as Narrative and Community in Ernest J. Gaines's *A Lesson Before Dying*," *Studies in the Literary Imagination* 49, no. 1 (Summer 2016): 129.

18.   Ernest J. Gaines, *A Lesson Before Dying* (New York: Vintage Contemporaries, 1993), 87-88; also see Zeitler, "'Mr. Joe Louis, Help Me,'" 129.

19.   100 U.S. 303 (1880).

20.   323 U.S. 214, 216 (1944).

21.   Gaines had initially planned to set his novel in the 1980s. Ernest J. Gaines, "Writing *A Lesson Before Dying,*" *Southern Review* 41 (2005): 773–74.

22.   Douglas A. Blackmon, *Slavery By Another Name: The Re-Enslavement of Black Americans From the Civil War to World War II* (New York: Doubleday, 2008). For an important book discussing the persistence of racial problems into the twenty-first century, especially as they relate to the criminal justice system, see Michelle Alexander, *The New Jim Crow: Mass Incarceration in the Age of Colorblindness* (New York: New Press, 2010).

23.   481 U.S. 279 (1987).

24.   For a detailed discussion of the story of the *McCleskey* case, see David C. Baldus et al., "*McCleskey v. Kemp*: Denial, Avoidance, and the Legitimization of Racial Discrimination in the Administration of the Death Penalty," in *Death Penalty Stories*, eds. John Blume and Jordan Steiker (New York: Foundation Press, 2009).

25.   "A Look at the 1940 Census," United States Census Bureau, accessed June 21, 2018, https://www.census.gov/newsroom/cspan/1940census/CSPAN_1940slides.pdf.

26.   481 U.S. at 319.

27.   For an excellent, detailed discussion of the Francis story, see Deborah W. Denno, "When Willie Francis Died: The 'Disturbing' Story Behind One of the Eighth Amendment's Most Enduring Standards of Risk," in Blume and Steiker, *Death Penalty Stories*.

28.   Gaines, "Writing *A Lesson Before Dying,*" 771.

29.   Laura Fries, "A Lesson Before Dying," *Variety*, May 21, 1999, https://variety.com/1999/tv/reviews/a-lesson-before-dying-1117499797/.

30.   Gaines, "Writing *A Lesson Before Dying,*" 776.

31.   Gaines, *A Lesson Before Dying*, 226-34.

32.   Stupp, "Living Death," 49.

33.   Ibid.

34.   Gaines, *A Lesson Before Dying*, 228.

35.   See the essays in Timothy Corrigan, ed., *Film and Literature: An Introduction and Reader*, 2nd ed. (London: Routledge, 2012).

36.   Robert Stam, "Beyond Fidelity: The Dialogics of Adaptation," in Corrigan, *Film and Literature*, 77.

37.   Yvonne Kozlovsky-Golan, *The Death Penalty in American Cinema: Criminality and Retribution in Hollywood Film* (London: I. B. Tauris, 2014), 86.

38.   Frank Herbert, *Dune* (New York: Ace, 1990), 620.

39.   Gaines, "Writing *A Lesson Before Dying,*" 774.

40.   Ibid.

41.   Stam, "Beyond Fidelity," 76.

42.   Gaines, "Writing *A Lesson Before Dying,*" 776.

43.   "*A Lesson Before Dying,*" Oprah.com, September 22, 1997, accessed June 6, 2018, http://www.oprah.com/oprahsbookclub/about-a-lesson-before-dying-by-ernest-gaines/all.

44.   Barbara D. Phillips, "TV: A Lesson on Death Row," *Wall Street Journal*, May 17, 1999.

45.   Ken Ringle, "'Lesson Before Dying': A Higher Education," *Washington Post*, May 22, 1999.

46.   Beyond television repeats, or viewings via DVD, Netflix, or other such on-demand services, the story of *A Lesson Before Dying* continues to attract new devotees through theater company productions, across the country, of Romulus Linney's play based on the novel. For example, in 2013 it was performed by the African American Repertory Theater in DeSoto, Texas. Irma P. Hall—one of the company's founders—reprised her role as Tante Lou. Lawson Taitte, "Irma P. Hall to Star in 'A Lesson Before Dying' at Desoto's African American Repertory Theater," *Dallas Morning News*, April 2, 2013.

Chapter Six

The Green Mile: An Extraordinary Look into Death Row

The Green Mile, which chronicles the encounters between Paul Edgecomb, supervisor of a prison's death row, and John Coffey, an inmate with extraordinary powers, originated as a six-part serial novel penned by Stephen King that was released between March and August 1996. That same year, the series won the Horror Writers Association's Bram Stoker Award for best novel before being consolidated into a single volume in 1997. Soon, however, the novel's reach spread even further when writer and director Frank Darabont (who several years earlier achieved critical success with *The Shawshank Redemption*, another prison movie based on a King novel) adapted *The Green Mile* for the big screen.

Opening on December 6, 1999, *The Green Mile* premiered as "a story which develops and unfolds, which has detail and space."[1] Unlike other Hollywood movies, it is lengthy—just over three hours, to be precise. Yet as film critic Roger Ebert notes, the extra time is needed as it "allows us to feel the passage of prison months and years" and, at the same time, allows for the story to fully develop—"[t]he movie would have been much diminished at two hours—it would have been a series of episodes without context."[2] Other critics, like *Variety's* Todd McCarthy, argue that the point of the movie still could have been reached without the lengthy journey.[3] Still, the length of the film aside, it clearly resonated with audiences. The film grossed $290 million worldwide[4] and was nominated for numerous awards—including at the Oscars, Golden Globes, and Screen Actors Guild Awards—for best picture, best writing, and outstanding supporting actor for Michael Clarke Duncan, who seamlessly played the role of John Coffey.[5]

Unlike other book-to-film adaptations that often lead to the simplest version of the story being told, Frank Darabont focused on being as true to

Stephen King's vision as possible: " . . . trying to mimic [his] voice; trying to speak in his patois—not just in terms of dialogue, but in terms of the characters."[6] He focused on incorporating the soul, as he remarked, into the film in a screenplay that took him exactly two months to write. At the same time, deliberate choices were made in respect to how the story was framed: "I love setting up questions about the movie that the audience is seeing. I love people not getting it until later. Because that makes for a much more satisfying storytelling experience for the viewer. . . . It's the more cerebral version of the set-up and pay-off."[7] Throughout the film, the characters and the storyline dance between sincerity and irony, all while facing challenges to their morality and compassion that appear contrary to the prison and death row setting that they find themselves in. Combined, this adds the necessary "texture" to the film that the book also had. What is perhaps most interesting, however, is that Darabont leaves the ultimate decision about the film's meaning (as well as that of John Coffey) to the audience: "The exciting thing about The Green Mile to me is that I can't sum it up. . . . I'm not sure what The Green Mile is about. All I know is that it's a hell of a story."[8]

While some reviews, like that of the *Guardian's* Philip French, highlight Biblical undertones of the movie's plot,[9] the reality is that this film provides audiences with numerous lessons relating to the use of the death penalty. Among the most critical of these are the execution of mentally challenged individuals and botched executions. Additionally, like *The Thin Blue Line* (discussed in chapter 2), *The Green Mile* also sheds valuable light on the issue of wrongful convictions.

"USUALLY, DEATH ROW WAS CALLED THE LAST MILE. WE CALLED OURS THE GREEN MILE."

When the film opens, it is 1999 at an assisted living facility somewhere in Louisiana. Audiences are soon introduced to Paul Edgecomb (Dabbs Greer portrays the elder version), a sharp, snappy resident with a pep in his step and an ease and friendliness about him. This good mood is seemingly short-lived as, during a showing of the movie *Top Hat* for the residents, he begins to cry. Soon, sitting on the facility's large veranda with his friend, Elaine, the rain pouring down around them, we learn why—the movie has taken him back to his younger years, a time that was pivotal in creating the man he is today.

Almost in an instant, the audience is transported back to 1935 to the Cold Mountain Penitentiary, also in Louisiana. Wide angles show a prison farm with row after row of inmates shackled together by the ankles, working on the yard. These "chain gangs" were popular in southern correctional institutions that often used inmates as laborers rather than bringing in outside contractors, thereby allowing the institutions to be more self-sufficient and

lecency principle to reach its conclusion. This time, however,
nd that there was a societal consensus against executing the
disabled. A majority of the states now banned such a practice,
a widespread lack of support from both the public and academ-
es. In the majority opinion (joined by Justice O'Connor, who
majority opinion in *Penry*), Justice John Paul Stevens noted

f their disabilities in areas of reasoning, judgment, and control of
lses, however, they do not act with the level of moral culpability that
zes the most serious adult criminal conduct. Moreover, their impair-
jeopardize the reliability and fairness of capital proceedings against
etarded defendants. [16]

tkins decision overruled *Penry*, thereby creating a categorical
n the execution of intellectually disabled individuals.
ne time, however, *Atkins* left the decision of what constituted
dation" or "intellectual disabilities" to the states. As a result,
uniform standard of what qualified as a threshold to determine
isability. [17] While an IQ of 70 was used by most states as a
other states set the threshold at a lower IQ or failed to identify a
shold at all. This led to the execution of a number of individuals
ne or even fully set mental retardation. In 2010, Virginia (which
numeric threshold) executed Teresa Lewis, a woman convicted
ng a murder for hire who had an IQ of 72, which is borderline
unctioning. [18] Similarly, Georgia, which also failed to set a nu-
ff, executed twice-convicted murderer Warren Hill in 2015 de-
t that with an IQ of 70, he had the mental functioning of an
old. [19]
he Supreme Court sought to address the issue of the IQ thresh-
greed to hear *Hall v. Florida*. Freddie Lee Hall, who had been
murder and sentenced to death, had an IQ of 71. [20] Following the
on, Florida law designated that persons with an IQ of 70 or
be considered intellectually disabled. Therefore, despite over-
idence that Hall was intellectually disabled, he was not consid-
under the Florida law. His appeals in the state courts were
denied and his death sentence upheld. The U.S. Supreme Court
t by having such a rigid threshold, the state "create[d] . . . an
risk that persons with intellectual disability will be executed,
e statute] is unconstitutional." [21] Striking down the law, Justice
Kennedy further noted that it failed to account for standard
asurement, adding that the law also required that Hall, like other

even draw a profit.[10] The camera picks up a truck driving through the prison's grounds, soon arriving at E block, which houses the prison's death row. Inside the warehouse-like building, the audience meets the younger Paul Edgecomb (portrayed by Tom Hanks) and the officers he supervises—Brutus "Brutal" Howard (David Morse), Dean Stanton (Barry Pepper), and Harry Terwilliger (Jeffrey DeMunn). The group is preparing to receive a new prisoner and they soon hear the call from outside the building. It also when we learn why it is called the green mile—"the floor was the color of faded limes."

When the car carrying the prisoner first pulls up, it appears as though the back wheels are flat; Brutus questions whether the car has a broken spring. The rear of the car, however, seems to spring back up, released from a tremendous weight, as the prisoner is removed from the vehicle. Close-ups of the prisoner's feet, walking toward the block in shackles, are shown, but the audience has yet to see his face. "Dead man. Dead man walking. We got a dead man walking here," Percy Wetmore (Doug Hutchison), another of the officers, chants as he leads the inmate toward, and then into, E block. Glimpses of the prisoner are offered to suggest to audiences his massive size (in the original novel, he is 6'8"), and looks of intimidation spread across the faces of the guards and the other prisoners alike.

"Am I going to have any trouble with you, big boy?" Paul asks. When he receives no answer, he prompts, "Can you talk?" The camera cuts to a close-up shot of the prisoner's massive hands, also bound by shackles, before slowly panning upward to finally reveal the prisoner's face. "Yessa boss, I can talk," the prisoner replies. A look of panic and terror resides on his face, but he is respectful and compliant. That does not stop Percy, a small man with a sadistic streak, from hitting the prisoner with his baton to get him into the cell. Paul, who takes an evenhanded approach to running his unit, does not tolerate Percy's actions and sends him away—but not before Percy smashes and breaks the finger of another inmate, Eduard Delacroix (or Del, as he is known to the block; this character is portrayed by Michael Jeter), with the same baton.

Paul then has the chains removed from the prisoner's hands and feet. "Your name is John Coffey," says Paul. The prisoner replies, "Yes sir, boss. Like the drink, only not spelled the same." John says he can only spell his name, suggesting that he may be illiterate or mentally challenged (a concern for a number of death row inmates). As Paul runs through the procedures of the prison, he asks John if there are any questions. Just one: "Do you leave the light on after bedtime? 'Cause I get a little scared of the dark sometimes . . . if it's a strange place." In that moment, John, with his bulging muscles and intimidating stature, is reduced to a childlike innocence, one that carries him through the rest of the film. When Paul confirms they leave the corridor lights on, John extends his hand. While the other guards get ready,

Paul extends his hand as well and the pair shake before the cell doors are shut and locked and John's time on death row begins. "I couldn't help it, boss," he tells Paul through the wrought iron bars. "I tried to take it back, but it was too late."

Intrigued by the admission, Paul begins to read John's case file; soon the film flashes between him and the crime as it plays out in the scene. It is dawn on the Detterick farm; the rooster crows in the background as a man walks from the house to the adjacent barn to begin his work. Shortly thereafter, while the camera holds still on the wide shot of the house and barn, a pair of blood-curdling screams overtakes the soundtrack. Mr. Detterick (played by William Sadler) runs back to the house to find his wife (Paula Malcomson), the one who was screaming, panicking that their daughters are gone. The couple's son finds a trail of blood on the back porch. This leads out through the field and into the neighboring woods.

After ordering his wife to call the police, Mr. Detterick loads his shotgun and heads out with his son in search of his daughters. He is soon joined by a mob of other angry white men armed with guns and pitchforks, the sound of hounds howling in the background as they search the land for any sign of the missing girls. On the shore of a lake, they find one of the missing girls' dolls laying against the rocks, its face and dress dirtied. They then hear the wails of a grown man in the distance and look up to see John Coffey ahead. His back is propped up against a log and he screams and cries, cradling the two young girls—their heads bloodied and their bodies lifeless—in his arms. After the men restrain the girls' father, who has taken to beating John, another man approaches. "I couldn't help it," John proclaims through the tears. "I tried to take it back, but it was too late." The man responds by putting the barrel of his shotgun up to John's throat: "Boy, you under arrest for murder."

Later in the film, Paul visits Burt Hammersmith (portrayed by Gary Sinise), who was John Coffey's original lawyer, seeking to find out about the inmate's history prior to the Detterick murders. Burt appears to be convinced of John's guilt (though he defended him because "[e]veryone is entitled to a defense"), though Paul does not believe that he is a violent man. "We had us a dog," Burt advises Paul, referencing John. "Just a sweet mongrel, you know the kind." Continuing, he notes that:

> In many ways, a good mongrel dog is like a Negro. You get to know it. Often you get to love it. It is of no particular use. But you keep it around because you think it loves you. If you're lucky, Mr. Edgecomb, you never have to find out any different.

These scenes suggest to the audience that John Coffey is treated in this manner for two distinct but inextricably intertwined reasons. First, one is given the impression that John Coffey is intellectually challenged and, there-

fore, he deserves to be "dealt with" di
that Coffey is "handled" in this way
perception that Coffey is just a bad, di
treatment than a "good mongrel dog"
mind using myriad stereotypical trope
race. Yet the use of those stereotypes i
encourage the viewer to challenge both
ic nature of them. As we will see, ho
quence of race does not drive the narr
very explicit way it does in *A Lesson B*
chapter). Instead, racial discriminatioı
Green Mile, allowing other issues to pla

standards of
the court fou
intellectually
and there was
ic communiti
authored the
that:

> Because (
> their impu
> characteri
> ments can
> mentally ı

"TELL THE TRUTH, BOSS, I DON'ı
NEVER I

In sum, the /
prohibition oı

At the saı
"mental retaı
there was no
intellectual d
cutoff point,
numeric thres
with borderli
did not use a
of orchestrati
intellectual f
merical cuto
spite the fac
eleven-year-

In 2014,
old when it a
convicted of
Atkins decis
below would
whelming ev
ered as such
subsequently
reasoned tha
unacceptable
and thus [th
Anthony M
errors of me

While Frank Darabont does not directly
intellectually challenged, there are a ı
addition to those referenced above) that
Darabont brings forth the important iss
disabled (formerly called mentally retaı
case of *Penry v. Lynaugh* in 1989 that t
ered whether it was constitutional to ex
Penry, who had the reasoning capabilit
based on the evolving standards of dec
retarded individuals violated the Eight
cruel and unusual punishment. [12] Writing
O'Connor reasoned that since only two :
a ban on the execution of mentally retard
al consensus needed to satisfy the princij
was not present. Accordingly, the court r
factor that may well lessen a defendant's
we cannot conclude *today* that the Eight
tion of any mentally retarded person of F
offense simply by virtue of his or her me
1989 the court refused to create a catego
were mentally retarded to prevent them fı

In *Atkins v. Virginia* (2002), the cour
of whether it was unconstitutional to exe
vidual. At the time of his crime, Daryl
which is significantly lower than the stai
intellectual disability. [15] As it did in *Penı*

defendants in a similar situation, be allowed to present evidence of their disability.[22]

In 2017, the Supreme Court again further clarified the standards related to intellectual disability. In *Moore v. Texas*, the court struck down a ruling by the Texas Criminal Court of Appeals (CCA) that relied on outdated guidelines from 1992 rather than the current standards used within the medical community.[23] Like *Hall*, the *Moore* opinion, authored by Justice Ruth Bader Ginsburg, found that the CCA erred in failing to consider the margin of error that would have further supported Bobby Moore's claim of intellectual disability. In lieu of outdated standards, the court reasoned that the current edition of the Diagnostic and Statistical Manual of Mental Disorders (DSM), published by the American Psychiatric Association, was a better guideline for determining intellectual disability.

While the standards of decency related to individuals with intellectual impairment certainly have evolved, the decisions in both *Hall* and *Moore* highlight another important consideration related to IQ and the death penalty—the Flynn effect. The Flynn effect refers to the idea that average intelligence scores (IQs) have increased steadily over time; therefore, when using such scores as a measure of intellectual functioning, such gains must be taken into account.[24] In other words, as the scores of standardized instruments, like the IQ test, rise, previous scores can become obsolete and individuals must be reexamined with more current instruments (which, when developed, standardize scores to an average of 100 to allow for comparisons between different tests) to determine their actual scores at a specific point in time that are relevant for making an assessment about intellectual functioning. With all of these considerations at play, it is reasonable to expect that the continued examination into the relationship between intellectual disabilities and the death penalty will find its way before the court in the future.

Although we are never explicitly told that John Coffey is intellectually challenged, that is certainly the impression that we, as viewers, are given. Consequently, the film acts as an important vehicle for considering the troubling relationship between mental culpability and capital punishment. Equally as bound up in stereotypical perceptions—in both the film and the real world—is the relationship between race and the death penalty. As we saw in the previous chapter, in a film such as *A Lesson Before Dying,* that relationship can be conveyed and understood, very openly and powerfully, in terms of human dignity and unequal treatment. The pervasive problem of racism is certainly present in *The Green Mile*, especially with regards to the attitudes of certain characters like Percy. Interestingly, however, ultimately the other prominent theme of the film applies and is conveyed in an egalitarian manner: any botched execution is brutal, whether the condemned is black or white, small and frail, or large and strong. It is the brutality of the botched execution that becomes its defining characteristic.

"ALL CREATURES GREAT AND SMALL..."[25]

As noted earlier, John Coffey's size is a defining characteristic. His stature becomes even more pronounced when Paul, Brutus, and Dean (and we, the audience, by extension) meet a tiny mouse inhabiting E block. Living inside the restraint cell that is being used for storage, the mouse appears from under the door, scampering along the green mile towards the men. "It ain't normal for a mouse to come up on people this way," Dean notes. When Brutus places a piece of a cookie on the floor, the mouse comes closer, accepting the treat while showing no fear of the humans. He eats it, then scurries back under the door into the restraint room. "Three grown men...outsmarted by a mouse," Brutus proclaims after the trio cleared out the room only to come up empty. "Yeah, that's the last we'll see of him," Paul remarks, referring back to the noise they made that likely scared the mouse off.

The next day, however, the mouse is back. This time, he approaches Harry, Percy, and Bill Dodge (Brent Briscoe), who are on shift. Harry and Bill again share food with the mouse, treating him with kindness and encouraging him to approach. Percy, on the other hand, uses the opportunity to try and kill him. "I'm going to stomp your life out," he yells at the mouse while chasing him down the corridor. When Paul and Brutus arrive to the commotion, they find Percy clearing the restraint room in search of the mouse, who again has retreated under the door. Paul uses the situation as a teaching moment: "Percy, do you want to think about what you're doing just now?" It was about more than trying to find the mouse—Harry points out that his actions scared the guards and the inmates alike, but Percy does not care. "So what? They aren't in cradle school, in case you didn't notice," he says. "Although you treat them that way half the time." Paul and Brutus point out that the inmates are under enough strain living on death row; they do not seek to contribute any more to that stress.

Later in the film, as Paul sits at his desk completing paperwork, he hears a laugh from down the mile. He grabs Brutus and Dean and makes his way to Del's cell. There, they see Del sitting—with the little mouse up on his shoulder. Del has gained the mouse's trust, and the mouse has gained his in return. As we learn, the mouse even has a name (which he has whispered into Del's ear). Audience—meet "Mr. Jingles." Soon, it becomes clear that Mr. Jingles is staying—Del has adopted him as a pet; the two play fetch with an old wooden spool in the cell, and Del shares some of his food with the mouse.

Percy, however, is having none of it. To him, the mouse is a disease, just like the inmates, and he views the prison as "a bucket of piss to drown rats in." He bides his time, waiting for the perfect moment to take care of Mr. Jingles. One day, when Paul and Brutus are sitting with Del, talking to him about taking the mouse to Florida, Percy gets his chance. Del throws the spool and it bounces outside of the cell. Thinking it is a turn at fetch, Mr. Jingles runs after it—and Percy stomps him to death. Del is heartbroken. Yet, this is not the end of the story for either Mr. Jingles or Percy.

There is something special about John Coffey, but it has nothing to do with his race, his intellectual capabilities, or his size. John Coffey has supernatural powers. When he puts these powers to work in the movie, he arguably administers justice for Mr. Jingles on two separate occasions. First, John brings the mouse back to life, as if Percy had never harmed him. In that critical moment, it did not matter how big John was or how small Mr. Jingles was. Life is life, and all creatures—great and small—deserved to live it.

If that is true, of course, then why did John Coffey murder two small girls? Unpacking the answer to that question requires us to fast forward to a scene that occurs much later in the movie, a scene which also marks the second occasion when John secures justice for Mr. Jingles. It is several days before John Coffey's scheduled execution day and he has just been returned to the prison after Paul, Brutus, and Harry snuck him out so he could use his powers to heal the warden's wife (Patricia Clarkson), who was suffering from a brain tumor (Dean was left behind to keep an eye on the other inmates and distract Percy, who has been locked up in a straightjacket in the restraint room). Now back on E block, Percy has been released and is putting his gear back on when John grabs him by the throat. He uses his powers to transfer the tumor he had pulled from the warden's wife to Percy, leaving him in a seemingly vegetative state. As Percy mindlessly walks toward the block's exit, he stops in front of the cell of William "Wild Bill" Wharton (portrayed by Sam Rockwell), a mass murderer who has been tormenting the guards and inmates alike since his arrival, and shoots him dead before collapsing.

Bewildered, Paul approaches John's cell, seeking answers as to what had just happened. "I punished them bad men," John says. "I punished them both." "Why?" Paul asks. John explains that when Wild Bill had grabbed his arm earlier, he had been able to see what the murderer had done. Confused, Paul continues to seek answers, when John outstretches his arm: "Take my hand, boss. You see for yourself." As the two lock hands, the visions start to flow. The audience (and Paul) is transported back to a replaying of the earlier seen involving the murders of the Detterick girls for which John was on death row. This time, however, the missing pieces are filled in—they had not been killed by John but instead by Wild Bill, who had been working for the family as a hand on the farm. Though the murders and the aftermath are not shown, it is clear that when John had been found, he was trying to heal the girls. John Coffey had been wrongfully convicted of murder.

We have seen justice obtained (again) for Mr. Jingles in the form of a death sentence given to Percy. At the same time, however, we are witnesses to injustice, in the form of the death sentence given to John. Life is life, and all creatures—great and small—might indeed deserve to live it, but sometimes life is simply not fair.[26] As *The Green Mile* demonstrates very vividly, neither is death, especially when administered by the state, using the electric chair.

"WE HAD THE ELECTRIC CHAIR. WE CALLED IT 'OLD SPARKY.'"

In the film, inmate Arlen Bitterbuck (portrayed by Graham Greene), convicted of murder, is the first to die. Under the watchful eye of the warden, Paul's team straps Arlen into the chair, places on a hood to cover his face, and tops his head with a moistened sponge before securing the electrode cap to his head. After the jolt is delivered, he is checked. His heart is still beating, although he appears unconscious. "Again," Brutus orders; a second jolt is delivered as a crowd looks on. Though the scene cuts in the midst of the second jolt being delivered, the audience learns it was a success as the next shot is of Arlen, deceased on a table, with Percy taunting him.

"What's up his ass?" Percy asks as Brutus wheels Arlen's body away. "You," Paul replies, matter-of-factly. Percy has been a thorn in everyone's side—he abuses the inmates (Del in particular) and cannot seem to gel with Brutus, Dean, or Harry. Yet, as the nephew of Louisiana's first lady, he seemingly gets away with whatever he wants because he knows that no one will fire him out of fear of dealing with his uncle, the governor (in this way, Percy mirrors Rick Hayes, the protagonist in *Last Dance*, as discussed in chapter 8, who also secured his position through relatives in high places). As the conversation between Paul and Percy unfolds, it is revealed that Percy has another offer at a different correctional facility that Paul suggests he take. Percy agrees to go—after Paul lets him run point on the next execution; if he will not let him do this, Percy indicates that he may well just stay on E block for the rest of his career. Against his better judgment, Paul eventually agrees, and the team works to train him in preparation for the next execution, which turns out to be Del's.

After Del is led into the execution room and strapped into the chair, Percy delivers the standard statement of charges and procedures, adding in a homophobic slur after Del expresses remorse for his crimes. As the hood is drawn over Del's face, Percy reaches down to wet the sponge—only he does not complete the task. After scanning to see if anyone is watching, he stands and places the dry sponge on Del's head before affixing the electrode cap. As the seconds tick down to the execution hour, Paul realizes the sponge is dry, but it is too late. Percy gives the order and electricity begins flowing through Del's body.

The electric chair was designed to deliver a jolt of between 500 and 2000 volts to the prisoner in order to stop their heart, effectively ending their lives. Before that would happen, they would be shaved where the electricity would make contact—through the top of the head via a metal skullcap-shaped electrode and on the prisoner's leg through a second terminal.[27] The prisoner then would be escorted to the chair, where they would be strapped in across their chest and groin region, with additional restraints for their arms and legs. For the device on their head, it would be attached over a saline-moistened sponge to help conduct the electricity and reduce the body's resistance to the current. (If the sponge was too wet, however, it ran the risk of short-circuiting the current.) A conductive gel also was used with the electrode placed on the leg. Just prior to the execution, the prisoner also would be blindfolded or have their face covered.

Upon the signal of the warden, the executioner would initiate the system, pulling down on a lever to connect the chair and the power supply.[28] The jolt would be delivered for approximately thirty seconds before the connection would be disconnected by turning off the machine. The prisoner would have to be left for several seconds to be cool enough so as to check them for signs of life; if there was still a heartbeat, an additional jolt would be administered, and the process repeated until they were pronounced dead. The body subsequently then had to be left for an additional amount of time for the internal organs to cool so that an autopsy could be performed.

The fact that these procedures were not properly followed for the execution of Del is nothing short of cruel and unusual punishment. Without the proper facilitation, the charge remains mainly in Del's head, eventually causing a large spark. As he screams in agony, his body begins to smoke. Paul rushes to end the execution but Brutus stops him—it is too late for Del, he advises, referencing the damage that is done to Del's body with each passing second. The lights flicker and the audience becomes increasingly uncomfortable, due in large part to the smell of Del's burning flesh that now permeates the room. Before long, blue streaks of fire run up and down his body; then, in a burst, his head is engulfed in flames. The audience rushes to flee the room as Percy tries to turn away, but Paul forces him to watch what he has done. Once it is clear that Del is finally dead, Brutus forces Percy to put the flames out on the body with the fire extinguisher, ending one of the most heinously botched executions possible.

THE ELECTRIC CHAIR IN PRACTICE

While the botching of Del's execution was the deliberate work of Percy, it does highlight many of the issues stemming from the use of the electric chair, an invention that made its debut on August 6, 1890, at Auburn Prison, located just west of Syracuse, New York. The device was invented in 1881 by Buffalo, New York dentist Alfred Southwick,[29] and later adopted by the state as a more humane alternative to hanging, which had become viewed as an archaic method of execution.[30] Yet before the electric chair was even used, it became the centerpiece of what was known as "the battle of the currents," a public fight between Thomas Edison and George Westinghouse. The two men had long been in competition in the electrical world: Edison was a proponent of direct current (DC), while Westinghouse's platform utilized alternating current (AC).[31] As a result, they often fought over customers and sought to prove that their equipment was superior. When the question arose as to whether DC or AC should be used for the purpose of execution, Edison (who also supported the development and use of the electric chair) campaigned for the latter and specifically recommended that a Westinghouse generator be used, the latest step in a series of effort to discredit his competition by showing that AC electricity was very good for one thing—killing people.[32]

In response, Westinghouse launched a counterattack to keep his products out of the death chamber, spending $100,000 in legal fees to ultimately take the case all the way to the U.S. Supreme Court.[33] His lawyers argued that using electricity to kill a person violated the Cruel and Unusual Punishment Clause of the Eighth Amendment in a petition for a writ of *habeas corpus* filed on behalf of William Kemmler, an illiterate axe murderer who had been condemned to die—and who was scheduled to be the first to be executed in New York's new electric chair. In a *per curiam* opinion handed down on May 23, 1890, the court held that the use of electricity to terminate an individual's life did not amount to cruel and unusual punishment and subsequently denied the petition.[34] As predicted by Westinghouse's lawyers, Kemmler's execution, which took place less than three months later, was botched.[35]

Despite the problems with Kemmler's execution, the use of this method continued.[36] Between 1900 and 2010, the electric chair was used to execute 4,374 prisoners.[37] Only 160 of these came after the use of the death penalty was reinstated following the *Gregg v. Georgia* decision in 1976.[38] Of the total number of executions carried out by electrocution, eighty-four of them (or approximately 1.92 percent of executions) were botched in some form.[39] While, at the time of this writing, lethal injection remains the primary method of execution, the use of the electric chair still is permitted by nine states.[40] Florida, Kentucky, and Virginia all allow an inmate to choose this method of execution, a request typically made in writing to the prison's warden. Alabama, Arkansas, Mississippi, Oklahoma, South Carolina, and Tennessee all authorize the use of the electric chair as an alternative method in the event that lethal injection is ever declared unconstitutional.

"IT'LL BE ALRIGHT FELLAS. THIS HERE'S THE HARD PART. I'LL BE ALRIGHT IN A LITTLE WHILE."

With the newfound awareness of John Coffey's innocence, Paul finds himself at a moral and professional crossroads. How can he bring himself to execute an innocent man? After further contemplation and a talk with his wife, Paul decides to talk to John to ask what he wants. John puts in his request for his final meal (meatloaf and mashed "taters") but declines the presence of a priest. Paul offers to take John out of the prison and help him escape; he questions how he can put to death one of God's true miracles (harkening back to John's supernatural powers) and have to answer for such actions later at the gates of heaven. John, ever the gentle giant, lays his hand upon Paul's: "You tell God, the father, it was a kindness you done. . . . I want it to be over and done with. I do. I'm tired, boss. . . . Mostly, I'm tired of people being ugly to each other." John does, however, have one request: he has never seen a movie before. Paul and his men are happy to oblige—they set up a theater in the block and John gets to watch the movie *Top Hat*. As Fred Astaire and Ginger Rogers dance across the screen, he looks on in awe and wonder, almost in a childlike state, calling them "angels, just like up in heaven."

Soon, judgment day has arrived: it is time for John to be executed. As he is led to the chair and strapped in, he asks Paul not to put the hood over his face before the sponge and skullcap are affixed. "Please boss, don't put me in the dark. I's afraid of the dark." Paul complies and, just before the execution commences, he reaches out and shakes John's hand, which already has been strapped to the chair. The lever is flipped, initiating the shock, but Paul, Brutus, Dean, and Harry cannot watch—their eyes are filled with tears and their hearts are heavy knowing that someone they came to know for who he was, not what he was wrongfully accused of, is gone.

That was Paul's last execution and we soon rejoin his elder self on the veranda in the present day. "I just couldn't do it anymore after that," he tells Elaine, noting that both he and Brutus had transferred into juvenile corrections to help children in need of guidance. It is in the last moments that the audience learns that John left Paul with something besides a life lesson—when he had shared the memories of the Detterick girls' murders, he had passed along a bit of his powers to Paul. You see, Paul looks like an average senior citizen, but the reality is that he is 108 years old in present time. He is not alone, however; Mr. Jingles also received a bit of the magic and is still alive as well.

The Green Mile, in all of its cinematic glory, teaches us many lessons about life and death. It shows that no matter one's size, all creatures—big and small—deserve to be treated with kindness and respect. Simultaneously, numerous issues with capital punishment, its application, and the electric chair as a method are brought to the forefront, masterfully interwoven with a story about a man who is nothing short of miraculous. Most importantly, however, *The Green Mile* teaches us that not everything is black and white.

NOTES

1. Roger Ebert, "The Green Mile Movie Review & Film Summary (1999)," RogerEbert.com, December 10, 1999, accessed December 5, 2018, https://www.rogerebert.com/reviews/the-green-mile-1999.

2. Ibid.

3. Todd McCarthy, "The Green Mile," *Variety*, November 28, 1999, accessed December 5, 2018, https://variety.com/1999/film/reviews/the-green-mile-1117759804/.

4. "The Green Mile (1999)—Financial Information," The Numbers, accessed December 5, 2018, https://www.the-numbers.com/movie/Green-Mile-The#tab=summary.

5. "The Green Mile (1999)—Awards," IMDB, accessed December 5, 2018, https://www.imdb.com/title/tt0120689/awards?ref_=tt_awd.

6. Daniel Argent and Erik Bauer, "Frank Darabont on The Green Mile," *Creative Screenwriting*, April 29, 2016, accessed December 24, 2018, https://creativescreenwriting.com/frank-darabont-on-the-green-mile/.

7. Ibid. Here, Darabont is referring to his choice to open the film with a short and ultimately incomplete scene of an angry mob on the hunt for something, which is unknown at the time, before moving into the actual movie.

8. Ibid.

9. Philip French, "The Green Mile," *Guardian*, February 27, 2000, https://www.theguardian.com/film/News_Story/Critic_Review/Observer_review/0,,141530,00.html. Similarly, Darabont also likens John Coffey to "a bit of a Christ figure." See Argent and Bauer, "Frank Darabont on The Green Mile."

10. Dennis Childs, *Slaves of the State: Black Incarceration From the Chain Gang to the Penitentiary* (Minneapolis: University of Minnesota Press, 2015).

11. See Trop v. Dulles, 356 U.S. 86, 101 (1958). The evolving standards of decency principle refers to the idea that public opinion—and, more importantly, its consensus—should be used to interpret the Cruel and Unusual Punishment clause of the Eighth Amendment. In doing so, the clause is not fixed in time but rather changes as public opinion changes, as what was acceptable when the Eighth Amendment was ratified in 1791 is not viewed as such today. See Matthew C. Matusiak, Michael S. Vaughn, and Rolando V. del Carmen, "The Progression of 'Evolving Standards of Decency' in U.S. Supreme Court Decisions," *Criminal Justice Review* 39, no. 3 (2014).

12. Penry v. Lynaugh, 492 U.S. 302 (1989).

13. Ibid., at 340 (italics added).

14. Atkins v. Virginia, 536 U.S. 304 (2002).

15. John Matthew Fabian, William W. Thompson, and Jeffrey B. Lazarus, "Life, Death, and IQ: It's Much More Than Just a Score: Understanding and Utilizing Forensic Psychological and Neuropsychological Evaluations in *Atkins* Intellectual Disability/Mental Retardation Cases," *Cleveland State Law Review* 59, no. 3 (2011).

16. 536 U.S. at 306–7.

17. Death Penalty Information Center, "State Statutes Prohibiting the Death Penalty for People with Mental Retardation," accessed December 9, 2018, https://deathpenaltyinfo.org/state-statutes-prohibiting-death-penalty-people-mental-retardation.

18. Alex Hannaford, "The Cruel and Unusual Punishment of Teresa Lewis," *Guardian*, August 22, 2010, https://www.theguardian.com/commentisfree/cifamerica/2010/aug/21/teresa-lewis-death-row.

19. Alan Blinder, "Georgia Executes Warren Lee Hill for Murder," *New York Times*, January 27, 2015, https://www.nytimes.com/2015/01/28/us/georgia-executes-warren-lee-hill-for-murder.html.

20. Over a forty-year period Hall had nine different IQ evaluations with scores ranging (after a sentencing court dropped the two lowest scores for evidentiary purposes) between 71 and 80. In 2010, Hall's IQ test was scored at 71. Hall v. Florida, 572 U.S. 701, 707 (2014).

21. Ibid., at 704.

22. Ibid., at 724. For additional discussion on the criticisms of IQ tests as measurements of intelligence, see, for example, Hans J. Eysenck, *The Structure and Measurement of Intelligence* (New York: Transaction Publishers, 2017).

23. Moore v. Texas, 137 S.Ct. 1039 (2017).

24. James R. Flynn, "Tethering the Elephant: Capital Cases, IQ, and the Flynn Effect," *Psychology, Public Policy, and the Law* 12, no. 2 (2006).

25. The phrase "All creatures great and small" is a line from the Anglican hymn "All Things Bright and Beautiful" by Mrs. Cecil Alexander in her *Hymns for Little Children*. The hymn references the equality of all of God's creatures in the eyes of the Lord. See Suzanne Byrd, "History of Hymns: 'All Things Bright and Beautiful,'" *Discipleship Ministries*, accessed December 10, 2018, https://www.umcdiscipleship.org/resources/history-of-hymns-all-things-bright-and-beautiful.

26. Racial disparity exists at all stages of the criminal justice process, including capital punishment; and, John Coffey's case highlights a phenomenon similar to that of Jefferson in *A Lesson Before Dying*. Namely, that in the pre-Civil Rights Movement South, a black man was more likely to be convicted if the victim was white. As mentioned above, however, race plays a far subtler, background role in *The Green Mile*. When raising the issue of wrongful convictions, a few words about race are essential. Blacks are seven times more likely than whites to be convicted of murder and 50 percent more likely to be innocent than offenders of other races convicted of the same crime. Samuel L. Gross, Maurice Possley, and Klara Stephens, *Race and Wrongful Convictions in the United States* (Irvine, CA: National Registry of Exonerations, 2017). This disparity further widens if the victim in the case was white—while just 15 percent of black murders involve a white victim, 31 percent of exonerations of blacks do. In reality, however, homicide is largely an intraracial crime, with whites more likely (84 percent) to kill whites and blacks more likely (93 percent) to kill blacks. Ibid. See also James Alan Fox, Jack Levin, and Kenna Quinet, *The Will to Kill: Making Sense of Senseless Murder*, 5th ed. (Thousand Oaks, CA: Sage, 2019).

27. Death Penalty Information Center, "Descriptions of Execution Methods," accessed December 8, 2018, https://deathpenaltyinfo.org/descriptions-execution-methods?scid=8&did=479.

28. Ibid.

29. Craig Brandon, *The Electric Chair: An Unnatural American History* (Jefferson, NC: McFarland, 1999).

30. In re Kemmler, 136 U.S. 436, 444 (1890).

31. Brandon, *The Electric Chair*, 67-88. See also Michael S. Rosenwald, "'Great God, He is Alive!' The First Man Executed By Electric Chair Died Slower Than Thomas Edison Expected," *Washington Post*, April 28, 2017, https://www.washingtonpost.com/news/retropolis/wp/2017/04/26/thomas-edison-the-electric-chair-and-a-botched-execution-a-death-penalty-primer/.

32. Brandon, *The Electric Chair*, 7.

33. Ibid., 10. Interestingly, the $100,000 spent by Westinghouse in the late 1800s would be close to $3 million in 2018, according to calculations using the Bureau of Labor Statistics CPI Inflation Calculator.

34. 136 U.S. at 449.

35. Brandon, *The Electric Chair*, 178–179. See also "Far Worse Than Hanging," *New York Times*, August 7, 1890.

36. For a detailed overview of the use of the electric chair since *Kemmler*, see Deborah W. Denno, "Is Electrocution an Unconstitutional Method of Execution? The Engineering of Death Over the Century," *William & Mary Law Review* 35, no. 2 (1994).

37. Austin Sarat, *Gruesome Spectacles: Botched Executions and America's Death Penalty* (Stanford, CA: Stanford Law Books, 2014).

38. Death Penalty Information Center, "Searchable Execution Database," accessed December 8, 2018, https://deathpenaltyinfo.org/views-executions.

39. Sarat, *Gruesome Spectacles*, 177.

40. Death Penalty Information Center, "Methods of Execution," accessed December 8, 2018, https://deathpenaltyinfo.org/methods-execution.

Chapter Seven

The Chamber: "Take a Deep Breath"

John Grisham is quick to condemn *The Chamber*, the 1996 cinematic version of his bestselling novel (published two years earlier). It "was not well done, and nobody went to see it." Indeed, he is "kind of happy nobody went to see it because it was so bad"; it was "a train wreck from the very beginning."[1] William Goldman, who wrote the screenplay, concurs; it was "a total wipe-out disaster . . . it was a terrible experience."[2] Grisham is a superstar author, and in 1996, he was on a tremendous roll. *The Chamber* was the fifth of his novels to be adapted for the silver screen within the space of three years,[3] and Goldman is an Oscar-winning screenwriter.[4] However, this was by no means their finest hour and the reviewers were only too happy to echo their concerns about the film. Roger Ebert decried the way in which "racism and hate language" were seemingly trotted out for nothing more than "the purpose of entertainment," Janet Maslin similarly criticized "the film's overheated tone," and Kenneth Turan summed up his colleagues' denunciations when he said that "'The Chamber' is like a balloon that all the air has leaked out of."[5] *The Chamber* is not considered to be one of Grisham's best books, but as Turan observed, even though the film was "the first of the five adaptations to seem embarrassed by the pulpiness of its material . . . It's ironic that this problem should arise on 'The Chamber,' because reviews of the book credit it as an attempt by Grisham to deal with important themes like capital punishment."[6]

The film (directed by James Foley[7]) failed largely because of its exaggerated focus on stereotypical characters that audiences had already had enough of. Moreover, this focus had the effect of making the gas chamber—which, as the book's title suggests, played an extremely important role in John Grisham's original story—almost a nonentity until the very end of the movie.

Through the use of passages such as the following, Grisham gives the gas chamber a central role in his novel:

> 'Sam, you there?' It was Gullitt.
> 'Yeah. I'm here.'
> 'Just saw you on channel four.'
> 'Yeah. I saw it.'
> 'You pissed?'
> 'I'm okay.'
> 'Take a deep breath, Sam. It's okay.'

> Among men sentenced to die in the gas chamber, the expression 'Take a deep breath' was used often and considered nothing more than an effort at humor. They said it to each other all the time, usually when one was angry. But when used by the guards it was far from funny. It was a constitutional violation. It had been mentioned in more than one lawsuit as an example of the cruel treatment dispensed on death row. [8]

For sixteen years, Sam Cayhall sat in his cell in the maximum security unit (death row) at the Mississippi State Penitentiary (generally referred to simply as "Parchman"). For sixteen years he lived within "the bowels of death itself," in close proximity to the "machinery of death" that would eventually call his name. [9] To be sure, the specter of execution does hang over the entire film. Oftentimes, however, that cloud of fear simply seems to exist because this is a film about capital punishment.

Nevertheless, *The Chamber* does have something very profound to tell us about cinematic portrayals of capital punishment. In the pages that follow, analysis of *The Chamber* spotlights two important and intertwined ways in which it depicts the process of litigating death: (a) the legal argument that a specific method of execution is "cruel and unusual" (this is related to twenty-first century, real-world developments); and (b) the way in which a lawyer's ability to defend his or her client in a capital case can be affected by political forces beyond the lawyer's control.

"HOW MUCH DO YOU KNOW ABOUT THE DEATH PENALTY?"

It is difficult to watch as Sam Cayhall (portrayed by Gene Hackman) is unceremoniously strapped into the chair, his excess weight unflatteringly bulging because of the tautness of the leather straps that restrain his extremities (including his head, which is secured to an imposing metal rod that runs from the floor to the ceiling of the gas chamber that he now sits within). Similarly, it is difficult to watch as the toxic fumes rise up, waiting for their all-too-conscious prey to reach its fatal respiratory breaking point by taking a deep breath. It is equally difficult to watch the consequences of that breath, which include a graphic display of the deadly effects of the hydrogen cyanide gas. [10] Yet, *The Chamber* makes it difficult for the viewer to take pity on the condemned. Cayhall is a proud fourth-generation Ku Klux Klan member; he is a racist, anti-Semitic, foul-mouthed bigot who dutifully heeded the call, in April 1967, to bomb the Indianola, Mississippi, office of Stanley Kramer, maiming that lawyer and killing his twin five-year-old sons. Sam Cayhall did not think twice about destroying the family of this "radical Jew lawyer with a beard and a bleeding heart, educated by Jews up North and now marching with and representing Negroes in the Mississippi Delta." [11] Towards the end of the film, Cayhall exhibits a modicum of remorse as his execution nears, but he still remains a despicable character.

The movie makes it far easier for audiences to sympathize with the other main character, Adam Hall (portrayed by Chris O'Donnell), a young and naïve, clean-cut, crusading attorney working at Kravitz and Bane, the Chicago-based, white-shoe law firm that has been representing Cayhall pro bono. Adam seems unfazed when E. Garner Goodman (Robert Prosky), one of the firm's partners, asks: "How much do you know about the death penalty?" As if his answer should immediately qualify him to successfully take on the case at this, the eleventh hour, Adam replies: "I've read everything there is." Adam is given the case but it comes with Goodman's sobering warning— "Then you know nothing."

The first death row meeting between Sam and Adam does not go well. When Sam finds out about Adam's lack of experience (that this is the lawyer's first capital case), his response is appropriately more colorful than Goodman's: "Oh great, the Jew bastards send a greenhorn to save me. I kill some of their people, and now they wanna kill me." Yet, it is the same thing that makes Adam's character appealing to the audience that helps to explain the lawyer's desire to take Sam's case and to endure his client's vitriolic verbal abuse. Adam Hall is Sam Cayhall's grandson.

"Three years at Michigan Law, and that sorry idea's the best you got?"

Sam is unimpressed with *all* of the legal strategies that Adam pursues on his behalf. He is unimpressed because he has become very familiar with all of them, spending countless hours studying law in the prison library and providing legal advice (including writing motions and petitions) for the other men on death row. "Three years at Michigan Law, and that sorry idea's the best you got?" is Sam's reaction when Adam explains he will be contending that execution by lethal gas is an unconstitutional "cruel and unusual punishment." This legal strategy fails in the film (as it actually did in the nation's courts at the time), but it is of no small consequence that, less than eighteen months after the release of *The Chamber*, Mississippi changed its death penalty laws, making lethal injection the sole method of execution and re-moving the gas chamber as a secondary option. [12] Thus, herein lies one of the most valuable aspects of the movie for modern audiences.

Sam's reaction to Adam's decision to follow the "cruel and unusual pun-ishment" strategy follows his first outburst regarding his impending fate. In the previous scene (which excessively dramatizes an otherwise miniscule part of the book's plot), Adam enters his hotel room. After Adam offloads a heavy pile of law books, the camera follows him to a pair of louvered bi-fold closet doors. Instinctively, as it joins Adam in facing the doors, the audience expects something to happen, but there is no sinister, brooding background music to generate a sense of foreboding. Similarly, there is no menacing Klansman waiting to punish Adam; Rollie Wedge (Sam's accomplice in the bombing, about whom we will hear more below) is nowhere to be seen, and everyone's hearts barely skip a beat when the doors are pulled back to the loud and sudden pop of a fake bomb "exploding" (the pop is the noise made by a balloon bursting). Adam is, however, visibly shaken and agitated when he angrily tells Sam about this warning he has received. Sam provides him with an abrupt reality check; he (as his lawyer should also be) is otherwise preoccupied with how "that gas they're gonna force me too sniff, makes your lungs explode and come flying out your mouth."

Sam is fully aware that, in 1984, Mississippi made lethal injection, rather than the gas chamber, its principal (or, perhaps, preferred) method of execu-tion; this fact offers him no comfort though because the change does not apply retroactively. Prisoners like Sam, sentenced to die before 1984, will still be marched to the gas chamber when their time comes. Unlike his grandfather, Adam still sees hope. He believes that the legislative change represented a concession by Mississippi that the gas chamber was a "cruel and unusual" method of execution. Sam's subsequent description of an exe-cution at Parchman, some years earlier (that prompted changes to the gas chamber), certainly seems to support Adam's conclusion. [13]

"CAN EXECUTIONS BE MORE HUMANE?" [14]

In 2002, Professor Deborah Denno, a noted expert on the death penalty, accurately observed that there was "a complete constitutional disregard for *how* inmates are executed." [15] From the 1980s through until the very early 2000s, federal courts, especially the U.S. Supreme Court, had been far more concerned with *who* was being executed. It takes time for lawsuits to work their way up through the judicial food chain though, and "[o]ften, cases failed to reach the Supreme Court because a new form of capital punishment replaced the older, more controversial form while challenges wound their way through the courts." [16] Had the Supreme Court been inclined to wade into the method-of-execution debate, it could have done so at around the same time that *The Chamber* hit movie theaters. The justices usually take a closer look at (and more often decide to hear) cases that raise questions upon which the lower circuit courts of appeal have issued conflicting rulings.[17] In 1996, the Supreme Court was confronted with two such rulings from the Fourth and Ninth Circuit courts (the former ruling that execution by lethal gas was constitutional, the latter holding that it was not). The high court vacated and remanded one of the cases because the issues had been mooted by a recent legislative change. However, it could have taken the other case had it been so inclined, recognizing that the lower courts were genuinely conflicted regarding the subject.[18]

Proving that judicial action is only one way of achieving social change, by the end of the twentieth century (within three years of the release of *The Chamber*), the majority of states that still retained the gas chamber as a method of execution either abolished it entirely in favor of lethal injection or relegated it to backup status.[19] This reduction in the gas chamber's "popularity" might lead one to conclude that *The Chamber* is similarly a relic of its time. However, as hinted at in the introduction to this book, the latest legislative (and particularly controversial) changes to capital punishment options suggest otherwise. Lethal injection replaced death by lethal gas as the preferred method of execution, but it was no less fraught with problems. There are significant problems associated with the three-drug cocktail typically used to execute an individual and there are numerous gruesome reports about recent botched attempts to execute individuals using lethal injection, attempts that run into myriad problems, including difficulties finding suitable veins[20] and complications resulting from the use of an alternative drug, the sedative midazolam.[21] Even though the use of midazolam is extremely controversial, states wishing to continue executing people using lethal injection increasingly find it necessary to seek alternatives. This is because pharmaceutical manufacturers, first overseas and then in the United States, have begun to refuse to produce the requisite drugs because they were being used in executions.[22] Concerned should the Supreme Court decide to rule that lethal injection was unconstitutional, beginning in 2015 several states (including Mississippi) also began adding the untested death-by-nitrogen-hypoxia to their lists of possible execution methods.[23]

INSTITUTIONALIZED (AND POLITICIZED) DIGNITY

In his memoir recounting his work on death row, the Reverend Joseph B. Ingle reflected upon the 1983 execution of Jimmy Lee Gray, one of the Parchman prisoners he ministered to. "Jimmy Lee Gray was dead. He had been killed by Governor William Winter acting in the name of the people of

Mississippi. He was the victim of a public, state-sanctioned murder. That was the issue, not the method of execution."[24] When analyzing the way in which the death penalty is treated by Hollywood in *The Chamber*, however, it is important to consider both the condemned prisoner *and* the method of execution. This is because, even if the latter was sacrificed in favor of characters (beyond just Sam and Adam) designed to invoke the "emotionalism and histrionics" that "have always been so characteristic of the debate" over capital punishment, the fact remains that this is a still very much a story about a particular way of killing people.[25] Nevertheless, as we have seen in recent years, in the real world versions of those debates, "how to kill" has taken center stage. Ingle's point remains an important one, and it allows us to return to the subject of the relationship between the death penalty and dignity.

Baze v. Rees

In 2008, the U.S. Supreme Court decided to hear a case involving the problems associated with lethal injection. In *Baze v. Rees*, the court upheld the constitutionality of execution by lethal injection using a specific set of three drugs: sodium thiopental (a sedative that rapidly induces unconsciousness akin to a person being in a coma), pancuronium bromide (a paralytic drug that stops respiration), and potassium chloride (which generates cardiac arrest).[26] The constitutional controversy stemmed from the inclusion of the second drug, pancuronium bromide. In separate cases, both in the early 1990s, Ralph Baze and Thomas C. Dowling were convicted of murder and placed on death row in Kentucky. They mounted a constitutional challenge to the specific combination of drugs used in the lethal injection process. It was pancuronium bromide that opened the door for the concept of dignity to enter the *Baze* dialogue about whether this punishment violated the Eighth Amendment. However, the concept of dignity upon which Chief Justice John Roberts focused in his plurality opinion was very different from the human concept of dignity that is the principal way in which the Supreme Court justices had previously discussed the relationship between dignity and the death penalty. "Woefully inadequate" was the label that Justice John Paul Stevens (in his concurring opinion in *Baze*) attached to the dignity argument made by the state of Kentucky and embraced by Roberts.[27]

Pancuronium bromide is part of a class of drugs derived from curare. Rather than anesthetizing the patient (animal or human) and causing it to temporarily lose its ability to feel, these drugs act as paralyzing agents. Consequently, in the administration of a lethal injection that uses the above-mentioned three drugs, the state runs the risk that the following might occur: If the sodium thiopental fails (for whatever reason) to place the condemned into a complete state of unconsciousness and the pancuronium bromide is then injected, the individual might well look like they are in a tranquil and peaceful coma-like state to witnesses and prison officials. However, they are actually in a conscious state of paralysis, unable to indicate that they are enduring the agonizing and tortuous sensation that their veins are burning as the lethal potassium chloride is injected into them.[28] This description might lead one to assume that the dignity discussion in *Baze* centered on *human* dignity. However, when it raised the concept, Kentucky instead focused on *institutional* dignity, contending that pancuronium bromide makes an aesthetic contribution to the execution process.

Chief Justice Roberts accepted Kentucky's institutional use of dignity. The "Commonwealth," he wrote, "has an interest in preserving the dignity of the procedure, especially where convulsions or seizures could be misperceived as signs of consciousness or distress."[29] Paralyzing the condemned apparently avoided "shocking the conscience" of those witnessing the execution. Roberts focused on Kentucky's interest in maintaining "the dignity of the procedure," which he said could not be met by a protocol that consisted of only drugs one and three.[30] The chief justice's reference to this type of dignity is illuminating, because it found very little explicit support in either the lower court opinions in the case, the briefs filed with the Supreme Court, or the points set forth during oral argument by Roy Englert arguing on behalf of Kentucky.[31] Indeed, during oral argument it was Roberts who initiated the dignity discussion by asking Donald Verrilli, the attorney for petitioners Baze and Dowling, whether he agreed that "an appropriate problem to be addressed by the execution protocol" is the "likelihood of involuntary muscle contractions." In light of the fact that the state perceived this to be a problem of aesthetics, Verrilli was unwilling to answer in the affirmative, to which Roberts responded that the state was concerned with "enhanc[ing]" the dignity, not only of the procedure as a whole, but also to the condemned."[32] In his opinion, Roberts ignored this; misstating the state's position, he focused on institutional dignity at the expense of individual dignity.

The dignity reasoning in *Baze* is instinctively problematic—it suggests that an institutional interest could trump something this valuable. This is inherently controversial because it provides a justification for institutional interests "to trump constitutional rights to such basic goods as health and the avoidance of excruciating pain."[33] Additionally, the plurality's emphasis on institutional dignity was problematic because it overlooked the extent to which institutional dignity and human dignity are inextricably intertwined. There is more to the concept of dignity than human self-determination. In terms of criminal justice, dignity can be thought of as a bicephalous concept because it is two-headed—one human, one institutional. This is appropriate because of the existence of two predominant theories of criminal punishment that mirror the philosophical bases of the two categories of dignity—deontology and consequentialism.

At the heart of deontology lies a belief that there are certain things that are morally right, and certain things that are morally wrong. Deontology evaluates an action's rightness without regard to its consequences. A deontological justification for a punishment is not determined by the societal benefit that will accrue, but rather by the degree to which an individual has done something to deserve the punitive treatment. As such, deontology emphasizes the importance of evaluating the culpability of the individual—because this will affect our evaluation of the extent to which the individual deserves a punishment.

By contrast, consequentialism views a legitimate punishment as one that is a means to achieving the ultimate goal of enhancing societal pleasure (or happiness) by reducing societal pain using the manner that has the fewest unpleasant effects. Consequentialist theories generally have no need to consider the identity of the individual who does something, because the rightness (or wrongness) of their action is not judged by their culpability. Similarly, consequentialism does not categorize actions as right or wrong. Rather, actions are judged by the value of their consequences. Therefore, this is a theory that frequently categorizes punishments by evaluating their effectiveness at deterring future crimes. A common criticism of this utilitarian approach is that it does not consider punishment to be an actual end, but rather a means to societal improvement. This, it is argued, provides little consideration of, or respect for the individual as a separate and distinct moral entity. If, "[t]hrough the imposition of just punishment, civilized society expresses its sense of revulsion toward those who, by violating its laws, have not only harmed individuals but also weakened the bonds that hold communities together," then it becomes easy to see why consequentialist defenses of capital punishment tend to emphasize institutional dignity.[34]

"ALL PROGRESS IS A NEGOTIATION"

The tension between human and institutionalized dignity is addressed in *The Chamber*. Indeed, it speaks directly to the second of the film's two main themes—namely, the politics of litigating capital cases. Unlike Grisham's novel, which makes copious references to dignity—primarily human dignity—the movie's script only uses the word once. Toward the end of the film, Rollie Wedge (played by Raymond J. Barry) pays Sam a visit, signing in as Sam's brother, Donnie Cayhall. Sam is not at all pleased to see his former accomplice, who has remained a free man all this time and who has come to caution him to keep his mouth shut. "You've been a good and loyal soldier, Sam," warns Wedge. "Go with the dignity that is yours." After Sam's execution, we briefly see the police arresting Wedge in a convenience store, but we know that Sam did not talk. We know that he maintained whatever semblance of dignity Wedge was referring to. Ironically, we know this because as the film progresses, it becomes increasingly clear that Sam's execution is little more than a pawn in a high stakes political scheme, a scheme designed to maintain the dignity of the state of Mississippi and the career of the Governor David McAllister (played by David Marshall Grant). This game (which is entirely absent from Grisham's book) is one that neither Adam nor his client ever had a shot at winning.

Whose Sovereignty?

Established by the Mississippi State legislature in 1956, the Sovereignty Commission had a broad anti-civil rights, pro-segregation, pro-states' rights agenda. Its stated "objective was to 'do and perform any and all acts deemed necessary and proper to protect the sovereignty of the state of Mississippi, and her sister states . . . ' from perceived 'encroachment thereon by the Federal Government or any branch, department or agency thereof.'"[35] This included providing financial aid and other material (and political) support to the White Citizens' Council, which formed two years earlier in the immediate aftermath of the U.S. Supreme Court's ruling in *Brown v. Board of Education* with the explicit goal of preserving white supremacy.[36] The 1988 movie *Mississippi Burning* (featuring Gene Hackman in a *very* different role from that which he played in *The Chamber*) is an Academy Award-winning cinematic portrayal of the violence and destruction wrought in pursuance of this goal.[37]

In *The Chamber*, by contrast, the subject matter feels like it is introduced into the story for nothing more than dramatic purposes (Grisham does not mention the Sovereignty Commission or the Citizens' Council in his novel). Nevertheless, it does become an important part of the plot and, ultimately, it speaks to the political barriers faced by Adam's lawyering. It is Nora Stark (Lela Rochon), Governor McAllister's African American aide, who educates Adam about the commission and the Citizens' Council, the latter which she describes as "[a] local group of respectable white people, professional types; pillars of their local community, who told the Klan what to do." Sam, she explains, is like all the other "poor, uneducated bigots, who couldn't find their butts with a map; the Citizens' Council used them to do their dirty work." The commission was disbanded in the mid-1970s; still, in *The Chamber*, two decades later, Governor McAllister is quick to remind Nora that any and "all progress is a negotiation."[38]

Readers of *The Chamber* are introduced to McAllister very early on, because he was the district attorney who secured (where two predecessors had failed) the capital conviction of Cayhall:

In 1979, two significant events occurred in the open but inactive Kramer bombing case. The first was the election of David McAllister as the district attorney in Greenville [the name of the town was changed to Indianola in the movie.[39]] At twenty-seven, he became the youngest D.A. in the state's history. As a teenager he had stood in the crowd and watched the FBI pick through the rubble of Marvin Kramer's office. Shortly after his election, he vowed to bring the terrorists to justice.[40]

But, McAllister is pursuing more than "justice." At the trial of Cayhall:

McAllister . . . performed brilliantly but had the obnoxious habit of spending all his spare time with the press. He was handsome and articulate and compassionate, and it became very clear that this trial had a purpose. Mr. McAllister had political ambitions on a grand scale.[41]

In the movie, the execution of Cayhall had exactly the same "purpose" attached to it. McAllister was now governor; McAllister presumably wanted to remain governor (or to pursue higher political office—we are not told anything about McAllister's aspirations, but it is clear he is ambitious).

At various points in the film, Adam gathers what he believes to be a body of compelling evidence proving that his client had indeed been a mere foot soldier, acting upon higher orders from both Wedge and prominent Mississippi civic and political leaders. This leads him on a last-ditch quest to find and confront Wedge at a Klan rally being held near Parchman. While this quest allows Adam to confirm Wedge's involvement in the bombing, he barely escapes with his life. Emphasizing Adam's naïveté, this confrontation does more harm than good for his client. It is this event that leads Wedge to visit Cayhall in prison (as mentioned above). More significantly though, it alerts McAllister to the fact that this interfering lawyer is getting far too close to the truth, the truth about who precisely it was that signed the Kramers's death warrant. In so doing, it dooms any chances that Adam will succeed with his mitigating circumstances legal strategy.

"Blood and death were served with Sunday breakfast"

It is Sam's alcoholic sister, Lee (portrayed by Faye Dunaway, whose performance the critics universally panned), who shows Adam a book about the history of KKK lynchings, a photograph in which has been highlighted by the Cayhall family because it depicts a young Sam posing with the crowd that has proudly gathered around a deceased African American man hanging from a tree. Angry emotions pouring out of him, Adam presents the book to Sam: "It ends with me. We've got four days left; this is our last appeal, it's called mitigating circumstances. Talk to me." During the jailhouse library conversation that follows, the camera intermittently cuts back and forth between Sam, Adam, and the African American guard, Sgt. Clyde Packer (Bo Jackson). The camera finally settles upon Sam, a sense of exhaustion and defeat etched across his face. It remains there as, in the background, one begins to hear Adam speaking: "Here's some synonyms for mitigating." This is the beginning of a monologue that Adam is delivering in front of a judge. As the film cuts to the courtroom, the camera slowly zooms in from a wide-angle view that places Adam front and center. He is dwarfed by the austerity of the proceedings as he pleads his client's case, arguing that the life that Sam Cayhall was born into predetermined his fate:

> He never knew he had any other recourse but hatred, and bigotry, and vio-
> lence . . . blood and death were served with Sunday breakfast . . . As the court
> is no doubt aware, my client is also my grandfather. And I would like now to
> tell you some warm and wonderful stories about our family, except I don't
> know any. In fact, I don't find my grandfather even remotely wonderful. But I
> know this. The very things that make him so monstrous are the very reasons
> that mitigate against this state murdering him. He was raised by his family, and
> *this* state, to become the man he became. By the time he was old enough to
> choose, he didn't have a choice.

There would be no last-minute reprieve for Sam Cayhall because, as the governor well knows, the order for the Cayhall Sunday breakfast of "blood of death" was, in 1967, placed by people whose identities it is in his political best interests to protect.

At an earlier point in the film, Sam *educates* Adam about the process and implications of unsealing the files of the Sovereignty Commission. As a prisoner on death row, Sam has the power to make this request. He declines to sign the requisite paperwork, knowing full well that the files probably contain enough mitigating information to force a gubernatorial commutation of his death sentence. This is a scene that underscores the gulf that exists between lawyer and client, between grandson and grandfather, and between the California-raised, Michigan Law-educated Adam and the born-into-a-Klan-family, Clanton, Mississippi, born-and-raised Sam. Both men know that the commission files might help Sam. Yet, it is only the latter who can see the real, more compelling truth, a truth that will trample all over even the most compelling legal argument: Governor McAllister *wants* Sam to request the opening of the files because "he's just fishing for what every politician wants; dirt on the enemies." Ultimately, in *The Chamber* those are the most important mitigating circumstances.

CONCLUSION: OVER-"TINKERING" WITH DEATH

There are numerous reasons why *The Chamber* was a critical and box office flop. One prominent explanation for its failure is the competition it faced. By the time the movie was released in the United States on October 11, audiences had been treated to a glut of Hollywood hits in 1996, including *Fargo*, *Twister*, *Mission Impossible*, *The Rock*, *Independence Day*, and *A Time to Kill* (the fourth Grisham adaptation to hit the silver screen since 1993). Additionally, in the weeks and months leading up to the release of *The Chamber*, moviegoers were being primed for two more cinematic successes (starring perhaps the two biggest male cinema heartthrobs of the mid-1990s). Coming soon, to a theater near them (released in November and December respectively), *Ransom* (Mel Gibson) and *Jerry Maguire* (Tom Cruise). Each grossed over $130,000,000.

Of arguably greater explanatory significance, however, is the fact that *The Chamber* was not the first 1996 movie to address capital punishment. Indeed, it was not even the second, or the third such film. That year, *The Chamber* played chronological fourth fiddle to *Dead Man Walking* (February 2), *Last Dance* (May 3), and *A Time to Kill* (July 24). As we saw in chapter 3, *Dead Man Walking* continues to be regarded as one of the best ever films about the death penalty. Cinematically, it was a very hard act to follow.[42] However, even its box office receipts paled in comparison with those of the other aforementioned 1996 films. This is representative of the fact that a film about capital punishment is never going to attract the huge audiences that, for example, flock to see a film about tornado chasers, or one about American-led world "forces" heroically launching a counterattack—on July 4, no less—against destruction-seeking extraterrestrials. If the average moviegoer thinks twice about going to the cinema to sit through a somber, moralizing film about a pending execution, it is the very rare individual who spends their hard-earned money to endure that cinematic experience multiple times in one year.

In February 1994, six weeks before the public announcement of his decision to retire from the U.S. Supreme Court, Justice Harry Blackmun penned a passion-filled opinion dissenting from the court's decision not to hear the capital case *Callins v. Collins*. In 1976, Blackmun was part of the majority in *Gregg v. Georgia*, which voted to lift the constitutional death penalty moratorium.[43] Over time, however, his views changed, and by 1994 he had finally reached an abolitionist conclusion about capital punishment. Blackmun would, for the rest of his time on the court, take the position that the death penalty was *per se* unconstitutional; he "fe[lt] morally and intellectually obligated simply to concede that the death penalty experiment has failed. It is virtually self-evident to me now that no combination of procedural rules or substantive regulations can ever save the death penalty from its inherent constitutional deficiencies." He would "no longer . . . tinker with the machinery of death."[44] One explanation for the failure of *The Chamber* is that by October 1996 Hollywood had "[*over*]-tinker[ed] with the machinery of death."[45]

For all its problems, though, *The Chamber* remains a useful and important (but not, perhaps, particularly powerful) cinematic treatment of two aspects of the capital punishment system—the trials and tribulations of death penalty lawyers, and the controversies associated with different methods of execution. "Take a deep breath" and ponder that.

NOTES

1. "A Conversation With Bestselling Author John Grisham," Diane Rehm Show, November 17, 2016, accessed May 13, 2018, https://dianerehm.org/shows/2016-11-17/a-conversation-with-bestselling-author-john-grisham.

2. William Goldman, *Which Lie Did I Tell?: More Adventures in the Screen Trade* (New York: Vintage, 2001), 125.

3. It was preceded, to cinemas, by *The Firm* (1993), *The Pelican Brief* (1993), *The Client* (1994), and *A Time to Kill* (1996).

4. In 1977, Goldman won the Best Adapted Screenplay Oscar for *All the President's Men*; and three of his screenplays made it on to the Writers Guild of America West "101 Greatest Screenplays" list (*Butch Cassidy and the Sundance Kid* (original screenplay, listed at number 11); *All the President's Men* (number 53); and *The Princess Bride* (adapted from Goldman's novel, listed at number 84). "101 Greatest Screenplays," Writers Guild of America West," accessed April 18, 2019, https://www.wga.org/writers-room/101-best-lists/101-greatest-screenplays/list.

5. Roger Ebert, "'Chamber' of Hate: Legal Thriller's Reliance on Racism Is Unsettling," *Chicago Sun-Times*, October 11, 1996; Janet Maslin, "A Racist and Killer or Just Misunderstood?," *New York Times*, October 11, 1996; Kenneth Turan, "A Familiar Walk to 'The Chamber,'" *Los Angeles Times*, October 11, 1996.

6. Turan, "A Familiar Walk." On Grisham's motives regarding writing *The Chamber*, see Nicholas Wroe, "Interview - A Life in Writing: John Grisham," *Guardian*, November 25, 2011.

7. Before *The Chamber*, Foley primarily directed Madonna's 1980s music videos. "James Foley—Filmography," IMDB.com, accessed May 23, 2018, https://www.imdb.com/name/nm0001226/?ref_=tt_ov_dr.

8. John Grisham, *The Chamber* (New York: Doubleday, 1994), 169.

9. Joseph B. Ingle, *Last Rights: 13 Fatal Encounters With the State's Justice* (Nashville: Abingdon Press, 1990), 121; Callins v. Collins, 510 U.S. 1141, 1145 (1994) (Blackmun, J., dissenting from the denial of certiorari).

10. Although the movie's depiction of the execution is very graphic, respectfully, Yvonne Kozlovsky-Golan goes too far when she says it "verges on the pornographic." Yvonne Kozlovsky-Golan, *The Death Penalty in American Cinema: Criminality and Retribution in Hollywood Film* (London: I.B. Tauris, 2014), 151.

11. Grisham, *The Chamber*, 2. In the movie, Kramer was clean-shaven.

12. "Mississippi and the Death Penalty," Mississippi Department of Corrections, accessed May 22, 2018, http://www.mdoc.ms.gov/Death-Row/Pages/Mississippi-Death-Penalty.aspx.

13. The description of this execution is a loosely veiled reference to the problem-riddled 1983 execution of Jimmy Lee Gray. See Scott Christianson, *The Last Gasp: The Rise and Fall of the American Gas Chamber* (Berkeley: University of California Press, 2010), 208-12; Donald A. Cabana, *Death at Midnight: The Confession of an Executioner* (Boston: Northeastern University Press, 1996), 7–8; Ingle, *Last Rights*, chapter 6. The UPI journalist Dan Lohwasser, who was one of the witnesses to the execution, wrote the most famous description of the

gruesome details of Gray's death. Dan Lohwasser, "Mississippi Child-Slayer Put to Death With Gas," *Tennessean*, September 2, 1983. His account was controversial because of its graphic nature. However, as Donald Cabana, the former warden of Parchman, observes, Lohwasser "could hardly have been accused of having an ax to grind. . . . Lohwasser [just] happened to be one of the journalists selected to witness the actual killing. As a former helicopter pilot in Viet Nam he was no stranger to violent death . . . " Cabana, *Death at Midnight*, 7–8.

14. Jack Shuler, "Can Executions Be More Humane?: A Law Professor Suggests an Untested Procedure as an Alternative to Lethal Injection," *Atlantic*, March 20, 2015.

15. Deborah W. Denno, "When Legislatures Delegate Death: The Troubling Paradox Behind State Uses of Electrocution and Lethal Injection and What It Says About Us," *Ohio State Law Journal* 63 (2002): 70 (italics added).

16. Linda E. Carter, Ellen S. Kreitzberg, and Scott Howe, *Understanding Capital Punishment Law*, 3rd ed. (New Providence, NJ: LexisNexis, 2012), 45.

17. A classic work addressing the reasons why the Supreme Court tends to grant certiorari in a case is H.W. Perry, Jr., *Deciding to Decide: Agenda Setting in the United States Supreme Court* (Cambridge, MA: Harvard University Press, 1991). Also see Ryan J. Owens and James Sieja, "Agenda-Setting on the U.S. Supreme Court," in *The Oxford Handbook of U.S. Judicial Behavior*, eds. Lee Epstein and Stefanie A. Lindquist (New York: Oxford University Press, 2017).

18. Fierro v. Gomez, 77 F.3d 301 (9th Cir. 1996), vacated and remanded by 519 U.S. 918 (1996); Hunt v. Nuth, 57 F.3d 1327 (4th Cir. 1995), *cert. denied* 521 U.S. 1131 (1997). See Carter, Kreitzberg, and Howe, *Understanding Capital Punishment Law*, 47.

19. Since 1976 (marked by the decision in *Gregg*), only eleven people have been put to death using hydrogen cyanide gas. The last such execution was carried out on March 3, 1999, in Arizona. This "lethal gas" form of capital punishment only remains an option (and not the primary option) in Arizona, California, Missouri, and Wyoming. "Methods of Execution," Death Penalty Information Center, accessed May 22, 2018, https://deathpenaltyinfo.org/methods-execution?scid=8&did=245#mo.

20. For example, see Roger Cohen, "Death Penalty Madness in Alabama," *New York Times*, February 27, 2018; Andrew Welsh-Huggins, "Ohio Calls Off Execution After Failing to Find Inmate's Vein," *Chicago Tribune*, November 15, 2017; Rhonda Cook, "Georgia Executes Brian Keith Terrell After Struggling to Find Vein," *Atlanta Journal and Constitution*, December 9, 2015.

21. For example, see *Associated Press*, "Alabama Death Row Inmate Ronald Bert Smith Heaved, Coughed for 13 Minutes During Execution," *Los Angeles Times*, December 9, 2016; Erik Eckholm, "Arizona Takes Nearly 2 Hours to Execute Inmate," *New York Times*, July 23, 2014; Jeffrey E. Stern, "The Cruel and Unusual Execution of Clayton Lockett," *Atlantic*, June 2015, accessed April 18, 2019, https://www.theatlantic.com/magazine/archive/2015/06/execution-clayton-lockett/392069/; Erica Goode, "After a Prolonged Execution in Ohio, Questions Over 'Cruel and Unusual,'" *New York Times*, January 17, 2014.

22. See, for example, Ed Pilkington, "British Drug Company Acts to Stop Its Products Being Used in US Executions," *Guardian*, May 15, 2013; Erik Eckholm, "Pfizer Blocks the Use of Its Drugs in Executions," *New York Times*, May 13, 2016.

23. See Shuler, "Can Executions Be More Humane?"; Nick Allen, "Michael Portillo Inspires Oklahoma to Consider Execution by Nitrogen," *Telegraph*, March 25, 2015; Austin Sarat, "The Trouble with Oklahoma's New Execution Technique," *Politico*, April 20, 2015, https://www.politico.com/magazine/story/2015/04/oklahoma-death-penalty-gas-chamber-117156.

24. Ingle, *Last Rights*, 135.

25. Cabana, *Death at Midnight*, 193.

26. 553 U.S. 35 (2008).

27. Ibid., at 73 (Stevens, J., concurring in the judgment).

28. Ty Alper, " Anesthetizing the Public Conscience: Lethal Injection and Animal Euthanasia," *Fordham Urban Law Journal* 35, no. 4 (2008): 822–24, 40–44.

29. 553 U.S. at 57.

30. Ibid., at 57–58.

31. Helen J. Knowles, "A Dialogue on Death Penalty Dignity," *Criminology & Criminal Justice* 11, no. 2 (2011): 125.

32. Baze v. Rees, 2008 WL 63222 (U.S.) (U.S.Oral.Arg., 2007), 10.

33. Michael C. Dorf, "How the Supreme Court's Lethal Injection Ruling Elevates Appearances over Reality," FindLaw, April 21, 2008, https://supreme.findlaw.com/legal-commentary/how-the-supreme-courts-lethal-injection-ruling-elevates-appearances-over-reality.html.

34. Paul G. Cassell, "In Defense of the Death Penalty," in *Debating the Death Penalty: Should America Have Capital Punishment? The Experts on Both Sides Make Their Case*, eds. Hugo Adam Bedau and Paul G. Cassell (New York: Oxford University Press, 2004), 198. Donald A. Cabana, the former warden at Parchman, provides a particularly chilling example of an inmate who was not at all deterred by the threat of the death penalty. This individual killed his cellmate (who just happened to be in the wrong place at the wrong time) *in order* that he would be convicted of murder and transferred from the general prison population to death row. He did so in order that he might be reunited with his former homosexual lover. Cabana, *Death at Midnight*, 123–24.

35. "Sovereignty Commission Online," Mississippi Department of Archives and History, accessed May 25, 2018, http://www.mdah.ms.gov/arrec/digital_archives/sovcom/scagencycasehistory.php.

36. 347 U.S. 483 (1954). Although there is nothing in the film noting this, the White Citizens' Council was formed in Indianola, where, in the movie, the Kramer bombing took place. Neil R. McMillen, *The Citizens' Council: Organized Resistance to the Second Reconstruction, 1954–1964* (Champaign: University of Illinois Press, 1994), 16–20.

37. It is important to note, however, that many of the reviews of the film were strongly negative, criticizing its glorification of the role of the FBI (including a fictional scene featuring the use of torture to solve the case), and its concomitant failure to discuss the role of civil rights activists. See, for example, Jack E. White, "Just Another Mississippi Whitewash," *Time*, January 9, 1989.

38. "Sovereignty Commission Online." The Citizens' Council also faded away during that decade, but modern incarnations still exist. For an excellent study of the Citizens' Council, see McMillen, *The Citizens' Council*.

39. The two towns, both real, are situated twenty-three miles apart.

40. Grisham, *The Chamber*, 20.

41. Ibid., 28.

42. Like *The Chamber, Last Dance* was a failure, grossing less than $6 million and garnering only one award nomination (a Worst New Star Razzie for the film's leading actress, Sharon Stone).

43. 423 U.S. 153 (1976).

44. 510 U.S. at 1145 (Blackmun, J., dissenting from the denial of certiorari).

45. Since the publication of Blackmun's *Callins* dissent, numerous authors in their discussions of capital punishment have employed the concept of "tinkering with death." See, for example, Alex Kozinski, "Tinkering with Death," *New Yorker*, February 10, 1997; Margareth Etienne, "Introduction: Tinkering With Death in Illinois," *University of Illinois Law Review* 2003, no. 4 (2003); "Tinkering with Death," *Boston Globe*, October 12, 2007; "The Supreme Court Keeps Tinkering With Death," editorial, *New York Times*, March 29, 2017, https://www.nytimes.com/2017/03/29/opinion/the-supreme-court-keeps-tinkering-with-death.html.

Chapter Eight

Last Dance: A Tango Between Life and Death

Opening on May 3, 1996, *Last Dance* (directed by Bruce Beresford) was seemingly doomed from the get-go. The movie debuted less than five months after *Dead Man Walking* (see chapter 3), which had opened to glowing reviews and went on to win numerous accolades (Susan Sarandon won both an Oscar and a Screen Actors Guild award for her performance and also was nominated for a Golden Globe; Sean Penn also was nominated for best leading performance by a male at all three awards shows). Sharon Stone, coming off the success of Martin Scorsese's *Casino*,[1] took the role of convicted killer Cindy Liggett in *Last Dance* to prove her seriousness as an actress. Yet, as *San Francisco Chronicle* movie critic Edward Guthmann pointed out in his review of the film, "Stone is no Sean Penn."[2]

The constant comparisons between *Last Dance* and *Dead Man Walking* made it all but impossible for the former to be assessed on its own merits. While, according to legendary film critic Roger Ebert, *Dead Man Walking* "reinvented the Death Row genre, saw the characters and the situation afresh, asked hard questions, and found truth in its dialogue," *Last Dance* was simply an unoriginal and poorly timed release.[3] *Rolling Stone* critic Peter Travers offered a similar appraisal: "Last Dance is a prison melodrama that embraces all the clichés that Dead Man Walking artfully dodged," going on to call the film "bogus, manipulative, and absurdly old-hat."[4] Anne Billson, movie critic for *The Telegraph* (UK), also called the film "a compendium of clichés;" she went on to raise the important question, "Why two depressing movies about death by lethal injection in a single year?", a further nod to *Last Dance*'s release on the heels of *Dead Man Walking*.[5]

Although these criticisms of *Last Dance* raise valid points, the reviews largely gloss over an important defining characteristic of the film—the fact

131

that the death row inmate is a woman. In framing the story around a female convict, writers Steven Haft and Ron Koslow cast a new light on an often-overlooked member of the death row community. Yet at the same time, *Last Dance* subtly tackles other issues related to the death penalty, including conditions of confinement, the qualifications of capital attorneys, and the moral and ethical quandaries that these individuals may find themselves in when helping inmates whose lives are on the line.

". . . YOU CAN ALL GO AHEAD AND KILL ME WITH A CLEAR CONSCIENCE."

By the time Rick Hayes (portrayed by Rob Morrow) meets Cindy Liggett, she has been serving twelve years on death row, convicted of a double murder that occurred in the course of a burglary when she was just nineteen years old. She is tough, angry, and untrusting of the attorney from the state's clemency division who is there to update her report as her death warrant looms. Moreover, she sees the issue as pointless—the governor (portrayed by Jack Thompson), who is the ultimate decision-maker as to whether clemency is granted, has never issued such a pardon for a death row inmate and Cindy does not expect the outcome of her case to be any different. She has effectively refused to fight to save herself, believing that she has no chance to do so.

Rick is the unlikely (yet, as the critics penned, seemingly cliché) protagonist of the story. Having blown into town in his Porsche just days before meeting with Cindy, he represents the privileged yin to her more disadvantaged yang. Rick's brother, John (portrayed by Peter Gallagher), serves as the governor's chief of staff. When Rick meets Sam Burns (played by Randy Quaid), the head of the clemency division, he is all but given his choice of jobs, despite the fact that he almost had been disbarred after a fraud allegation and his resumé has a noticeable gap from when he took a few years off after his father's death, years that were dominated by partying. As John helps him move into his new apartment, an Armani suit hangs for all to see, pressed and ready to be worn at the first society gala.

When Rick first meets with Cindy, he seems confused as to why she is unwilling to cooperate. "What have you got to lose?" he asks her. The update to the report is routine, yet she believes that nothing will change the outcome of her situation. She states, "You go ahead and make your damn report. Then you go ahead and give it to the governor, and you let him give it serious consideration, and then you can all go ahead and kill me with a clear conscience." After taking him to task about going by Rick ("What's wrong with Richard?" she asks, to which he replies, "What's wrong with Rick?"), Cindy requests to be taken back to her cell. As Rick leaves the prison after their first meeting, he declares to Sam, "Oh man, she is a pisser." Sam responds with a chuckle, "Sounds like she sure as hell had your number."

As the movie plays on, Rick finds himself more invested in Cindy's case. He believes that he can get new information out of her and presses Sam to continue to work with her. Sam comments that she will not cooperate, particularly in light of the fact that her death warrant had been served the night before, but Rick persists. He visits Cindy again, who continues to turn down the help. "Look, even if I get clemency, it means life in here with no parole, and that's no life. I'm not begging for mercy I'm not gonna get," she declares before again abruptly ending their meeting. Soon, however, Rick has a breakthrough, finding a way to connect with Cindy by talking to her about her younger brother, her mother, and her love of drawing. He seemingly wins her over when a picture of the Taj Mahal that she had requested (she wants to draw it and though it is complex, she has "23.5 hours a day to get it right") appears in the mail.

Throughout the film, it becomes clear that this will not be an easy case for Rick—the odds clearly are stacked against him. Not only is the governor openly against clemency, he has a personal connection to one of the victim's fathers, who pushed for Cindy getting the maximum penalty (the family of the other victim, as we later learn, does not want her to be executed but refuses to offer a statement to the court). Further, both the governor and the district attorney who originally prosecuted the case believed it to be an open-and-shut case against Cindy and refuse to hear any new evidence to the contrary. With the clock counting down, audiences are left to wonder if Rick will be able to save Cindy before it is too late.

WOMEN ON DEATH ROW

Like many areas of the American criminal justice system, women are largely underrepresented on death row and in the number of people who have been executed. According to the Death Penalty Information Center, just sixteen women have been executed since the capital punishment moratorium was lifted following *Gregg v. Georgia* in 1976.[6] These individuals represent just 1.1 percent of all completed executions post-*Gregg*; this is despite the fact that women accounted for nearly 51 percent of the population according to the most recent U.S. Census report.[7] White females have been executed at a rate of three to one as compared to black females, and all but two put to death by lethal injection.[8]

Statistics on homicide (effectively those cases that would be eligible for capital punishment) indicate that women commit just a fraction of the offenses. In the 2017 Uniform Crime Report compiled by the Federal Bureau of Investigation, for example, of the 12,108 murders in which the offender's sex was identified, just under 12 percent—1,443 cases—were perpetrated by women.[9] At the end of the same year, however, women comprised just under two percent of the more than 2,700 inmates on death row.[10] Of course, it is unlikely that all 1,443 cases were disposed of within the calendar year. Regardless, even when taking this into account and adjusting for the fact that a greater proportion of capital-eligible crimes are committed by men, women are still significantly underrepresented on death row.[11]

Interestingly, the murders committed by the fictional Cindy Liggett both confirm and contradict patterns related to homicide offending, both by women and more generally. In his analysis, Victor Streib found that among death row inmates, convictions for felony-murder are most common.[12] The double homicides committed by Cindy occurred during the commission of a home invasion burglary. Additionally, despite common misperceptions that homicide is an interracial crime, meaning that members of one race murder members of another (with priority given to white victims who are killed by black offenders),[13] the opposite is the true and also is the case in *Last Dance*. Both of Cindy's victims were white, as was she.

Where the film departs, however, is in the relationship between the offender and victim. Through Cindy's flashbacks to the night of the crime, it becomes clear to the audience that she knew at least one of her victims, Debbie Hunt—they had gone to school together. Yet for female homicide offenders sentenced to death, the majority of their victims are intimate partners (for example, husbands and boyfriends) or children.[14] Additionally, while most homicides (both generally and while occurring during the commission of a felony) are committed with a gun,[15] Cindy uses a blunt object that happens to be available in the room. Further, while most homicides by females are planned in advance,[16] Cindy's act is more spontaneous, prompted by her victims awakening from their sleep as she burglarized the house, similar to Karla Faye Tucker, who killed two people in 1983 during a robbery (she subsequently was executed in 1998, just two years after *Last Dance* premiered).

EQUAL PROTECTION AND DISPARITY AMONG THE SEXES

In his concurrence in *Furman v. Georgia* in 1972, Justice Thurgood Marshall opined:

> There is also overwhelming evidence that the death penalty is employed against men and not women. Only 32 women have been executed since 1930, while 3,827 men have met a similar fate. It is difficult to understand why women have received such favored treatment since the purposes allegedly served by capital punishment seemingly are equally applicable to both sexes.[17]

While the *Furman* decision is often reviewed in the context of racial disparity in the application of the death penalty, the concurrence from Justice
Marshall shows that such inequity also extends to differences between the
sexes. In fact, since the *Gregg* decision four years later, 1,469 men have been
executed in the same time frame that the sixteen women mentioned earlier
were put to death.[18]

Some scholars, like Andrea Shapiro, have gone so far as to suggest that
the inequity among the sexes in sentencing capital-eligible crimes amounts to
a constitutional violation.[19] They point to the Equal Protection Clause of the
Fourteenth Amendment, ratified in 1868, which indicates that all U.S. citizens shall be afforded the same rights and protections by the states.[20] Since,
however, women are sentenced to capital punishment and executed at a rate
that is disproportional to men, the use of the death penalty continues to be an
arbitrary and capricious practice even in light of legal challenges that sought
to remedy such issues.[21] The only way to overcome such challenges, Shapiro
argues, is to abolish the death penalty altogether.[22]

There are three underlying theories as to why women are less likely to be
sentenced to capital punishment as compared to their male counterparts.[23]
The first—the chivalry theory—suggests that prosecutors and jurors stereo-
type women as passive and weak.[24] As such, both groups are reluctant to
impose the death penalty on women that they view as needing male protection or those who are viewed as less capable of making rational and appropriate decisions; this leads to them being held to a lower moral standard.[25]
Conversely, the "evil woman" theory suggests that women who do not fit the
"traditional" views of femininity, such as prostitutes, lesbians, and women of
color, are more likely to be sentenced to the death penalty.[26] In this perspective, women like Aileen Wuornos, a lesbian prostitute who killed seven men
in Florida, are viewed as violating society's sense of what is "ladylike behavior" and consequently do not need the protection of chivalrous individuals.[27]
Finally, there is a consideration by jurors of "future dangerousness," even in
instances, such as capital cases, where the offender is not likely to be released.[28] Since women tend to be physically smaller than males and considered weaker than the opposite sex, they are viewed as less dangerous and, by
extension, less deserving of the death penalty.[29] Ironically, though Cindy
Liggett defies the foundations of the "evil woman" theory (unlike the other
inmates on her block, including Reggie, portrayed by Diane Sellers), she still
was sentenced to death. Similarly, though Rick assumes a chivalrous role in
trying to save her life, chivalry alone was not enough to spare her from death
row in the first place.

IT'S NO CAMP CUPCAKE, BUT IT'LL DO[30]

One of the biggest criticisms of *Last Dance*, aside from the subpar script, was the inaccurate portrayal of the conditions of death row. Indeed, the conditions of confinement on death row—which Patrick Hudson calls "institutionalized hell"[31]—have long been a source of concern for inmates.[32] These individuals often are left in small cells (some no larger than fifty square feet), sometimes for twenty-four hours per day. Everything is done in their cell and they are devoid of contact with anyone other than the guard who brings them food or transports them elsewhere in the prison. They have nothing else to do but contemplate their crimes while effectively living in isolation.

The resulting consequences of long-term subjecting to these conditions is what is known as the "death row phenomenon" or "death row syndrome."[33] Individuals exposed to such conditions have been found to experience increased levels of stress, feelings of hopelessness and depression, and to exhibit suicidal tendencies.[34] Further, given the lengthy appeals process and time between conviction and execution (in 2013, this was an average of 15.5 years[35]), these issues often are further exacerbated by the constant exposure to the conditions of death row. As such, whether the prolonged exposure to death row conditions is a violation of the cruel and unusual punishment clause of the Eighth Amendment or, more broadly, human rights under international law has regularly been a topic of conversation among capital punishment scholars.[36]

The prison where Cindy Liggett is housed, however, is seemingly devoid of many of these characteristics. Her cell appears larger and is not dark and dingy, but instead light and clean. Her walls appear almost freshly painted, adorned with pictures she has drawn during her time in the prison (other inmates have opted for different forms of art therapy, including needlework, stitching upbeat phrases like "Think Happy Thoughts"). She also regularly converses back and forth with others in her cellblock, sharing a sisterhood of sorts as they gossip about letters with pen pals and, later when the mood turns more serious, how Cindy is processing her upcoming execution. Despite attempts to act the cliché jailbird parts, the other women of death row appear as more of a sorority than hardened criminals. This is further pronounced when Reggie, one of the more vocal inmates, shaves her head for Cindy's execution as a show of protest; as Cindy is led out of the block to another prison for death watch, the other women clank their cups against the bars in solidarity.

THE RIGHT TO A (QUALIFIED) ATTORNEY

When Rick Hayes arrives in the unknown southern city and begins his crusade to save Cindy Liggett, it is clear that he is at a deficit, legally speaking. While he had successfully completed law school and passed the bar, he clearly is wet behind the ears with little experience of actual practice. In his minimal time as an attorney, he had nearly been disbarred, casting doubts as to whether he should even be practicing (fortunately for him, as noted above, he had family in high places who were able to secure him a job). All of this aside, he had no experience dealing with a capital case. Through hard work and long nights posted on his couch reading case files with a beer in one hand and a slice of pizza in the other, it appears that Rick might find a way to success (or at least he hopes to). Yet the question for audiences always remains—is he actually an *effective* attorney for Cindy?

The 1963 landmark Supreme Court decision *Gideon v. Wainwright* is perhaps one of the most well-known decisions pertaining to the Sixth Amendment's guarantee of legal representation. Clarence Earl Gideon, who had been identified by an eyewitness and subsequently charged with breaking and entering a pool hall in Florida with the intent to commit larceny (money was stolen out of a cigarette machine; a record player was also taken in the theft), appeared alone in court, too poor to hire an attorney, and requested that the Florida Circuit Court provide him with representation. It was declined and he was subsequently convicted. He then petitioned his case to the U.S. Supreme Court on the grounds that his Sixth Amendment rights had been violated. In a unanimous opinion in favor of Gideon, the court held that any defendant who cannot afford to retain counsel on their own has the right to have an attorney appointed to them by the state courts in any criminal proceeding.[37] Writing for the majority, Justice Hugo Black noted that:

> From the very beginning, our state and national constitutions and laws have laid great emphasis on procedural and substantive safeguards designed to assure fair trials before impartial tribunals in which every defendant stands equal before the law. This noble ideal cannot be realized if the poor man charged with a crime has to face his accusers without a lawyer to assist him.[38]

While *Gideon* may be the most well-known case, the right to have appointed counsel had been established thirty-one years earlier for capital defendants in the case of *Powell v. Alabama* (1932). After nine black youths were accused of raping two white women, their cases were expedited through the legal system; the boys subsequently were tried in three separate hearings, convicted, and sentenced to death within a single day. While Alabama law at the time required that defendants in capital cases be provided counsel, they failed to provide a reasonable amount of time for the attorneys to meet with the defendants and prepare an adequate defense. Writing for the majority, Justice George Sutherland indicated that the defendants' due process rights as well as their right to counsel, had been violated when they were not given the opportunity to adequately prepare for their hearings.[39]

While both *Powell* and *Gideon* confirm the right to an attorney for defendants accused of both capital and non-capital crimes, they also require that this representation be effective. Where these decisions fall short, however, is in failing to lay out any standards for said representation. Instead, they assume that the appointed attorney is competent and therefore effective. Yet given that upwards of 90 percent of capital defendants are indigent, meaning that they require court-appointed counsel because they cannot afford a lawyer, determining such effectiveness is of particular importance when lives are on the line.[40]

THE ESTABLISHMENT OF THE
INEFFECTIVE COUNSEL THRESHOLD

It was not until the 1984 case of *Strickland v. Washington* that the test to determine whether counsel is in fact effective was created.[41] In a majority opinion authored by Justice Sandra Day O'Connor, the court reasoned that in order to reach a successful claim of ineffective counsel, a defendant must pass a two-pronged test. First, the defendant must be able to prove that their counsel was deficient, meaning that the conduct fell below an "objective standard of reasonableness."[42] Second, the defendant must be able to show that the errors made were prejudicial to their case. In other words, were it not for the actions or errors of their defense attorney, the outcome of the case would have been different for the defendant. Taken together, the two-pronged test established in *Strickland* provide a bare minimum set of standards that defense attorneys must meet. Satisfying the first prong of the test in particular is extremely difficult to do because of the objectivity—and consequent subjectivity—of "reasonableness"; consequently, it is nearly impossible to successfully satisfy both parts of the *Strickland* test. As a result, most post-conviction claims of ineffective counsel fail.[43]

Ineffective counsel can occur as a result of institutional barriers.[44] Preparing an adequate capital defense can require several thousand hours of work; yet given that indigent defendants often are represented by public defenders who have very heavy caseloads, that time may not always be available, thereby impeding their ability to mount a successful defense. Though recommendations have been made by the American Bar Association to remedy this issue,[45] the reality is that most capital defendants still are represented by attorneys whose number of clients far exceed the national caseloads standards.[46] Another barrier to effective representation is the lack of available funding to support the attorneys beyond just their compensation. This can impact their ability to bring on support staff to help with legal research, access investigators and experts, and provide basic resources like technology or other office equipment.[47]

These barriers have led to a number of issues for capital defendants. According to one study by the Innocence Project, among the most common ineffective assistance of counsel claims raised are allegations of defense attorneys failing to present defense witnesses to establish an alibi, failing to seek DNA or other testing that would exclude the defendant, failing to object to evidence or statements introduced by the prosecution or move for a suppression, and a failure to interview witnesses during trial preparation or conduct cross-examination during the hearing.[48] Defense attorneys have also been accused of failing to present their own expert testimony, failing to investigate claims, and failing to object to a witness identification.[49] Even more egregious and overt errors include capital defense attorneys who have been found to fall asleep during the trial,[50] arrive at court and attempt to defend the accused while intoxicated,[51] and even to represent clients while they themselves were convicted offenders.[52] Yet despite all of these issues that have resulted in convictions and subsequent impositions of capital punishment sentences, a significant majority of claims of ineffective assistance of counsel are rejected by the courts for failing to meet the threshold established in *Strickland*.[53] Further, while the aforementioned issues largely occur in the context of the guilt phase, similar concerns also have been raised during the sentencing phase of the bifurcated trial proceeding.[54]

Sadly, Cindy Liggett is no exception to this issue. A crucial fact—that she was high on crack continuously for two days before the murders, a fact that could have mitigated the *mens rea*, or guilty intent, of the crime—was never presented by her lawyers at trial. Her co-offender, Doug (played by Don Harvey), took a plea deal for a reduced sentence in exchange for testifying that they had only drunk beer and smoked marijuana. He later confessed to Rick and signed an affidavit that the district attorney in the case had told him to make this statement and then suppress evidence, further highlighting that ineffectiveness does not only occur at the defense table in the courtroom. As her execution draws near, Rick attempts to use this fact—citing ineffective counsel—as grounds for a stay of execution.

"I DO NOT WANNA DIE, OK? BUT IF I DO, IT'S GONNA BE ON MY TERMS."

While Cindy Liggett initially seems resolved to her impending execution being carried out, her statement above highlights the importance of death row inmates being able to die with dignity. Yet, as her relationship with Rick

Hayes underscores, representing death row inmates also can present moral and ethical challenges for attorneys. [55] In particular, attorneys who represent capital defendants and death row inmates are required to act in a way that protects their client's interests, which may conflict with their own value system that typically opposes the idea of the death penalty. [56]

In her examination of capital defense attorneys, Christy Chandler offers two models through which to view the capital attorney-client relationship. [57] The first of these is the "paternalistic model," in which the attorney guides the client toward what they believe to be in that individual's best interest. In doing so, however, the attorney risks overriding the wishes of the client. [58] The second form the relationship may take, called the "autonomous model," prioritizes the client's decision-making authority above what the attorney believes to be right. [59] Such autonomy can effectively tie the hands of the lawyer, who believes that life in prison is a better outcome for their client than the death penalty, and wishes to pursue any means necessary to save their client's life. [60] Of these two models, the American Bar Association appears to lean more toward the client's autonomy, noting that "a lawyer shall abide by a client's decisions concerning the objectives of representation." [61]

As *Last Dance* plays on, it is clear that the relationship between Rick and Cindy follows a paternalistic model. Despite Cindy's numerous requests to leave her report alone and allow the chips to fall as they may, Rick seems determined not to give up until all avenues have been exhausted. In many ways, the story in *Last Dance* is more about his redemption than her saving. He is the black sheep of the family, always finding himself in older brother John's shadow, but he believes that if he saves Cindy, despite everyone telling him that it cannot be done, then he can prove to everyone that he can do something right instead of always messing up.

Even after their first several meetings, once Rick is finally able to break down Cindy's walls and she starts sharing information, it is clear that the continued search for a way to override her death sentence is his pursuit, not hers. When he finally uncovers the truth about what had happened the night of the murders, namely that she had been high on crack during and prior to the burglary, Cindy urges him to leave it be.

> Cindy: "You listen to me, Rick. You have done more for me than anyone ever has."
> Rick: "Look, it is not over, okay? There is a judge on the federal court of appeals—"
> Cindy: "No. I have screwed up a lot of things in my life. This one, I wanna do right."

Despite this conversation, Rick continues to pursue the case, first revisiting Doug in prison and getting his amended statement. He then seeks out the federal judge he mentioned to Cindy (Judge Gorman, portrayed by Ted Manson), who is away on a fishing trip. After taking a seaplane and then a boat out to where the judge is located, Rick brings him a motion for a stay of execution and pleads with him to review Cindy's case and the new evidence. When the judge acknowledges his familiarity with the case, Rick presses him for when they can expect to hear from him. Judge Gorman responds that he will radio his ruling back from the ranger's station once he has read the documents. When Rick returns to the prison and lets Cindy know he found the judge, he seems all but confused as to why she is not happier, instead asking him to stay with her through the execution.

Death Row Volunteering

While the differentiation between the paternalistic and autonomous models often is clear (for example, it is clear that Rick adheres to the former strategy), the line between these gets blurred when the client indicates that they wish to halt their *habeas corpus* appeals and proceed to execution. Known as "death row volunteering" or "elected execution," this allows capital inmates to die "on their own terms." Oftentimes, the decision to suspend their appeals and move forward with the execution is a product of the conditions they face on death row and the subsequent effects of these conditions (the "death row syndrome" discussed earlier). This decision also may be influenced by a desire to die with grace and dignity, to end the suffering their drawn-out appeals can bring to their or the victim's families, or even to leave the world in a blaze of glory.[62]

In the context of capital punishment, death row volunteering accounts for approximately 10 percent of executions carried out. In the post-*Gregg* era, the first execution to be carried out as a function of volunteering was Gary Gilmore in 1977 (who, coincidentally, also was the first person to be executed after the death penalty resumed operation). Since then, 148 individuals (at the time of this writing) have halted their appeals and expedited their death sentences.[63] Of these, just three were females—Christina Riggs (2000), Lynda Block (2002), and—perhaps the most famous woman to be executed—Aileen Wuornos (2002).[64] As with capital punishment more broadly, as discussed earlier, females also are underrepresented among death row volunteers.

When a client wishes to effectively end their life through state-assisted suicide, this can present even greater moral and ethical challenges for their attorney. Unless the inmate is incompetent to waive their appeals, their lawyer has a responsibility to abide by their client's wishes—even if that means ending their own life.[65] Since, however, there is a lack of case law (as well as a lack of formal training[66]) to guide the lawyer's actions regarding how best to handle such situations, many view it as a moral and ethical responsibility to attempt to discourage their clients from halting appeals.[67] In the most extreme sense, it may be viewed in the context of "don't let go of the hand of a drowning person," which can help to explain why some lawyers, like Rick, hold on and push forward even when the outcome is grim.[68]

"EVERYONE GAVE UP ON HER." (WELL, ALMOST EVERYONE)

Before long, the day of reckoning for Cindy Liggett has arrived. Outside the prison where she is awaiting execution, the media have gathered to report every detail, as have the protestors—some wish to see Cindy pay for her crimes with her life, others—including the cliché gaggle of nuns singing *Amazing Grace*—plead for mercy. Inside, she sits on death watch with Rick, who has spent every moment with her since returning from seeing Judge Gorman. The question remains: will all of Rick's efforts pay off? Will Cindy's life be spared?

As the clock ticks down, Cindy receives a visit from her brother Billy (portrayed by Skeet Ulrich), whom Rick has arranged to have come and see her from the jail where he was serving time for a low-level offense. Having been the one to originally turn her in to police for the crimes, Billy apologizes and Cindy comforts him, offering him absolution and assuring him that he did the right thing. As they wait to hear if the judge will issue a stay, the execution chamber is prepped—close-up shots of the belts being readied to strap her in, the chairs where the witnesses will sit carefully staged in perfectly uniform rows, the tray of supplies being laid out, and the syringes filled and carefully placed in the machine that will be used to administer them; Cindy's final meal, including a burger and fries, filet mignon, an egg, and cake ("I decided to stop watching my weight," she quips) arrives in her cell.

Soon, the final moments have arrived. Cindy says her goodbyes to Rick and Billy, who then are escorted out of the cell (Billy is taken to a waiting room where he sits with Sam while Rick, as promised, joins others in the dimly lit execution viewing room to stay with Cindy until the very end). She puts on the dress Rick had bought for her before being led down the hall to the chamber by the warden, several armed guards, and other officials. There, she is strapped to the table, the IVs that will deliver the drugs inserted into her arms, and the curtain opened. The system is initiated with closeups on the buttons that soon will be pressed, bringing an end to Cindy's life.

In that moment, the red light on the phone begins to blink and after receiving news, the warden orders everyone to stand down. It seems as though Judge Gorman has come through and Cindy will be spared. She is unstrapped from the table and makes her way back to the cell, where Rick rejoins her, seemingly relieved that he stopped the execution. That relief, however, is short-lived—the original prosecutor has appealed the case to a special panel of the federal court of appeals, who lifted the stay. After Cindy orders Rick to just let her go, the process is carried out. Cindy Liggett has been executed by lethal injection. As Rick told John earlier in the movie, "Everyone gave up on her." Rick, however, does not give up on Cindy. He stayed by her side until the very end; bowing his head, he recognized that despite his best efforts, he simply could not save her.

Last Dance, in spite of its clichés, shows the gut-wrenching and often heartbreaking process of defending inmates on death row. For attorneys like Rick, it is impossible not to be invested in clients whose lives are on the line, particularly when representing them challenges their morality and ethics. For inmates like Cindy, it is equally difficult not to give up or decide not to fight when the deck seems so heavily stacked against them. The movie not only highlights these issues, but also shows how, in the final moments, both lawyers and their clients perform a last dance, a final goodbye, before the music ends.

NOTES

1. In *Casino*, Stone played the role of Ginger, wife of mob boss Sam Rothstein (portrayed by Robert De Niro). She won a Golden Globe and scored an Oscar nomination for this role.

2. Edward Guthmann, "'Last Dance' Trips Over Wasted Chance/Death Row Drama Misplays Sharon Stone's Role," *San Francisco Chronicle,* May 3, 1996, https://www.sfgate.com/movies/article/Last-Dance-Trips-Over-Wasted-Chance-Death-Row-2983820.php.

3. Roger Ebert, "Last Dance Movie Review & Film Summary (1996)," RogerEbert.com, May 3, 1996, accessed November 11, 2018, https://www.rogerebert.com/reviews/last-dance-1996.

4. Peter Travers, "Last Dance—Rolling Stone," *Rolling Stone*, May 3, 1996, accessed November 11, 2018, https://www.rollingstone.com/movies/movie-reviews/last-dance-123193/.

5. Anne Billson, "Dead Woman Outstaying Her Welcome," *Telegraph*, August 24, 1996, https://www.telegraph.co.uk/culture/4703463/Dead-woman-outstaying-her-welcome.html.

6. "Searchable Execution Database," Death Penalty Information Center, accessed November 11, 2018, https://deathpenaltyinfo.org/views-executions.

7. Lindsey M. Howden and Julie A. Meyer, *Age and Sex Composition: 2010* (Washington, DC: U.S. Census Bureau, U.S. Department of Commerce, 2011), accessed November 11, 2018, https://www.census.gov/prod/cen2010/briefs/c2010br-03.pdf.

8. "Searchable Execution Database." See also Harry Greenlee and Shelia P. Greenlee, "Women and the Death Penalty: Racial Disparities and Differences," *William & Mary Journal of Women and the Law* 14, no. 2 (2008).

9. "FBI Expanded Homicide Data Table 3—Murder Offenses By Age, Sex, Race, and Ethnicity, 2017," Crime in the United States (FBI Uniform Crime Report), accessed November 11, 2018, https://ucr.fbi.gov/crime-in-the-u.s/2017/crime-in-the-u.s.-2017/topic-pages/tables/expanded-homicide-data-table-3.xls.

10. Deborah Fins, *Death Row USA, Winter 2018: A Quarterly Report by the Criminal Justice Project of the NAACP Legal Defense and Educational Fund, Inc.* (Washington, DC: NAACP Legal Defense and Educational Fund, 2018), accessed November 11, 2018, https://www.naacpldf.org/wp-content/uploads/DRUSAWinter2018_.pdf.

11. Victor L. Streib, "Death Penalty for Female Offenders, January 1, 1973 Through December 31, 2012," accessed November 11, 2018, https://deathpenaltyinfo.org/documents/FemDeathDec2012.pdf. See also Elizabeth Rapaport, "Some Questions About Gender and the Death Penalty," *Golden Gate University Law Review* 20, no. 3 (January 1990); Victor L. Streib,

"Gendering the Death Penalty: Countering Sex Bias in a Masculine Sanctuary," *Ohio State Law Journal* 63 (2002).

12. Victor L. Streib, "Rare and Inconsistent: The Death Penalty For Women," *Fordham Urban Law Journal* 33, no. 2 (2006).

13. James Alan Fox, Jack Levin, and Kenna Quinet, *The Will to Kill: Making Sense of Senseless Murder*, 5th ed. (Thousand Oaks, CA: Sage, 2019).

14. "Women and the Death Penalty—Background," Death Penalty Information Center, accessed November 11, 2018, https://deathpenaltyinfo.org/women-and-the-death-penalty#Background.

15. "FBI Expanded Homicide Data Table 8—Murder Offenses by Weapon, 2013-2017," Crime in the United States (FBI Uniform Crime Report), accessed November 11, 2018, https://ucr.fbi.gov/crime-in-the-u.s/2017/crime-in-the-u.s.-2017/topic-pages/tables/expanded-homicide-data-table-8.xls.

16. Fox, Levin, and Quinet, *The Will to Kill*.

17. Furman v. Georgia, 408 U.S. 238, 365 (1972) (Marshall, J., concurring).

18. "Searchable Execution Database," Death Penalty Information Center, accessed November 11, 2018, https://deathpenaltyinfo.org/views-executions. Interestingly, at the time the movie was made, the numbers were even more striking. In the twenty years between the *Gregg* decision and the film's release, just one woman—Velma Barfield—was executed.

19. Andrea Shapiro, "Unequal Before the Law: Men, Women, and the Death Penalty," *Journal of Gender, Social Policy & The Law* 8, no. 2 (2006).

20. U.S. Const. XIV § 1.

21. 408 U.S. at 238; Gregg v. Georgia, 428 U.S. 153 (1976). See also Elizabeth Rapaport, "The Death Penalty and Gender Discrimination," *Law and Society Review* 25, no. 2 (1991).

22. Shapiro, "Unequal Before the Law," 470.

23. It should be noted that while such disparity exists at the sentencing phase, men and women are largely treated the same at earlier phases of the judicial process, including plea negotiation, the decision to prosecute, and conviction. See Shapiro, "Unequal Before the Law," 452.

24. Ibid., 456. See also Steven F. Shatz and Naomi R. Shatz, "Chivalry is Not Dead: Murder, Gender, and the Death Penalty," *Berkeley Journal of Gender, Law & Justice* 27, no. 1 (2012): 106.

25. Shapiro, "Unequal Before the Law," 456–57.

26. Ibid., 458–59; Shatz and Shatz, "Chivalry is Not Dead," 106.

27. Ibid., 459.

28. Shatz and Shatz, "Chivalry is Not Dead," 106–7.

29. Ibid.

30. Camp Cupcake is the nickname given to the women's federal prison in Alderson, WV, which has housed, among other well-known inmates, Martha Stewart. See Aleski Tzatzev, "CAMP CUPCAKE: Take a Tour of America's Cushiest Prison," *San Francisco Gate*, June 6, 2013, https://www.sfgate.com/technology/businessinsider/article/CAMP-CUPCAKE-Take-A-Tour-Of-America-s-Cushiest-4584222.php.

31. Patrick Hudson, "Does the Death Row Phenomenon Violate a Prisoner's Human Rights Under International Law?" *European Journal of International Law* 11, no. 4 (2000): 835.

32. Mark D. Cunningham and Mark P. Vigen, "Death Row Inmate Characteristics, Adjustment, and Confinement: A Critical Review of the Literature," *Behavioral Sciences and the Law* 20, no. 1–2 (2002).

33. Amy Smith, "Not 'Waiving' But Drowning: The Anatomy of Death Row Syndrome and Volunteering for Execution," *Boston University Public Interest Law Journal* 17 (2008); Florencio J. Yuzon, "Conditions and Circumstances of Living on Death Row—Violative of Individual Rights and Fundamental Freedoms? Divergent Trends in Judicial Review in Evaluating the 'Death Row Phenomenon,'" *George Washington Journal of International Law and Economics* 30 (1996).

34. John H. Blume, "Killing the Willing: 'Volunteers,' Suicide and Competency," *Michigan Law Review* 103, no.5 (2005); Richard W. Garnett, "Sectarian Reflections on Lawyers' Ethics and Death Row Volunteers," *Notre Dame Law Review* 77, no. 3 (2002); Kathleen L. Johnson,

"The Death Row Right to Die: Suicide or Intimate Decision?" *Southern California Law Review* 54, no. 3 (1980); Matthew T. Norman, "Standards and Procedures for Determining Whether a Defendant is Competent to Make the Ultimate Choice—Death: Ohio's New Precedent for Death Row Volunteers," *Journal of Law and Health* 13 (1998); J. C. Oleson, "Swilling Hemlock: The Legal Ethics of Defending a Client Who Wishes to Volunteer for Execution," *Washington and Lee Law Review* 63, no. 1 (2006); Melvin I. Urofsky, "A Right to Die: Termination of Appeal for Condemned Prisoners," *Journal of Criminal Law and Criminology* 75, no. 3 (1984).

35. "Time on Death Row," Death Penalty Information Center, accessed November 11, 2018, https://deathpenaltyinfo.org/time-death-row.

36. See Kathleen M. Flynn, "The 'Agony of Suspense': How Protracted Death Row Confinement Gives Rise to an Eighth Amendment Claim of Cruel and Unusual Punishment," *Washington and Lee Law Review* 54 no. 1 (Winter 1997).

37. Gideon v. Wainwright, 372 U.S. 335 (1963).

38. Ibid., at 344.

39. Powell v. Alabama, 287 U.S. 45, 51 (1932).

40. Christina Swarns, "The Uneven Scales of Capital Justice," *American Prospect*, June 18, 2004, http://prospect.org/article/uneven-scales-capital-justice.

41. Andrea D. Lyon, "The Capital Defense Attorney," in *America's Experiment With Capital Punishment: Reflections on the Past, Present, and Future of the Ultimate Penal Sanction*, 3rd ed., eds. James R. Acker, Robert M. Bohm, and Charles S. Lanier (Durham, NC: Carolina Academic Press, 2014).

42. Strickland v. Washington, 466 U.S. 668, 688 (1984).

43. Lyon, "The Capital Defense Attorney," 387.

44. Ibid., 377.

45. American Bar Association, "Guidelines for the Appointment and Performance of Defense Counsel in Death Penalty Cases," *Hofstra Law Review* 31 (2003): 913–1090.

46. National Right to Counsel Committee, *Justice Denied: America's Continuing Neglect of Our Constitutional Right to Counsel* (Washington, DC: The Constitution Project, 2009), accessed November 17, 2018, https://constitutionproject.org/wp-content/uploads/2012/10/139.pdf.

47. Kate Taylor, *System Overload: The Cost of Under-Resourcing Public Defense* (Washington, DC: Justice Policy Institute, 2011), accessed November 17, 2018, http://www.justicepolicy.org/uploads/justicepolicy/documents/system_overload_final.pdf.

48. Emily M. West, *Court Findings of Ineffective Assistance of Counsel Claims in Post - Conviction Appeals Among the First 255 DNA Exoneration Cases* (Washington, DC: The Innocence Project, 2010), accessed November 17, 2018, https://www.innocenceproject.org/wp-content/uploads/2016/05/Innocence_Project_IAC_Report.pdf.

49. Ibid.

50. Muniz v. Smith, 647 F.3d 619 (6th Cir. 2011).

51. People v. Garrison, 47 Cal. 3d 746 (1989).

52. State v. Wille, 595 So. 2d 1149 (La. 1992).

53. West, *Court Findings*.

54. The decision in Gregg, 428 U.S. at 153, created the bifurcated trial, which separated the guilt and penalty phases in an attempt to overcome the arbitrary application of the punishment as identified in Furman, 408 U.S. at 238.

55. See, generally, Jaclyn Schildkraut, "An Inmate's Right to Die: Legal and Ethical Considerations in Death Row Volunteering," *Criminal Justice Studies* 26, no. 2 (2013).

56. C. Lee Harrington, "A Community Divided: Defense Attorneys and the Ethics of Death Row Volunteering," *Law & Social Inquiry* 25, no. 3 (2000).

57. Christy Chandler, "Voluntary Executions," *Stanford Law Review* 50, no. 6 (1998).

58. Welsh S. White, "Defendants Who Elect Execution," *University of Pittsburgh Law Review* 48, no. 3 (1987).

59. Chandler, "Voluntary Executions," 1900.

60. Ibid., 1901.

61. American Bar Association. *Rule 1.2: Scope of Representation & Allocation of Authority Between Client & Lawyer.* Model Rules of Professional Conduct, August 16, 2018, accessed November 18, 2018, https://www.americanbar.org/groups/professional_responsibility/publications/model_rules_of_professional_conduct/rule_1_2_scope_of_representation_allocation_of_authority_between_client_lawyer/.

62. Richard G. Strafer, "Volunteering for Execution: Competency, Voluntariness and the Propriety of Third Party Intervention," *Journal of Criminal Law and Criminology* 74, no. 3 (1983).

63. "Searchable Execution Database."

64. Aileen Wuornos gained fame—or, perhaps more correctly, infamy—as the first woman in the U.S. ever to fit the FBI's definition of a serial killer. Numerous books and films were written about her story, including the film *Monster* (2003), for which Charlize Theron won an Oscar, a Golden Globe, and a Screen Actors Guild Award (among other national and international recognitions) for best lead actress. See IMDB, "Monster—Awards," accessed January 12, 2019, https://www.imdb.com/title/tt0340855/awards?ref_=tt_ql_op_1.

65. Jane L. McClellan, "Stopping the Rush to the Death House: Third-Party Standing in Death-Row Volunteer Cases," *Arizona State Law Journal* 26, no. 1 (1994).

66. Harrington, "A Community Divided," 862.

67. Ibid., 877.

68. Attorney #17, as quoted in ibid., 869.

Chapter Nine

Monster's Ball: Understanding the Broader Impact

Monster's Ball has been referred to as "the best script that couldn't get made."[1] Its writers, Will Rokos and Milo Addica, were struggling actors looking to craft themselves breakout roles to launch their careers. The pair had met fifteen years earlier when they acted together in a play in New York. They kept in touch after the engagement ended, and later spent eight months, holed up in Addica's California apartment, writing the script for *Monster's Ball*. Their writing process was anything but conventional: the movie ultimately is sparse in dialogue and was the product more of improvised acting than traditional screenwriting. Yet in the end, they found a commonality in their own lives: the troubled relationship between fathers and sons. That, coupled with an exploration of a cycle of violence between them, served as the foundation of the film's script.

Once completed, the pair began shopping the script around Hollywood. It drew the attention of Robert DeNiro, Tommy Lee Jones, and Marlon Brando for the lead role, and Oliver Stone and Sean Penn for directing. The film initially was optioned by Atlas Entertainment, who cut some of the pivotal points of the script before letting it go. First Line Features, who also wanted changes, then picked it up: specifically, they wanted a happier ending for the characters despite the fact that this would strip the film of its intended meaning. The company also wanted to bring in DeNiro to play the film's protagonist, Hank Grotowski, and Penn to direct, but that venture became too costly to pursue, so First Line Features dropped their option. Lawrence Bender, a producer known for works such as *Reservoir Dogs, Pulp Fiction, Good Will Hunting,* and the *Kill Bill* movies, also picked up the film, but it again went nowhere.[2]

Frustrated but unwilling to give up, Rokos and Addica connected with Lee Daniels, who later produced *Lee Daniels' The Butler* and the hit television show *Empire*. Unlike the previous options, Daniels wanted the film to have the ending the writers envisioned. He took the film to Lions Gate Entertainment, where director Marc Forster (later known for *Finding Neverland, Stranger than Fiction,* and *World War Z*) signed on.[3] The film had a modest budget of $4 million,[4] yet it still drew in its own star power: Billy Bob Thornton signed on to play Hank, and Halle Berry was cast as Leticia Musgrove, a role she pursued after reading the script.[5] She went on to win both an Oscar and a Screen Actors Guild Award for the role.[6] The film was also nominated for an Academy Award for best writing for an original screenplay, ultimately losing out to *Gosford Park*.[7] Some movie critics, including Roger Ebert and the *Guardian*'s Philip French, offered praise for the film. Ebert, who gave the film four stars, noted that it "has the complexity of great fiction," going on to call the screenplay "subtle and observant" and Thornton and Berry's performances "powerful." [8] French called the movie "a fine tradition in Death Row dramas," adding it to a list of best examples of the genre with *Dead Man Walking, The Green Mile,* and *Last Dance,* all discussed earlier in this book.[9] Not all critical response, however, was as positive as those reviews offered by Ebert and French; for many, *Monster's Ball* ultimately became a movie "people love to hate."[10]

While many of the other chapters in this book deal with legal and constitutional issues stemming from the use of the death penalty, *Monster's Ball* instead tackles one of the moral questions associated with capital punishment from a different perspective: how do state-sanctioned executions impact people beyond just those condemned to die? The movie provides a unique opportunity to consider this question by examining the stories of those who carry out the executions and those who lose loved ones to such events. Specifically, attention is paid to the effect that taking the life of a condemned prisoner has on the corrections staff and ways in which they work to mitigate their reactions. The impact of having a loved one on death row or losing them to execution is examined by considering both the family unit, and children in particular. Through such inquiries, the broader collateral damage caused by the death penalty is highlighted.

"IT'S A JOB. LET'S DO OUR JOB RIGHT."

Monster's Ball utilizes a unique format in which "each scene is a vignette rather than a linear slice of narrative."[11] The film is set in Georgia, and opens with Hank asleep in bed, a fan spinning overhead, the blades circling like hands on a clock. On the opposite side of the screen, a series of what appear to be flashbacks pulse in and out, as if to give the audience insight into his dreams (or, perhaps more aptly, his nightmares). A chronic insomniac, he rises in the middle of the night, heads to the bathroom, and vomits (this is out of sight of the audience as the camera holds steady on a long shot of the hallway leading to the home's kitchen). After getting dressed, Hank heads to a local diner, where he is greeted by his regular waitress who brings him his usual—a cup of black coffee and a bowl of chocolate ice cream with a plastic spoon. She chats with him, asking how his son is.

In the next vignette, we meet Sonny (portrayed by Heath Ledger), Hank's son, who is in a local motel room, smoking a cigarette and staring at himself in the mirror. There is soon a knock at the door; it is Vera (played by Amber Rules), a local prostitute. Sonny hands her the money, offers her a drink of Wild Turkey, and the pair have sex. Afterwards, Vera looks back at Sonny in the same mirror from the bathroom and asks, "What's the matter, honey? You look so sad." He tells her that he is fine and invites her to get something to eat and talk. Declining this invitation, she leaves the motel room, with nothing more than a: "Take care, Sonny."

The scene cuts once again, this time to Hank arriving home. As he comes in, he sets down the mail and the paper. "Morning, Pop," he says, introducing the audience to his father, Buck (portrayed by Peter Boyle). Buck is in poor health, relying on a walker and an oxygen tank to get through the day. He spends his time collecting stories about executions, which he saves in a scrapbook. His attention shifts over breakfast with Hank as he notices several young black boys walking on his property. He launches into a racist rant, punctuated with the statement "There was a time when they knew their place." As Hank goes outside with his shotgun, Sonny arrives home and is ordered to tell the boys, who he appears friendly with, to get off the property. When he refuses to comply, Hank fires off a shot into the air, sending the boys running, and then a second round. "You watch your ass, alright," Hank warns Sonny before returning to the house. Sonny's sensitivity toward the boys, just like with Vera, makes him particularly vulnerable, a trait that is unsuitable for his job at the prison; it is also something that makes him an outcast within his own family.

Now dressed in his corrections uniform, Hank leaves the house to head to the prison, leaving Buck behind. As he drives off the property, he is confronted by the boys' father, Ryrus Cooper (played by Mos Def), who tells Hank that there is no need to threaten the boys. "Next time you want to play cowboy," Ryrus states, "I'm over here all the time." He then takes his boys and goes back to his house. The exchange summarizes the ongoing racial tensions between blacks and whites in the South, an underlying theme throughout this film and others highlighted in this book.

Now at the prison, the scene opens with one of the guards, Dappa (portrayed by Anthony Bean), strapped into the electric chair; he struggles and is able to free himself from one of the straps while the other guards, including

Hank and Sonny, look on. The team is preparing for the upcoming execution of Lawrence Musgrove, who has been on death row for the past eleven years. "You see what you did, Sonny?" Hank comments. "I'm sorry, that was my mistake," Sonny, looking disappointed, replies. "It won't happen again." Hank orders the team to keep practicing until they get it right.

After working their shift at the penitentiary, Hank and several other pris- on guards sit around a table sharing drinks at the local bar. Their colleague Sonny sits alone at the bar, smoking a cigarette and drinking a beer. Hank walks over, pays for his drink, and reminds Sonny of the importance of doing the job correctly: "Just like I said, no more mistakes, alright? I want to make damn sure that nobody makes any mistakes, especially you." In this moment it is clear that despite choosing to follow in his father's footsteps, the expec- tations for Sonny are higher than the other guards, possibly so high that he will never be able to make Hank proud of him.

Back at the table, one of the other guards proclaims, "[H]e'll be a man tomorrow," referencing Sonny and suggesting that this will be his first time assisting with an execution. "In England," explains Hank, "they go so far as to give the guy a party the night before. They call it the Monster's Ball." Is that what is happening in this scene? The answer to that question remains unclear; but one thing is certain—the audience now has insight into the title of the film. [12]

The audience later finds itself in a car with two of the movie's other characters. A pair of close-up shots gives viewers some context: the tempera- ture gauge of the car, with the needle on the hottest setting, and the hands of a black woman, with a simple gold wedding band adorning the left ring finger, grip the steering wheel. The view switches to outside the car: it is a rusty old Ford, with smoke coming from the exhaust pipe, making its way down a long, empty stretch of road. Its occupants, the woman and her young son, arrive at the state penitentiary. Inside, they are scanned through the gates, though the audience has yet to see their faces (similar to the way in which viewers are introduced to John Coffey in *The Green Mile*, as discussed in Chapter 6). The camera then switches to a wide-angle view of a room; the boy is sitting at a picnic-style table with a man, the prisoner, who has his back to the camera. Guards flank the corner of the room while the woman stares out the window.

It soon becomes apparent that the man is Lawrence and he is saying his goodbyes to his son Tyrell (played by Coronji Calhoun), a heavy boy with a solemn look on his face and a sadness in his eyes. Lawrence tells his son that he will leave him his drawings and his clothes. Tyrell seems confused: "I'm not going to see you after this?" Lawrence tells him no, but Tyrell doesn't seem to understand.

Lawrence: "'Cause I'm a bad man."

Tyrell: "Who says?"
Lawrence: "I do. But I want you to know something . . . You ain't me . . .
You're everything that's good about me. You're the best of what I am, that's
what you are. The man you see sitting here today, you ain't."

Leticia, the boy's mother, joins Lawrence and Tyrell at the table. She seems
frustrated, even as Tyrell boasts to his father about winning a school award
for his drawing (a shared passion between the two). The car is leaking radia-
tor fluid and she is on the verge of losing the family home because she can no
longer afford to make the payments. The strain of being a single parent and
sole provider is clearly weighing on Leticia and she lashes out at Lawrence:
"Only reason I'm here is so you could say goodbye to your son. I've been
coming here for damn near eleven years, Lawrence, and I'm tired. I'm tired
of coming here." Visiting time ends; Lawrence hugs Tyrell and tells him that
he will call. Before the guards escort him back to his cell, Lawrence apologizes to Leticia for hurting her.

With no outstanding appeals, the execution is going to take place that
night. As Hank preps his team about what to expect, the camera cuts back
and forth between the group and shots of Lawrence packing up his belongings in his cell. After the corrections officers join together in prayer, the
camera cuts between Leticia and Tyrell, who are now back at home waiting
for Lawrence's call, and Sonny putting handcuffs on Lawrence with Hank
overseeing and leading him to the deathwatch cell. The stress is palpable:
Leticia is chain-smoking, while Tyrell has taken to eating candy he has
hidden throughout the house. Feeling imprisoned in her own home, Leticia
decides to seek various forms of relief by leaving for a short time in order to
buy some alcohol. Also imprisoned, but in a cell, with nowhere to go but to
his death, Lawrence breaks into a panic attack, but resumes drawing once he
regains his composure; his last meal goes virtually untouched. The drawing
is his principal sustenance during his final hours on earth.

Back at the house, Leticia realizes that Tyrell has been eating chocolate
(readers are encouraged to consider the physical and metaphorical role that
food plays in this movie) and she beats him, berating him and calling him a
"fat little piggy." She raids his stash, forces him on a scale, and continues to
hit him when the number nears two hundred pounds. After knocking him to
the floor, she helps the crying boy up, a distraught look on her face, and goes
back to waiting for Lawrence's call (though it never comes as the warden
does not believe it is a good idea).

The time for the execution has arrived. At the prison, two rows of perfectly lined chairs sit empty, waiting for witnesses. Lawrence is prepped for the
electric chair: his pants leg is cut off, his head and leg shaven in anticipation
of the electrodes. The curtain to the execution chamber is closed as witnesses
file in. Lawrence places on a diaper in case he soils himself before the guards

lead him to the chamber. Just before entering, Sonny breaks from the line and throws up, but the march to the electric chair continues. Lawrence is strapped into the chair, the electrodes attached, and the curtain opened. When asked for his final words, Lawrence responds, "Push the button." With that, the hood is lowered, the lever is flipped, and Lawrence Musgrove is executed.

THE EXECUTIONER

In an op-ed for the *New York Times,* Semon Frank Thompson, the former superintendent at the Oregon State Penitentiary, discussed the effect that executing inmates had on him and his staff.[13] He highlighted the tremendous burden he and others faced knowing that they had to take a life, regardless of whether they were morally opposed to it. It produced anxiety and sleepless nights. After executing two men, both convicted killers, some of the corrections officers left their positions; others expressed a desire not to be involved in further executions. It also led to alcohol and drug abuse, depression, and even suicide. A number of research studies have provided findings that echo Thompson's observations. These studies note that having to execute individuals also may lead to persistent stress or guilt, hallucinations or nightmares, emotional withdrawal, physical symptomology (for example, fainting spells) or illness, sleeplessness, and even secondary trauma or posttraumatic stress disorder (PTSD).[14] Despite the potential ways that carrying out an execution can affect people charged with the task, those individuals see their job as one that must be done with professionalism.[15] Many corrections officers working on death row believe that it is their responsibility to treat the inmates with decency, dignity, and care regardless of the offenses they may have committed.[16]

Part of what enables corrections officers to carry out a death sentence (and for some, multiple executions) are the strategies they use to cope with what they are exposed to.[17] This is not to suggest that they do not experience strain or struggle as a result of their job; instead, it highlights the importance of implementing and maintaining positive coping mechanisms in order to be able to do it. Religious beliefs, Biblical references, and conversations with clergy have been found to help some executioners, while others may find support from their peers, prison administration, or the criminal justice system as a whole.[18] These supports, however, may only provide so much of a buffer; corrections officers who work on executions may often find themselves at a moral crossroads, attempting to reconcile their jobs with a perceived loss of humanity that ultimately can lead to more questions than answers.[19] In such instances, moral disengagement—the process of regulating one's actions against a personal value system in order to protect their well-being—may be used by the corrections officers to overcome such objections so that they can continue to perform their job functions;[20] dissociation or diffusion of responsibility also may help to achieve this end.[21]

Back in the prison's bathroom, Sonny is trying to pull himself together when Hank bursts in: "Do you know what you did?" he repeats over and over. "You fucked him up. You fucked up that man's last walk!" Hank repeatedly hits Sonny, berating him in a manner that bears similarity to how Leticia attacked Tyrell because of his compulsive overeating. Sonny is punched in the face and knocked to the ground before the other guards come in and break up the fight; Hank threatens them that he will take their jobs if they ever interfere again.

The film cuts from Sonny, looking distressed in the bathroom, to him lying on his bed back at the house. Hank bursts into his room, seemingly ready for another round. This time, however, Sonny is not having it. He grabs a gun and forces Hank out of his room and downstairs to the living room. "You hate me, don't you?" Sonny asks Hank after the pair stare one another down for a few moments. "Yeah, I hate you. I always did," he responds. With a blank look on his face, Sonny counters, "Well I always loved you;" he then turns the gun on himself.

At Sonny's funeral, it becomes clear just how disconnected Hank was from his son: "All I want to hear is that dirt hitting that box," he remarks when the preacher asks if he wants a specific passage read. "He was weak," Buck added. In that moment, the complex relationship between fathers and sons is very pronounced, yet so is the toll that being an executioner can take on a person. The day after burying Sonny, Hank quits his job as a corrections officer and burns the uniform that had defined him for so long.[22]

THE FAMILY OF THE CONDEMNED

Just as it does with the executioners, capital punishment takes a significant toll on the family members of the condemned. As it is depicted in *Monster's Ball*, this burden disproportionately falls to mothers as most death row inmates (unlike Cindy Liggett in *Last Dance*) are men. These women find themselves in a difficult situation: they now must act as both parents and serve as the breadwinner of the family as the sole source of financial support.[23] Given, however, that prisoners' families do not have access to the same resources as murder victims' next of kin, they may have to work multiple jobs just to make ends meet.[24]

In some cases, the family member may be unable to work for a number of reasons: they may spend time sitting through the capital trial,[25] visiting their loved ones in prison,[26] or dealing with the impact of the trauma caused by having a loved one on death row.[27] Consequently, the loss of income may lead to trouble meeting basic needs such as food and clothing, and these individuals may even wind up losing their residences.[28] Moreover, both monetary and time constraints also may make it difficult for the family to visit the prisoner in the first place, which can have profound psychological impacts on both parties.[29]

Aside from the mounting financial burden, researchers have found that family members of individuals on death row experience numerous health issues both before and after the execution of a loved one. Included among these are diabetes,[30] heightened blood pressure,[31] emphysema or other breathing difficulties,[32] migraines,[33] and digestive issues.[34] Heart attacks[35] or other cardiological issues,[36] cancer,[37] organ failure,[38] and even death[39] are among the most extreme health issues faced by these individuals. Individuals with loved ones on death row also may experience bouts with sleeplessness,[40] alcohol or drug abuse,[41] or eating disorders.[42]

Various issues related to mental health also have been linked to individuals who have loved ones on death row or who have experienced the execution of a family member. One of the most common is depression, which has been consistently reported in family members of death row prisoners by scholars they are working with.[43] The depression may be accompanied by feelings of hopelessness,[44] chronic sadness,[45] anger or irritability,[46] functional impairment,[47] and an inability to feel pleasure.[48] In the most extreme instances, the depression may manifest into suicidal ideation/action[49] or PTSD.[50] Moreover, this symptomology often is not short-lived, instead sometimes lasting for many years. Collectively, these challenges—both physical and psychological—all may compound into what is known as "bereavement overload," whereby an individual faces too many problems or issues at one time, issues that make coping with their situation all but impossible to deal with.[51]

In many ways, Leticia Musgrove exemplifies the typical family member of a death row prisoner. The sentencing of her husband has rendered her the sole provider of the family. In the days following Lawrence's execution, she loses her job at a local burger joint (though she quickly finds new employment at the diner Hank frequents) and soon after is evicted from her house. She relies on cigarettes and alcohol as a crutch and exhibits signs of anger and irritability toward both Lawrence and Tyrell, as well as a short fuse and little patience for her son.[52] In fact, virtually the only positive emotion Leticia shows toward Tyrell comes when a hit-and-run driver (whose identity the audience never learns) strikes him as they walk home together from the diner in the rain one night.[53] As the sheet is drawn over Tyrell at the hospital, letting Leticia know her son is dead, she is beside herself with grief, inconsolable over the loss of her "baby." Now without both her son and her husband, Leticia is left to deal with her feelings on her own, even more isolated from the world around her.

Children of Death Row Prisoners

While Leticia appears to be the stereotypical wife of a death row inmate, Tyrell seemingly defies what is known about children of these individuals. Aside from his compulsive overeating, Tyrell is a quiet, well-behaved child. Despite Leticia's outbursts, for which he often bears the brunt, he remains respectful of his mother. Like his father, who it appears he has a positive relationship with (for as much as anyone can have a positive relationship with someone who is largely absent from their life), he spends his time drawing just as Cindy Liggett did in *Last Dance* (see chapter 8).

Unlike Tyrell, children of death row prisoners and those individuals who have been executed often exhibit greater emotional and behavioral problems when compared to their peers whose parents are not incarcerated.[54] The loss of their parent to death row impacts the overall stability of the household, which can lead to the traumatization of the child.[55] Such trauma is compounded further once the parent is executed.[56] Consequently, children of death row inmates may be anxiety-ridden or aggressive, exhibit signs of grief, experience social isolation, or engage in criminal behavior themselves.[57] Like their custodial parents, they also may engage in suicide attempts or exhibit other signs of depression, PTSD, or other mental health concerns.[58] Further, unlike Tyrell, who is allowed to hug his father as he said goodbye before the execution, most states have no contact rules in place for visitation with death row inmates even when those inmates are parents, which can lead to additional psychological harm for the child.[59]

CONCLUSION: "I HAVEN'T FELT ANYTHING IN SO LONG."

After Tyrell is killed, Hank drives Leticia home, yet this fateful evening is only the first of many times their paths cross. Days later, as Hank is driving into town, he sees Leticia walking alongside the road (her car no longer works, and she is left without transportation) and gives her a ride into town. Both reeling from the losses of their sons and the aftereffects of their own personal experiences with death row, they seem to be trying to make any sense they can of the world. Hank buys a local gas station; Leticia continues to work at the diner, scrimping and saving in hopes that she can soon buy reliable transportation and save her home. In their own way, they each exhibit what scholars refer to as "psychological numbness"—they go through the motions but seemingly have lost the ability to feel anything.[60]

One evening, presumably during one of his insomnia episodes that takes him to the diner, Hank offers Leticia a ride home after her shift ends. Once at her place, she invites him in, and, after several drinks, the pair engage in a steamy sexual encounter in an attempt to drown out their pain: "I want you to make me feel good. Just make me feel good," Leticia exclaims over and over.

Ironically, before they begin to have sex, Leticia shows Hank the drawings that her husband did while he was incarcerated. She then tells him, "He got himself electrocuted over there in Jackson [where the penitentiary was located]." In that moment, Hank appears to realize that he was her husband's executioner, though he does not let on to Leticia.

As their relationship continues to develop, Hank gives Sonny's truck to Leticia; she buys him a new Stetson using money she got from pawning her wedding ring.[61] When she brings the hat by the house, Buck makes a series of racist sexual innuendos to her. Hank responds by moving Buck into a nearby nursing home. This is one of the ways in which he tries to earn Leticia's forgiveness (he also names his new gas station after her). When the sheriff's department evicts Leticia from her home, she moves in with Hank, seemingly leaving their troubles behind them.

As they prepare for bed that first night living together, an exchange between the pair shows how their relationship provides for both of them in different ways in the aftermath of their grief:

> Hank: "I want to take care of you."
> Leticia: "Good… 'cause I really need to be taken care of."

Soon, however, the fantasy of their situation is replaced by its reality. That same evening, when Hank runs out to get ice cream for them, Leticia heads up to Sonny's room, where Tyrell's belongings have been stored. While looking at photos of both boys, she stumbles across the pictures Lawrence drew of Sonny and Hank the night of his execution. In that moment, Leticia realizes she is sleeping with (and now living with) the man who put her husband to death. When Hank returns from the store, she greets him, shell-shocked, but says nothing about making the connection between him and Lawrence's execution. Yet with no other options, isolated and without any family, Leticia is forced to continue as normal. As she looks longingly for answers in the night sky, Hank says with a sigh, "I think we're going to be alright."

As Celeste Fisher and Carol Wiebe note, "While the relationship between Hank and Leticia happens by chance, its foreground is a sense of loneliness and loss, a sense of their mutual, desperate need."[62] For him, it is absolution from his job as an executioner (and its associated trauma) and his failure as a father to Sonny. For her, the need stems from losing everything and being left with nothing, including (unbeknownst to Hank) the relationship she thought would be her saving. Ultimately, however, that common need stems from being "the individuals who, in the end, will bear the burden of surviving the execution."[63]

Monster's Ball, in its various forms of rawness, shows the impact of capital punishment on the people the condemned leave behind in some form.

Some have even gone so far as to argue that, aside from the legal and constitutional challenges for prisoners raised throughout this book, the use of capital punishment also produces similar statutory violations for families of the condemned.[64] Ironically, only a small body of research exists that considers the impact on members of the prisoner's family (with greater focus on the spouses and parents as opposed to their children) and even less explores the impact these events have on the people who carry them out. Yet the research that does exist indicates that when the condemned is finally executed, it is not only their last moments, but the last moments of "a more normal life" those around them have; for once that last breath is taken, life after execution is never the same for the people left behind.[65]

NOTES

1. David S. Cohen, *Screen Plays: How 25 Scripts Made It to a Theater Near You—For Better or Worse* (New York: Harper Collins, 2008), 235.

2. Ibid.

3. Ibid.

4. "Monster's Ball (2001)—Financial Information," The Numbers, accessed January 31, 2019, https://www.the-numbers.com/movie/Monsters-Ball#tab=summary.

5. Cohen, *Screen Plays*, 240.

6. "Monster's Ball—Awards—IMDB," IMDB, accessed January 31, 2019, https://www.imdb.com/title/tt0285742/awards?ref_=tt_awd.

7. "The 74th Academy Awards | 2002: Winners and Nominees," Academy of Motion Picture Arts and Sciences, accessed January 31, 2019, https://www.oscars.org/oscars/ceremonies/2002?qt-honorees=0#qt-honorees.

8. Roger Ebert, "Monster's Ball Movie Review & Film Summary (2002) | Roger Ebert," RogerEbert.com, accessed January 31, 2019, https://www.rogerebert.com/reviews/monsters-ball-2002.

9. Philip French, "Monster's Ball—Review," *Guardian*, June 8, 2002, https://www.theguardian.com/theobserver/2002/jun/09/features.review67.

10. Sharon P. Holland, "Death in Black and White: A Reading of Marc Forster's *Monster's Ball*," *Signs* 31, no. 3 (Spring 2006): 793. Conversely, the film review site Rotten Tomatoes found an 85 percent positive review rating for the film. *See* "Monster's Ball (2002)," Rotten Tomatoes, accessed March 19, 2019, https://www.rottentomatoes.com/m/monsters_ball.

11. Holland, "Death in Black and White," 804.

12. Cohen, *Screen Plays*, 237.

13. Semon Frank Thompson, "What I Learned From Executing Two Men," *New York Times*, September 15, 2016, https://www.nytimes.com/2016/09/18/opinion/sunday/what-i-learned-from-executing-two-men.html.

14. Kelly L. Brown, and Melissa Benningfield, "Death Row Correctional Officers: Experiences, Perspectives, and Attitudes," *Criminal Justice Review* 33, no. 4 (2008); Amanda Gil, Matthew B. Johnson, and Ingrid Johnson, "Secondary Trauma Associated With State Executions: Testimony Regarding Execution Procedures," *Journal of Psychiatry & Law* 34, no. 1 (2006); Walter C. Long and Oliver Robertson, *Prison Guards and the Death Penalty* (London: Penal Reform International, 2015), accessed February 2, 2019, https://cdn.penalreform.org/wp-content/uploads/2015/04/PRI-Prison-guards-briefing-paper.pdf; Michael J. Osofsky and Howard J. Osofsky, "The Psychological Experience of Security Officers Who Work with Executions." *Psychiatry* 65, no. 4 (2002); Michael J. Osofsky, Albert Bandura, and Philip G. Zimbardo, "The Role of Moral Disengagement in the Execution Process," *Law and Human Behavior* 29, no. 4 (August 2005).

15. Brown and Benningfield, "Death Row Correctional Officers," 526; Long and Robertson, *Prison Guards and the Death Penalty*, 2; Osofsky and Osofsky, "The Psychological Experience of Security Officers," 367.

16. Osofsky and Osofsky, "The Psychological Experience of Security Officers," 367.

17. Ibid.

18. Ibid.

19. Ibid.

20. Long and Robertson, *Prison Guards and the Death Penalty*, 2; Osofsky, Bandura, and Zimbardo, "The Role of Moral Disengagement," 372, 382.

21. Osofsky and Osofsky, "The Psychological Experience of Security Officers," 367.

22. One of the guards spoken to by Sister Helen Prejean in *Dead Man Walking* shares a number of similarities with Hank, including insomnia. The guard also took an early retirement, though unlike Hank, he died shortly after from a heart attack likely induced by the stress of his former career. Similarly, in *The Green Mile*, both Paul Edgecomb and Brutus Howard left their positions on death row in favor of working in juvenile corrections after witnessing John Coffey's execution.

23. Michael L. Radelet, Margaret Vandiver, and Felix M. Berardo, "Families, Prisons, and Men with Death Sentences: The Human Impact of Structured Uncertainty," *Journal of Family Issues* 4 no. 4 (1983); Susan F. Sharp, *Hidden Victims: The Effects of the Death Penalty on Families of the Accused*. (Piscataway, NJ: Rutgers University Press, 2005).

24. Sharp, *Hidden Victims*, 44.

25. Sandra Joy, *Grief, Loss, and Treatment for Death Row Families: Forgotten No More* (Lanham, MD: Lexington Books, 2014).

26. Ibid.

27. Sharp, *Hidden Victims*, 13, 14.

28. Ibid., 21.

29. Radelet, Vandiver, and Berardo, "Families, Prisons, and Men With Death Sentences," 599.

30. Elizabeth Beck et al., "Seeking Sanctuary: Interviews With Family Members of Capital Defendants," *Cornell Law Review* 88, no. 2 (January 2003).

31. Ibid. *See also* Sharp, *Hidden Victims*, 32, 38, 51, 103.

32. Beck et al., "Seeking Sanctuary," 407; Sharp, *Hidden Victims*, 120.

33. Sharp, *Hidden Victims*, 38, 103, 120.

34. Ibid., 51, 103.

35. Beck et al., "Seeking Sanctuary," 407.

36. Sharp, *Hidden Victims*, 103.

37. Ibid., 51.

38. Ibid., 32.

39. Ibid., 103.

40. Beck et al., "Seeking Sanctuary," 411; Sharp, *Hidden Victims*, 66.

41. Sharp, *Hidden Victims*, 103.

42. Ibid., 120.

43. Sandra J. Jones and Elizabeth Beck, "Disenfranchised Grief and Nonfinite Loss as Experienced by the Families of Death Row Inmates," *Omega* 54, no. 4 (2007). *See also* Beck et al., "Seeking Sanctuary," 406; Joy, *Grief, Loss, and Treatment*, 105; Sharp, *Hidden Victims*, 103.

44. Sharp, *Hidden Victims*, 109.

45. Beck et al., "Seeking Sanctuary," 406; Jones and Beck, "Disenfranchised Grief," 289.

46. Ibid.; Jones and Beck, "Disenfranchised Grief," 290.

47. Ibid.

48. Ibid.

49. Elizabeth Beck, Sarah Britto, and Arlene Andrews, *In the Shadow of Death: Restorative Justice and Death Row Families* (New York: Oxford University Press, 2007). See also Beck et al., "Seeking Sanctuary," 406; Jones and Beck, "Disenfranchised Grief," 290.

50. Rachel King and Katherine Norgard, "What About Our Families? Using the Impact on Death Row Defendants' Family Members as a Mitigating Factor in Death Penalty Sentencing

Hearings," *Florida State University Law Review* 26 no. 4 (1999). See also Beck, Britto, and Andrews, *In the Shadow of Death*, 135; Beck et al., "Seeking Sanctuary," 405, 410.

51. Sharp, *Hidden Victims*, 24.

52. See also Beck et al., "Seeking Sanctuary," 407.

53. Coincidentally, Hank finds himself driving past Leticia as she cradles Tyrell's listless body and screams for help. Though he initially continues driving, Hank ultimately reverses the car and takes Leticia and Tyrell to the nearby hospital.

54. Joy, *Grief, Loss, and Treatment*, 223; Sharp, *Hidden Victims*, 106.

55. Beck et al., "Seeking Sanctuary," 394–95; Joy, *Grief, Loss, and Treatment*, 223, 225.

56. Joy, *Grief, Loss, and Treatment*, 235.

57. See, generally, Elizabeth Beck and Sandra J. Jones, "Children of the Condemned: The Loss of a Father to Death Row," *Omega* 56 no. 2 (2007). See also Beck et al., "Seeking Sanctuary," 394-395; Joy, *Grief, Loss, and Treatment*, 240, 245.

58. Beck and Jones, "Children of the Condemned," 208–9.

59. Sharp, *Hidden Victims*, 173. *See also* Beck and Jones, "Children of the Condemned," 201–2; Long and Robertson, *Prison Guards and the Death Penalty*, 3.

60. Beck et al., "Seeking Sanctuary," 411.

61. Hank's original hat was in the back seat of his car the night he stopped to help Leticia and Tyrell. When he loaded the injured boy into the car, the hat was covered with blood; he later asked someone at the hospital to throw it out for him.

62. Celeste Fisher and Carol Wiebe, "Race, Sex, and Redemption in *Monster's Ball*," *Ethnic Studies Review* 26 no. 2 (2003): 69.

63. Ibid., 70.

64. Rachel King, "No Due Process: How the Death Penalty Violates the Constitutional Rights of the Family Members of Death Row Prisoners," *Boston University Public Interest Law Journal* 16, no. 2 (2007). King argues that the physical, psychological, and emotional harms caused to family members, including children, is a constitutional violation. Through established case law, she highlights how the U.S. Supreme Court previously has identified a "right to family" that is infringed upon through the use of capital punishment.

65. Sharp, *Hidden Victims*, 109.

Conclusion

That's a Wrap

Famously, Willie Francis twice endured the following ordeal:

> You get a funny crawling feeling when you walk out of that death cell to go out and die. I tried to think about all the other condemned men who had left this same cell and in cells all over the world to go out and be punished. I wondered what they had thought about . . . All the other prisoners were staring out from their cell doors. I didn't hear anybody say anything but I could tell by their faces they all felt sorry for me. I saw the man who shaved my head. He was frowning in a funny sort of way, and as I stepped into the elevator and turned around, I saw him wave his little finger at me.[1]

After the State of Louisiana botched his execution in May 1946 (which led to an appeal that went all the way up to the U.S. Supreme Court), it succeeded in carrying out the death sentence when it executed Francis one year later. This kind of drama is just one of the myriad aspects of capital punishment that make it an attractive subject for the silver screen. As we have seen, however, cinematic portrayals of capital punishment are by no means created equal, and many fail to capture the interest and imagination of audiences. In part, this is because—as discussed in the introduction to this volume—the death penalty is something about which there is considerable public ambivalence. The results of a 2018 Quinnipiac University poll made it very clear that public opinion continues to send a decidedly "mixed message" about questions relating to the death penalty, "question[s] that . . . [have] moral and religious implications," and that are likely to influence American electoral politics at all levels (local, state, and federal) for the foreseeable future.[2]

The goal of movies more broadly is to attract a large enough audience to generate a profit for those who provide the money to make them; filmmakers do not want to antagonize potential ticket buyers (or television and streaming viewers). It is a simple fact of life that "[f]ilms are expensive to make," and, therefore, "[i]t is unlikely that filmmakers would take a stance too far outside the mainstream of existing political and cultural beliefs because the likelihood of recouping the investment would be negligible."[3] The only consensus of opinion about capital punishment is that there is no consensus of opinion about capital punishment. Therefore, given the high failure rate of movies, the enterprise of making films about the death penalty can be particularly financially risky. As we have seen, *The Chamber* (discussed in chapter 7) failed at the box office, while *Dead Man Walking* (discussed in chapter 3) succeeded; and *Last Dance* (chapter 8) suffered in part from coming so close on the heels of another capital punishment film, prompting one to ask whether it suffered from "capital punishment audience fatigue."

In his book about politics and film, Daniel P. Franklin observes that "[p]ublic beliefs probably form a sort of philosophical and moral range within which film content is acceptable."[4] The movies discussed in this book demonstrate that there are numerous ways to capture the drama of the death penalty on the silver screen in a manner that an audience finds "acceptable." Take Willie Francis's story for example. Were a film to be made about it, would it focus on Willie's life, on the crime he committed, on his trial and execution, on his life on death row, on his lawyers, on his victims, or on his Supreme Court appeal? If the films analyzed in this book are anything to go by, the answer would be that filmmakers could pick and choose from all of the above options and succeed in making a profitable film.

It is, however, clear that a particularly potent way of filming the death penalty is to focus on individual stories and creating characters for the audience to root for rather than taking a position for or against the death penalty. *Dead Man Walking* in particular speaks to this point. It comes the closest of all the films in this book to opposing the death penalty itself (rather than illuminating issues that might be reformed or regulated in a different manner) because it is based on the book written by Sr. Helen Prejean, who is clearly an advocate for the abolition of capital punishment. Nevertheless, the movie is driven by the individual stories of the principal characters—Sr. Helen, Matthew Poncelet, and Earl Delacroix.

This prompts us to ask one important question—is serious cinematic treatment of the most profound moral and sociopolitical aspects of capital punishment sacrificed at the altar of individual characters' stories? The answer is surely yes. This, however, is not necessarily a bad thing. For, as we have endeavored to show, while a film might principally be driven by such stories, woven into those stories—through the use of various cinematic styles and techniques—are important observations about the nature of the death penalty (and its administration in the United States) itself. Consequently, there is great educational value in analyzing such films.

In *Murder in Coweta County* (chapter 1), Sheriff Lamar Potts heroically brings wealthy and politically powerful John Wallace to justice. Yet the film is about far more than the true story of a crusading sheriff succeeding against a corrupt system.[5] It sheds light on, and therefore facilitates a dialogue about the importance of the rule of law and holding everyone—irrespective of their financial resources—equally accountable to that rule of law (despite the fact that, as both supporters and opponents of the death penalty agree, the legal system is far from perfect).

Systemic imperfections associated with capital punishment in the United States are thrown into stark relief in several of the films discussed in this book. Take, for example, *The Green Mile* (chapter 6) and *The Chamber* as discussed earlier. Although *The Chamber* was released in 1996, it asks the audience an important question that is front and center in a large percentage of twenty-first century debates about the death penalty: What particular methods of execution constitute "cruel and unusual punishment" in violation of the Eighth Amendment to the U.S. Constitution? Currently, only a handful of states allow the use of the gas chamber, all either if the offender chooses it or if lethal injection is declared unconstitutional.[6]

Nine states currently authorize the use of the electric chair as a form of execution (although, in each of those states, lethal injection is the primary method).[7] *The Green Mile* provides an impactful illustration of the problems associated with electrocution. At the same time, the film also forces us to confront many other issues related to the death penalty, particularly the persistent influence of judgments driven by stereotypes. Although *The Green Mile* takes place well before the Supreme Court's 2002 decision banning the execution of intellectually disabled inmates, it asks the audience to consider that aspect of capital punishment, as well as the issue of racial discrimination. It does so by using a principal character—John Coffey—who is portrayed as (a) a black man with neither family nor history, and (b) a saintly character who uses magical powers to help whites in crisis, in this case by curing their illnesses.[8]

Although films about capital punishment have largely avoided the question of whether the judicial system is so rife with racial disparity as to invalidate the death penalty, race remains an important theme raised in many of the movies discussed this book, most prominently in *A Lesson Before Dying* (chapter 5). Set in 1940s Louisiana, it follows the story of Jefferson, a black man who has been convicted of a crime he did not commit. His white lawyer's unsuccessful defense was that Jefferson was so stupid that he could not have committed the murder. The historical backdrop against which this film is set is emphasized by the fact that all the characters in the movie correctly assume that as a black man accused of killing a white man, Jefferson's life will not be spared. Instead of legally exonerating Jefferson, the movie teaches the audience a powerful lesson, the same lesson Jefferson finally learns—that rather than being the "hog" that his defense attorney and others called him, he is instead a human being with dignity and self-worth.

Last Dance (chapter 8) also asks the audience to consider the issue of effectiveness of counsel. Cindy Liggett's original lawyers failed to introduce important mitigating evidence at her trial and, a dozen years later, Rick Hayes takes up her appeals—but this is his first capital case and his previous career has been less than distinguished. Nevertheless, this and the other issues subtly tackled by the film (including conditions of confinement and the moral and ethical quandaries that these individuals may find themselves in when helping inmates whose lives are on the line) are not what set this film apart from the others discussed in this book. *Last Dance* examines the process by which Cindy, one of the small percentage of death row inmates who are female, accepts her fate as she moves toward execution.

Both the documentary *The Thin Blue Line* (chapter 3) and the movie *The Life of David Gale* (chapter 4) raise awareness of the most serious consequence of the systemic imperfections associated with capital punishment—sending innocent men and women to death row and then to their state-sanctioned deaths. In *The Thin Blue Line*, director Errol Morris prefers to tell the story of Randall Dale Adams rather than argue that such mistakes are common enough to support ending capital punishment. Still, the evidence uncovered in his documentary led to the overturning of Adams's conviction, something that did not happen in the fictional *The Life of David Gale.*

Analysis of *Monster's Ball* (chapter 9) brings this book to a close by forcing us to confront the fact that capital punishment affects numerous different groups of individuals—in this case, prison guards and the families of the condemned prisoners. It is a poignant reminder of the complexity of the criminal justice system at the heart of which lies "the machinery of death,"[9] a system that ultimately generates far more questions than answers.

The death penalty continues to be a debatable and contentious issue. It is a subject that divides politicians, judges, and the public alike. In the United States it is also, as Yvonne Kozlovsky-Golan observes, a subject that exposes a deep "paradox." The country is "[j]ustly proud of its robust democratic institutions and its pledge to guarantee the freedom of all citizens," but "it is also a hotbed of intense political violence, the most striking expression of which—a festering wound which continues to bleed—is the death penalty."[10] It is our hope that this book has raised awareness of some of the more important aspects of this paradoxical and controversial subject, and the questions that they generate when lights, cameras, and executions come together to create cinematic portrayals of capital punishment.

NOTES

1. Quoted in Jason Stupp, "Living Death: Ernest Gaines's *A Lesson Before Dying* and the Execution of Willie Francis," in *Demands of the Dead: Executions, Storytelling, and Activism in the United States*, ed. Katy Ryan (Iowa City: University of Iowa Press, 2012), 56.

2. "Most U.S. Voters Back Life Over Death Penalty," Quinnipiac University Poll, March 22, 2018, https://poll.qu.edu/national/release-detail?ReleaseID=2530. For one particular way in which the death penalty is influencing national electoral politics debates, see Tim Arango, "Democrats Rethink the Death Penalty, and Its Politics," *New York Times*, April 7, 2019, https://www.nytimes.com/2019/04/07/us/politics/death-penalty-democrats.html.

3. Mark Sachleben, *World Politics on Screen* (Lexington: University Press of Kentucky 2014), 23.

4. Daniel P. Franklin, *Politics and Film: The Political Culture of Film in the United States* (Lanham, MD: Rowman and Littlefield, 2006), 8.

5. The most prominent example of this theme is the 1973 film *Walking Tall*, based on the life of real-life Tennessee Sheriff Buford Pusser. The success of that movie led to two sequels, a 1978 television remake, a 1981 television series, and a 2004 reboot that was followed by two sequels of its own.

6. "Methods of Execution," Death Penalty Information Center, accessed April 30, 2019, https://deathpenaltyinfo.org/methods-execution.

7. Ibid.

8. The "magical Negro" is a fairly common image in film. For a critical evaluation of its use, see Cerise L. Glenn and Landra J. Cunningham, "The Power of Black Magic: The Magical Negro and White Salvation in Film," *Journal of Black Studies* 40, no. 2 (November 2009).

9. Callins v. Collins, 510 U.S. 1141, 1145 (1994) (Blackmun, J., dissenting from the denial of certiorari).

10. Yvonne Kozlovsky-Golan, *The Death Penalty in American Cinema: Criminality and Retribution in Hollywood Film* (London: I.B. Tauris, 2014), 235.

Bibliography

Acker, James R. "Snake Oil With a Bite: The Lethal Veneer of Science and Texas's Death Penalty." *Albany Law Review* 81, no. 3 (2018): 751–805.

Adams, Randall, William Hoffer, and Marilyn Mona Hoffer. *Adams v. Texas*. New York: St. Martin's Press, 1991.

Alexander, Michelle. *The New Jim Crow: Mass Incarceration in the Age of Colorblindness*. New York: New Press, 2010.

Alper, Ty. "Anesthetizing the Public Conscience: Lethal Injection and Animal Euthanasia." *Fordham Urban Law Journal* 35, no.4 (2008): 817–55.

American Bar Association. "Guidelines for the Appointment and Performance of Defense Counsel in Death Penalty Cases." *Hofstra Law Review* 31 (2003): 913–1090.

Arens, Edmund. *"Dead Man Walking*: On the Cinematic Treatment of Licensed Public Killing," *Contagion: Journal of Violence, Mimesis, and Culture* 5 (Spring 1998): 14–29.

Bailly, Lionel. *Lacan: A Beginner's Guide*. London: Oneworld Publications, 2009.

Baldus, David C., George Woodworth, John Charles Boger, and Charles A. Pulaski, Jr. *"McCleskey v. Kemp*: Denial, Avoidance, and the Legitimization of Racial Discrimination in the Administration of the Death Penalty." In Blume and Steiker, *Death Penalty Stories*, 229–75.

Barnes, Margaret Anne. *The Tragedy and the Triumph of Phenix City, Alabama*. Macon, GA: Mercer University Press, 1999.

———. *Murder in Coweta County*. Gretna, LA: Pelican Publishing, 1976.

Bartley, Numan V. *The New South 1945–1980: The Story of the South's Modernization*. Baton Rouge: Louisiana State University Press, 1995.

Bates, Peter. "Truth Not Guaranteed: An Interview With Errol Morris." *Cinéaste* 17, no. 1 (1989): 16–17.

Baumgartner, Frank R., and Tim Lyman. "Louisiana Death-Sentenced Cases and Their Reversals: 1976-2015." *Journal of Race, Gender & Poverty* 7 (2016): 58–75.

Beck, Elizabeth, Brenda Sims Blackwell, Pamela Blime Leonard, and Michael Mears. "Seeking Sanctuary: Interviews With Family Members of Capital Defendants." *Cornell Law Review* 88, no. 2 (January 2003): 382–418.

Beck, Elizabeth, Sarah Britto, and Arlene Andrews. *In the Shadow of Death: Restorative Justice and Death Row Families*. New York: Oxford University Press, 2007.

Beck, Elizabeth, and Sandra J. Jones. "Children of the Condemned: The Loss of a Father to Death Row." *Omega* 56 no. 2 (2007): 191–215.

Bedau, Hugo Adam. "Background and Developments." In *The Death Penalty in America: Current Controversies*, edited by Hugo Adam Bedau, 3–35. New York: Oxford University Press, 1997.

Bedau, Hugo Adam, and Paul G. Cassell. *Debating the Death Penalty: Should America Have Capital Punishment? The Experts on Both Sides Make Their Case*. New York: Oxford University Press, 2004.

Bergman, Paul, and Michael Asimow. *Reel Justice: The Courtroom Goes to the Movies*. Kansas City, MO: Andrews and McMeel, 1996.

Blackmon, Douglas A. *Slavery By Another Name: The Re-Enslavement of Black Americans From the Civil War to World War II*. New York: Doubleday, 2008.

Blocher, Joseph. "The Death Penalty and the Fifth Amendment." *Northwestern University Law Review Online* 111, no. 1 (2016): 1–17.

Blume, John H. "Killing the Willing: 'Volunteers,' Suicide and Competency." *Michigan Law Review* 103, no.5 (2005): 939–1009.

Blume, John H., Sheri Lynn Johnson, and Scott E. Sundby. "Competent Capital Punishment Representation: The Necessity of Knowing and Heeding What Jurors Tell Us About Mitigation." *Hofstra Law Review* 36, no. 3 (Spring 2008): 1035–66.

Blume, John H., and Jordan Steiker, eds. *Death Penalty Stories*. New York: Foundation Press, 2009.

Brandon, Craig. *The Electric Chair: An Unnatural American History*. Jefferson, NC: McFarland, 1999.

Brennan, William J., Jr. "The Constitution of the United States: Contemporary Ratification." In *Interpreting Law and Literature: A Hermeneutic Reader*, edited by Sanford Levinson and Steven Mailloux, 13-24. Evanston, IL: Northwestern University Press, 1988.

———. "In Defense of Dissents." *Hastings Law Journal* 37 (1986): 427–38.

Brown, Kelly L., and Melissa Benningfield. "Death Row Correctional Officers: Experiences, Perspectives, and Attitudes." *Criminal Justice Review* 33, no. 4 (2008): 524–40.

Bullock, Charles S., III, and Mark J. Rozell, eds. *The New Politics of the Old South: An Introduction to Southern Politics*, 6th ed. Lanham, MD: Rowman & Littlefield, 2017.

Cabana, Donald A. *Death at Midnight: The Confession of an Executioner*. Boston: Northeastern University Press, 1996.

Cardozo, Benjamin N. *Law and Literature and Other Essays and Addresses*. New York: Harcourt, Brace, 1931.

Carpenter, Andrew Elliott. "*Chambers v. Mississippi*: The Hearsay Rule and Racial Evaluations of Credibility." *Washington and Lee Race and Ethnic Ancestry Law Journal* 8, no. 1 (2002): 15–33.

Carter, Linda E., Ellen S. Kreitzberg, and Scott Howe. *Understanding Capital Punishment Law*, 3rd ed. New Providence, NJ: LexisNexis, 2012.

Cassell, Paul G. "In Defense of the Death Penalty." In Bedau and Cassell, *Debating the Death Penalty*, 183–217.

Chandler, Christy. "Voluntary Executions." *Stanford Law Review* 50, no. 6 (1998): 1897–1927.

Chase, Anthony. *Movies on Trial: The Legal System on the Silver Screen*. New York: The New Press, 2002.

Childs, Dennis. *Slaves of the State: Black Incarceration From the Chain Gang to the Penitentiary*. Minneapolis: University of Minnesota Press, 2015.

Christianson, Scott. *The Last Gasp: The Rise and Fall of the American Gas Chamber*. Berkeley: University of California Press, 2010.

Cicchini, Michael D. "The Battle Over the Burden of Proof: A Report From the Trenches." *University of Pittsburgh Law Review* 79, no. 1 (Fall 2017): 61–104.

Clark, Leroy D. "All Defendants, Rich and Poor, Should Get Appointed Counsel in Criminal Cases: The Route to True Equal Justice." *Marquette Law Review* 81 (1997): 47–78.

Cohen, David S. *Screen Plays: How 25 Scripts Made It to a Theater Near You—For Better or Worse*. New York: Harper Collins, 2008.

Corrigan, Timothy, ed. *Film and Literature: An Introduction and Reader*, 2nd ed. London: Routledge, 2012.

Cunningham, Mark D., and Mark P. Vigen. "Death Row Inmate Characteristics, Adjustment, and Confinement: A Critical Review of the Literature." *Behavioral Sciences and the Law* 20, no. 1–2 (2002): 191–210.

Denno, Deborah W. "When Willie Francis Died: The 'Disturbing' Story Behind One of the Eighth Amendment's Most Enduring Standards of Risk." In Blume and Steiker, *Death Penalty Stories*, 17–94.

———. "When Legislatures Delegate Death: The Troubling Paradox Behind State Uses of Electrocution and Lethal Injection and What It Says About Us." *Ohio State Law Journal* 63 (2002): 63–260.

———. "Is Electrocution an Unconstitutional Method of Execution? The Engineering of Death Over the Century." *William & Mary Law Review* 35, no. 2 (1994): 551–692.

Dionisopoulos, George N. "To Open a Door and Look Inside: *Dead Man Walking* as a Prima Facie Case." *Western Journal of Communication* 74, no. 3 (2010): 292–308.

Dow, David R. "Fictional Documentaries and Truthful Fictions: The Death Penalty in Recent American Film." *Constitutional Commentary* 17, no. 3 (Winter 2000): 511–44.

Dworkin, Ronald. *Taking Rights Seriously*. Cambridge, MA: Harvard University Press, 1977.

Ebert, Roger. *Roger Ebert's Video Companion*. Kansas City, MO: Andrews McMeel, 1998.

Etienne, Margareth. "Introduction: Tinkering With Death in Illinois." *University of Illinois Law Review* 2003, no. 4 (2003): 1073–75.

Eysenck, Hans J. *The Structure and Measurement of Intelligence*. New York: Transaction Publishers, 2017.

Fabian, John Matthew, William W. Thompson, and Jeffrey B. Lazarus, "Life, Death, and IQ: It's Much More Than Just a Score: Understanding and Utilizing Forensic Psychological and Neuropsychological Evaluations in *Atkins* Intellectual Disability/Mental Retardation Cases." *Cleveland State Law Review* 59, no. 3 (2011): 399–430.

Fisher, Celeste, and Carol Wiebe. "Race, Sex, and Redemption in *Monster's Ball.*" *Ethnic Studies Review* 26 no. 2 (2003): 68–80.

Flynn, James R. "Tethering the Elephant: Capital Cases, IQ, and the Flynn Effect." *Psychology, Public Policy, and the Law* 12, no. 2 (2006): 170–89.

Flynn, Kathleen M. "The 'Agony of Suspense': How Protracted Death Row Confinement Gives Rise to an Eighth Amendment Claim of Cruel and Unusual Punishment." *Washington and Lee Law Review* 54 no. 1 (Winter 1997): 291–333.

Fox, James Alan, Jack Levin, and Kenna Quinet. *The Will to Kill: Making Sense of Senseless Murder*, 5th ed. Thousand Oaks, CA: Sage, 2019.

Franklin, Daniel P. *Politics and Film: The Political Culture of Film in the United States*. Lanham, MD: Rowman and Littlefield, 2006.

Fujiwara, Chris. "Beyond a Reasonable Doubt and the Caesura." In *A Companion to Fritz Lang*, edited by Joe McElhaney, 161–75. Malden, MA: John Wiley & Sons, 2015.

Gaines, Ernest J. *A Lesson Before Dying*. New York: Vintage Contemporaries, 1993.

———. "Writing *A Lesson Before Dying.*" *Southern Review* 41 (2005): 770–77.

Garnett, Richard W. "Sectarian Reflections on Lawyers' Ethics and Death Row Volunteers." *Notre Dame Law Review* 77, no. 3 (2002): 795–830.

Gershman, Bennett L. "*The Thin Blue Line*: Art or Trial in the Fact-Finding Process?" *Pace Law Review* 9 (1989): 275–317.

Gewirth, Alan. "Human Dignity as the Basis of Rights." In *The Constitution of Rights: Human Dignity and American Values*, edited by Michael J. Meyer and William A. Parent, 10–28. Ithaca, NY: Cornell University Press, 1992.

Gil, Amanda, Matthew B. Johnson, and Ingrid Johnson. "Secondary Trauma Associated with State Executions: Testimony Regarding Execution Procedures." *Journal of Psychiatry & Law* 34, no. 1 (2006): 25–35.

Gleiberman, Owen. "A View to a Kill." *Entertainment Weekly*, January 19, 1996, 36.

Glenn, Cerise L., and Landra J. Cunningham. "The Power of Black Magic: The Magical Negro and White Salvation in Film." *Journal of Black Studies* 40, no. 2 (November 2009): 135–52.

Goldman, William. *Which Lie Did I Tell?: More Adventures in the Screen Trade*. New York: Vintage, 2001.

Gottschalk, Marie. *The Prison and the Gallows: The Politics of Mass Incarceration in America*. New York: Cambridge University Press, 2006.

Grant, Jonathan, ed. *Donald L. Grant, The Way it Was in the South: The Black Experience in Georgia*. Athens: University of Georgia Press, 2001.

Greenlee, Harry, and Shelia P. Greenlee. "Women and the Death Penalty: Racial Disparities and Differences." *William & Mary Journal of Women and the Law* 14, no. 2 (2008): 319–35.

Grisham, John. *The Chamber*. New York: Doubleday, 1994.

Gross, Samuel L., Maurice Possley, and Klara Stephens. *Race and Wrongful Convictions in the United States*. Irvine, CA: National Registry of Exonerations, 2017.

Grundmann, Roy, Cynthia Lucia, and Tim Robbins. "Between Ethics and Politics: An Interview with Tim Robbins." *Cinéaste* 22, no. 2 (1996): 4–9.

Halberstam, David. *The Fifties*. New York: Villard, 1993.

Harrington, C. Lee. "A Community Divided: Defense Attorneys and the Ethics of Death Row Volunteering." *Law & Social Inquiry* 25, no. 3 (2000): 849–81.

Hatch, Virginia Leigh, and Anthony Walsh. *Capital Punishment: Theory and Practice of the Ultimate Penalty*. New York: Oxford University Press, 2016.

Heller, Deborah L. "Death Becomes the State: The Death Penalty in New York State—Past, Present and Future." *Pace Law Review* 28 (2008): 589–615.

Herbert, Frank. *Dune.* New York: Ace, 1990.

Higginbotham, A. Leon, Jr. *In the Matter of Color—Race & the American Legal Process: The Colonial Period*. New York: Oxford University Press, 1978.

Holland, Sharon P. "Death in Black and White: A Reading of Marc Forster's *Monster's Ball*." *Signs* 31, no. 3 (Spring 2006): 785–813.

Hood, Roger, and Carolyn Hoyle. *The Death Penalty: A Worldwide Perspective*, 5th ed. New York: Oxford University Press, 2015.

Hudson, Patrick. "Does the Death Row Phenomenon Violate a Prisoner's Human Rights Under International Law?" *European Journal of International Law* 11, no. 4 (2000): 833–56.

Hutner, Gordon, ed. *Selected Speeches and Writings of Theodore Roosevelt*. New York: Vintage, 2014.

Ingle, Joseph B. *Last Rights: 13 Fatal Encounters with the State's Justice*. Nashville: Abingdon Press, 1990.

Johnson, Kathleen L. "The Death Row Right to Die: Suicide or Intimate Decision?" *Southern California Law Review* 54, no. 3 (1980): 575–631.

Johnson, Sheri Lynn. "The Color of Truth: Race and the Assessment of Credibility." *Michigan Journal of Race & Law* 1 (1996): 261–346.

Jones, Sandra J., and Elizabeth Beck. "Disenfranchised Grief and Nonfinite Loss as Experienced by the Families of Death Row Inmates." *Omega* 54, no. 4 (2007): 281–99.

Joy, Sandra. *Grief, Loss, and Treatment for Death Row Families: Forgotten No More*. Lanham, MD: Lexington Books, 2014.

Kauffman, Kent. *Movie Guide for Legal Studies*. New York: Pearson, 2010.

King, Rachel. "No Due Process: How the Death Penalty Violates the Constitutional Rights of the Family Members of Death Row Prisoners." *Boston University Public Interest Law Journal* 16, no. 2 (2007): 195–253

King, Rachel, and Katherine Norgard. "What About Our Families? Using the Impact on Death Row Defendants' Family Members as a Mitigating Factor in Death Penalty Sentencing Hearings." *Florida State University Law Review* 26 no. 4 (1999): 1119–76.

Knowles, Helen J. "A Dialogue on Death Penalty Dignity." *Criminology & Criminal Justice* 11, no. 2 (2011): 115–28.

Kozinski, Alex. "Tinkering with Death." *New Yorker*, February 10, 1997.

Kozlovsky-Golan, Yvonne. *The Death Penalty in American Cinema: Criminality and Retribution in Hollywood Film*. London: I. B. Tauris, 2014.

La Fontaine, Eugenia T. "A Dangerous Preoccupation With Future Danger: Why Expert Predictions of Future Dangerousness in Capital Cases Are Unconstitutional." *Boston College Law Review* 44, no. 1 (2002): 207–43.

Lawes, Lewis Edward. *Life and Death in Sing Sing*. New York: Doubleday, 1929.

Liebman, James S. *The Wrong Carlos: Anatomy of a Wrongful Execution*. New York: Columbia University Press, 2014.

Lyon, Andrea D. "The Capital Defense Attorney." In *America's Experiment With Capital Punishment: Reflections on the Past, Present, and Future of the Ultimate Penal Sanction,*

3rd ed., edited by James R. Acker, Robert M. Bohm, and Charles S. Lanier, 375–92. Durham, NC: Carolina Academic Press, 2014.

Manweller, Mathew. "Film Review Essays." *Contemporary Justice Review* 7, no. 3 (September 2004): 335–41.

Matusiak, Matthew C., Michael S. Vaughn, and Rolando V. del Carmen. "The Progression of 'Evolving Standards of Decency' in U.S. Supreme Court Decisions." *Criminal Justice Review* 39, no. 3 (2014): 253–71.

McClellan, Jane L. "Stopping the Rush to the Death House: Third-Party Standing in Death-Row Volunteer Cases." *Arizona State Law Journal* 26, no. 1 (1994): 201–41.

McMillen, Neil R. *The Citizens' Council: Organized Resistance to the Second Reconstruction, 1954-64*. Champaign: University of Illinois Press, 1994.

McMillen, Sally G., Elizabeth Hayes Turner, Paul Escott, and David Goldfield, eds. *Major Problems in the History of the American South*. 3rd ed. Vol. II: *The New South*. New York: Cengage Learning, 2011.

Moore, Dot. *No Remorse: The Rise and Fall of John Wallace*. Montgomery, AL: NewSouth Books, 2011.

Morris, Errol, and Peter Bates. "Truth Not Guaranteed: An Interview with Errol Morris." *Cinéaste* 17, no. 1 (1989): 16–17.

Nichols, Bill. *Engaging Cinema: An Introduction to Film Studies*. New York: W. W. Norton, 2010.

Norman, Matthew T. "Standards and Procedures for Determining Whether a Defendant is Competent to Make the Ultimate Choice—Death: Ohio's New Precedent for Death Row Volunteers." *Journal of Law and Health* 13 (1998): 103–40.

Norris, Robert J. *Exonerated: A History of the Innocence Movement*. New York: New York University Press, 2017.

O'Brien, John. "Ernest J. Gaines." In *Conversations With Ernest Gaines*, edited by John Lowe, 25–38. Jackson: University Press of Mississippi, 1995.

Oleson, J. C. "Swilling Hemlock: The Legal Ethics of Defending a Client Who Wishes to Volunteer for Execution." *Washington and Lee Law Review* 63, no. 1 (2006): 147–230.

"An Oral Interview with Judge W. A. Bootle, Part I." *Journal of Southern Legal History* 7 (1999): 117–99.

Osofsky, Michael J., Albert Bandura, and Philip G. Zimbardo. "The Role of Moral Disengagement in the Execution Process." *Law and Human Behavior* 29, no. 4 (August 2005): 371–93.

Osofsky, Michael J., and Howard J. Osofsky. "The Psychological Experience of Security Officers Who Work With Executions." *Psychiatry* 65, no. 4 (2002): 358–70.

Owens, Ryan J., and James Sieja. "Agenda-Setting on the U.S. Supreme Court." In *The Oxford Handbook of U.S. Judicial Behavior*, edited by Lee Epstein and Stefanie A. Lindquist, 169–85. New York: Oxford University Press, 2017.

The Oxford American Dictionary and Language Guide. New York: Oxford University Press, 1999.

Parkinson, David. *100 Ideas That Changed Film*. London: Laurence King, 2012.

Paternoster, Ray, and Jerome Deise. "A Heavy Thumb on the Scale: The Effect of Victim Impact Evidence on Capital Decision Making." *Criminology* 49, no. 1 (2011): 129–61.

Perry, H. W., Jr. *Deciding to Decide: Agenda Setting in the United States Supreme Court*. Cambridge, MA: Harvard University Press, 1991.

Pojman, Louis P. "Why the Death Penalty Is Morally Permissible." In Bedau and Cassell, *Debating the Death Penalty*, 51–75.

Potera, Carol. "ANA Expands Opposition to Capital Punishment." *American Journal of Nursing* 117, no. 6 (2017): 13.

Prejean, Helen. *Dead Man Walking: The Eyewitness Account of the Death Penalty That Sparked a National Debate*. New York: Vintage Books, 2013.

———. *The Death of Innocents: An Eyewitness Account of Wrongful Executions*. New York: Vintage Books, 2005.

———. Foreword to Robbins, *Dead Man Walking: The Shooting Script*, xi.

Radelet, Michael L., Margaret Vandiver, and Felix M. Berardo. "Families, Prisons, and Men with Death Sentences: The Human Impact of Structured Uncertainty." *Journal of Family Issues* 4 no. 4 (1983): 593–612.

Rapaport, Elizabeth. "The Death Penalty and Gender Discrimination," *Law and Society Review* 25, no. 2 (1991): 367–83.

———. "Some Questions About Gender and the Death Penalty." *Golden Gate University Law Review* 20, no. 3 (January 1990): 501–65.

Robbins, Tim. *Dead Man Walking: The Shooting Script.* New York: Newmarket Press, 1997.

Rogers, Alan. *Murder and the Death Penalty in Massachusetts.* Amherst: University of Massachusetts Press, 2008.

Sachleben, Mark. *World Politics on Screen.* Lexington: University Press of Kentucky, 2014.

Sarat, Austin. "The Cultural Life of Capital Punishment: Responsibility and Representation in *Dead Man Walking* and *Last Dance.*" *Yale Journal of Law and the Humanities* 11, no. 1 (January 1999): 153–90.

———. *Gruesome Spectacles: Botched Executions and America's Death Penalty.* Stanford, CA: Stanford Law Books, 2014.

Schildkraut, Jaclyn. "An Inmate's Right to Die: Legal and Ethical Considerations in Death Row Volunteering." *Criminal Justice Studies* 26, no. 2 (2013): 139–50.

Schrader, Paul. "Notes on Film Noir." *Film Comment* 8, no. 1 (Spring 1972): 8–13.

Shapiro, Andrea. "Unequal Before the Law: Men, Women, and the Death Penalty." *Journal of Gender, Social Policy & The Law* 8, no. 2 (2006): 427–70.

Shapiro, Carole. "Do or Die: Does *Dead Man Walking* Run?" *University of San Francisco Law Review* 30, no. 4 (1996): 1143–66.

Sharp, Susan F. *Hidden Victims: The Effects of the Death Penalty on Families of the Accused.* Piscataway, NJ: Rutgers University Press, 2005.

Shatz, Steven F., and Naomi R. Shatz. "Chivalry is Not Dead: Murder, Gender, and the Death Penalty." *Berkeley Journal of Gender, Law & Justice* 27, no. 1 (2012): 64–112.

Sherwin, Richard K. "Law Frames: Historical Truth and Narrative Necessity in a Criminal Case." *Stanford Law Review* 47, no. 1 (November 1994): 39–83.

Shuler, Jack. "Can Executions Be More Humane?: A Law Professor Suggests an Untested Procedure as an Alternative to Lethal Injection." *Atlantic*, March 20, 2015.

Silvio, Lucy. "Raking in the Money?" *America* 8 (March 1996): 10–11.

Smith, Amy. "Not 'Waiving' But Drowning: The Anatomy of Death Row Syndrome and Volunteering for Execution." *Boston University Public Interest Law Journal* 17 (2008): 237–54.

Stam, Robert. "Beyond Fidelity: The Dialogics of Adaptation." In Corrigan, *Film and Literature,* 74–88.

Steiker, Carol S., and Jordan M. Steiker. *Courting Death: The Supreme Court and Capital Punishment.* Cambridge, MA: Belknap Press, 2016.

Strafer, Richard G. "Volunteering for Execution: Competency, Voluntariness and the Propriety of Third Party Intervention," *Journal of Criminal Law and Criminology* 74, no. 3 (1983): 860–912.

Streib, Victor L. "Gendering the Death Penalty: Countering Sex Bias in a Masculine Sanctuary." *Ohio State Law Journal* 63 (2002): 433–74.

———. "Rare and Inconsistent: The Death Penalty For Women." *Fordham Urban Law Journal* 33, no. 2 (2006): 101–32.

Stupp, Jason. "Living Death: Ernest Gaines's *A Lesson Before Dying* and the Execution of Willie Francis." In *Demands of the Dead: Executions, Storytelling, and Activism in the United States,* edited by Katy Ryan, 45–58. Iowa City: University of Iowa Press, 2012.

Thompson, Carlyle V. "From a Hog to a Black Man: Black Male Subjectivity and Ritualistic Lynching in Ernest J. Gaines's *A Lesson Before Dying.*" *CLA Journal* XLV, no. 3 (2002): 279–310.

Urofsky, Melvin I. "A Right to Die: Termination of Appeal for Condemned Prisoners." *Journal of Criminal Law and Criminology* 75, no. 3 (1984): 553–82.

Warden, Rob. "How and Why Illinois Abolished the Death Penalty." *Law and Inequality* 30, no. 2 (2012): 245–86.

Welsh-Huggins, Andrew. *No Winners Here Tonight: Race, Politics, and Geography in One of the Country's Busiest Death Penalty States*. Athens, OH: Ohio University Press, 2009.

White, Jack E. "Just Another Mississippi Whitewash." *Time*, January 9, 1989.

White, Welsh S. "Defendants Who Elect Execution." *University of Pittsburgh Law Review* 48, no. 3 (1987): 853–77.

Wright, Daniel B., and Melanie Hall. "How a 'Reasonable Doubt' Instruction Affects Decisions of Guilt." *Basic and Applied Social Psychology* 29, no. 1 (2007): 91–98.

Yant, Martin. *Presumed Guilty: When Innocent People Are Wrongly Convicted*. Buffalo, NY: Prometheus Books, 1991.

Yuzon, Florencio J. "Conditions and Circumstances of Living on Death Row—Violative of Individual Rights and Fundamental Freedoms? Divergent Trends in Judicial Review in Evaluating the 'Death Row Phenomenon.'" *George Washington Journal of International Law and Economics* 30 (1996): 39–73.

Zeitler, Michael. "'Mr. Joe Louis, Help Me': Sports as Narrative and Community in Ernest J. Gaines's *A Lesson Before Dying*." *Studies in the Literary Imagination* 49, no. 1 (Summer 2016): 129–40.

Index

About the Authors

Bruce Altschuler is professor emeritus at the State University of New York at Oswego and the author or co-author of seven books, most recently, *Seeing Through the Screen: Interpreting American Political Film*, and numerous articles in professional journals.

Helen J. Knowles is associate professor of political science at the State University of New York at Oswego. She is the author of *The Tie Goes to Freedom: Justice Anthony M. Kennedy on Liberty*, and the co-editor (with Steven B. Lichtman) of *Judging Free Speech: First Amendment Jurisprudence of US Supreme Court Justices*. She has also published numerous articles about various aspects of politics, and political history in legal and political science journals.

Jaclyn Schildkraut is associate professor of criminal justice at the State University of New York at Oswego. She is the co-author of *Mass Shootings: Media, Myths, and Realities* (with H. Jaymi Elsass) and *Columbine, 20 Years Later and Beyond: Lessons from Tragedy* (with Glenn W. Muschert), and the editor of *Mass Shootings in America: Understanding the Debates, Causes, and Responses*. She has published numerous research works on the topics of school and mass shootings both in social science journals and edited volumes.